GOODBYE Uncle Bengy, HELLO Uncle Sam

A Journey to Citizenship

Pastor:
Thanks for your help
& support
Enjoy the read
Joseph & Dian

JOSEPH R McLAREN

ISBN: 1466267356
ISBN-13: 9781466267350
Library of Congress Control Number: 2011915485

CreateSpace, North Charleston, SC

Contents

INTRODUCTION

The purpose of writing this book is not the illusion that I have reached the pinnacle of my career or accomplishments. Instead, it is a reflection on the environments that have shaped my outlook on life.

My story presents the dynamic perspective of a boy influenced by events, places, and people. It chronicles life behind the all-inclusive resort curtain that many tourists see when they visit paradise, and the life of a man as a new citizen in America.

From the perspective of an outsider looking in, and now an insider looking out, the influence of the US is unquestionable. In a democracy, citizens have a responsibility to remain vigilant and informed. The government we employ reflects the populace's ability to gather and process information for decision-making. My story illustrates how mundane activities, such as working, attending school, traveling, dating, and seeking love and acceptance inform that outlook. Learning is continuous, and I am constantly reminded that choices are not always black or white, but shades of gray. I view doubts, not as signs of weakness, but as humbling recognition that no one person has all the answers. With this in mind, I offer my perspective.

Finally, while I am grateful for the privilege of living in the USA, I am forever thankful for my experience with the Jamaican spirit that I affectionately refer to as Uncle Bengy. This spirit is the big bark in the little dog that says, "Yeah man, no problem!"

CHAPTER 1: **JAMAICA**

i.

"Congratulations! Your application has been recommended for approval. At this time, it appears that you have established your eligibility for naturalization." A smile crested on the stoic face of the interviewing officer as he extended a welcoming handshake. Similar words of congratulations have been uttered to privileged millions ready to join the family of citizens of the United States of America. I had correctly answered the required civics questions, and the final requirement was attendance at a swearing-in ceremony one month later.

This was my second attempt at citizenship. Two years before, my first attempt failed almost simultaneously with my six years of marriage to a US citizen. I had since reapplied as a permanent resident seeking citizenship, rather than as a spouse of a US citizen. My eligibility for citizenship was actually realized eight years after my initial application for a green card, and thirteen years after I came to the United States to attend business school. The process took five years longer than the normal processing time of three years—the normal time *if* the overburdened immigration agency functioned with no errors or processing delays. The numerous stumbling blocks and processing delays had caused me to wonder if the country of my birth, which I affectionately call Uncle Bengy, was imploring me to reconsider. I also wondered, did Uncle Sam want me?

My "thank you" to the immigration officer revealed no emotions. I was not sure how to feel. My mind was racing. I was relinquishing my Jamaican citizenship and the rights to the land of my birth at a time when—based on recent economic reports—the American dream was becoming a nightmare.

The jobs report continued to be dismal. In February 2009, six hundred and fifty-one thousand people—myself included—had lost their jobs, thus pushing the unemployment rate even higher. The stock market continued its bearish run with the Dow falling below 7,000, which was half its previous high of 14,000 in October of 2007. Homeowners' foreclosure filings mounted several percentage points higher than the previous year. The accepted economic comparison was the Great Depression of the 1930s.

A month earlier, America witnessed a historic first when Barack Obama was inaugurated the forty-fourth president of the United States. His election campaign lasted nearly two years. As a candidate, Obama challenged Americans to have the "audacity of hope." So, audaciously, I joined his campaign, despite the fact that I was not yet a citizen and could not vote. President Obama inherited a collapsing financial system, mounting deficits, and a ballooning national debt. In addition, Uncle Sam was involved with two wars—Afghanistan and Iraq, plus other smaller involvements in the Global War on Terrorism. Previous congresses and the Bush Administration had made no attempt to pay for these wars and continued to finance them through borrowing and supplemental spending, circumventing the regular budget process. Oil prices were on the rise. The US auto industry was in freefall, and two of the three American bastions—General Motors and Chrysler—filed for bankruptcy. As the baby boomers neared retirement, health care, social security, and other rising costs threatened to overwhelm the entitlement system.

Immigration reform was a hotly-debated topic. The country struggled with the question of what should be done with over ten million illegal immigrants. Political pandering and name-calling seemed an acceptable alternative to problem solving and serious policy discussions. Many feared that America was on the decline, and a large dosage of hope plus strong leadership was necessary to restore the country's status as a beacon of hope. Against this backdrop, I became a US citizen and started a mental review of my life that led to my oath. I recalled events and experiences that had challenged me and shaped my life. The mental rewind continued as far back as I could remember, to a country surrounded by the refreshing Caribbean Sea—Jamaica.

ii.

Jamaica is approximately the size of "the constitution state," Connecticut. Its size bears no comparison to the heart and spirit of its people. This spirit is serenaded by the likes of singers Harry Belafonte and the Legend (Bob Marley). It is captured and immortalized not only by Marcus Garvey, but also by the notorious drug gang—The Jamaican Posse. Luther and Maud Powell inspired that spirit in their son, Secretary of State Colin Powell. It is demonstrated by the can-do attitude of Olympian sprinter Usain "Lightning" Bolt.

These personalities, not only capture the color and spirit of the Jamaican people, but also the essence of the United States of America—a catalyst for the realization of dreams and the pursuit of happiness. It is an illustrative coincidence that the Latin of the United States motto—"E pluribus unum"—translates almost identically to the Jamaica's motto: "Out of many, one people."

CHAPTER 2: **CEDAR SPRINGS**

i.

I was born in Grandma Mary's home. Like everyone else, I learned to simply call her Meme. Meme's two-bedroom white concrete house was perched on the side of a hill. Except for the zinc roof glistening in the sun, it was largely hidden from view by numerous leafy pimento trees that provided Meme a source of income.

We didn't live with Meme. However, the different houses that my parents rented were in close proximity, and Meme and I formed a close bond as I grew up. We had several discussions. One discussion topic centered on the concept of "having out one's lot," one of the reasons for the number of children that a woman bore. Children were viewed as a pension strategy. The greater the number of children, the higher the likelihood of at least one child becoming successful and taking care of his or her aging parents.

Many years later when I attended business school, I came to appreciate this strategy as diversifying one's portfolio: "Don't put all your eggs in one basket." During our discussions, I asked Meme if it would have been better to have fewer children and work hard to ensure that they succeeded. Financial success increases the likelihood that a child can better help with parents' care. At the time, Jamaica did not have entitlement services for the old. I was instructed that such family planning concepts were not popular in those days.

Unlimited procreations also made sense when many hands were needed on the farm. This concept is a legacy held over from slavery, when owners encouraged procreation to increase property. I came up with another conclusion. With no electricity, no TV, and few entertainment activities after dark, the only reliable recreational activity left for many was sex. That observation earned my grandmother's indignation the first time I suggested it, and I later avoided repeating my theory in her presence.

Whether the reason was blessing from God, strategic, recreational, or a relic from slavery, large families were the norm in rural Jamaica. My birth was another addition to an already large family. Because there are several ways to rank my position, psychologists would be challenged in determining my likely behavior based on birth order. By the time I learned to count, my family was already established. I was ninth in a tally of ten for my mother, eleventh in the tally of twelve—adding two from my father's previous marriage.

To further complicate this sibling algebraic expression, I am first in the union of my father and mother. When my mother's "lot" ended, there were ten children. At the end of the biological parenting process, there were seven boys and six girls. These thirteen children are the products of three mothers and six fathers.

After eight children and in her late thirties, Mom was still an attractive woman. When she met Dad, many of her children were already adults. Jenny, Marlene, Beverly, Errol, Mikey, Ricky, Collin, and Conroy preceded me. Kenny followed me as the last of my mother's children. My eldest sister, Jenny, was already getting ready to start her own business and family when I came along.

At age forty, Dad was a roamer escaping his former life and looking to start a new one. He was very strong and fell into the good graces of my uncle Soldier. They formed a bond sawing wood together. From cutting down trees with an axe to manfully ripping the tree trunks into boards, sawing was tedious and labor intensive.

At least two men were required to manually operate the six-foot blade. Mom's brother, whom everyone called Soldier, was impressed with Big Mac's skill sawing and invited him to church. Soon Big Mac was dating my mother and not long after, I was born.

I was raised with strong Judeo-Christian principles that encouraged abstinence before marriage—a precept encouraged and observed by both parents—despite the fact that I was born only two months after they were married.

I enjoyed watching Big Mac work and listening to the songs and dances that he and Uncle Soldier made up. Those songs harmonized with the tempo and rhythm made by the saw ripping the wood. As children we got close to the action, since there were no hard hats or concerns about safety regulations. At times we even tried to muscle the blade before being asked not to touch it. Despite this allure, I concluded that I would not follow my father into the sawing profession.

The profession of a pastor was more appealing. Pastors had cars and travelled around to different churches and people looked up to them. My father didn't own a vehicle since the profession of lumberman did not derive enough income for such "luxury." I did not emphasize distinctions among cars, but rather among modes of transportation. While I enjoyed riding the donkey or the mule, I preferred the bus for distance, and any car was preferred over the crowded buses.

The cars the pastors drove were modest European cars that did not require conversion for the left-hand drive roads. Often, pastors would offer us rides on our way to church. When Pastor Melbourne engaged me in conversation as we rode in his car, I was sure I wanted to become a pastor.

Big Mac was not disturbed by my decision to seek an alternative profession. He was thrilled at the thought of me joining the ministry. My lack of interest in Big Mac's profession did not deter my effort to fight with the hungry mosquitoes and follow him to work. Not only did I love to watch him work, but the thought of eating "big man lunch" was added motivation.

For lunch, Big Mac and Soldier boiled or roasted a combination of yams, breadfruit, plantain, dumplings, and salt fish (codfish). They made a wood fire and set the pot that they carried with them on three stones above the fire.

The flour dumplings were the main attraction. They were kneaded tightly, usually by Big Mac's large hands, and then flattened. We called these dumplings "cartwheels" because of their size, which was wide enough to rival the wheels we made from wood for our toy trucks. It became a well-established fact: Big Mac made big dumplings.

The name Big Mac emerged before many Jamaicans had any concept of what a burger was—since the fast-food chain McDonald's was yet to be introduced to that market. Years later, when I first learned of McDonald's Big Mac, I surmised it had to be huge to be named after my dad.

ii.

Big Mac appeared oblivious to his strength. Ironically, church was the place where many people marveled, in agony, at his strength. During greetings, his large and rough hands would engulf visitors, pastors, and the delicate hands of petite women. The handshakes caused grimaces, screams, sheepish smiles, and sighs of relief when they ended. When playing with Kenny and me, Big Mac balanced us in the palm of each hand and lifted us above his head for weight training. At the end of the exercise, my brother and I compared bellies to see who had the more discernable palm and fingerprint from Big Mac's hand.

Big Mac's strength came on full display one Sabbath (Saturday) morning on our way to church. Big Mac, Mom, Kenny, Conroy, and I had almost completed the two-mile journey after we had left grandmother's house. We had walked this way several times, and I knew each occupant of the dozen houses scattered along the sides of the hilly terrain along the way. Only two of those households attended the same church. We inched along the graveled road that snaked its way along the side of the mountain of the Cedar Springs district.

In the distance, I could see and hear Ms. Regina's son, who was nicknamed "Myson," complaining and making threats. Animals had eaten and damaged his crop, and he was sure those animals belonged to Big Mac. He insisted that there would be consequences if Big Mac passed his house without paying for the damages. Myson's crop was valuable. However, at the time, I could not understand why anyone would make such a fuss about a crop that no one ate, but burned. They didn't even make a big bonfire with it; they made joints like cigarettes and burned, or rather smoked, them. Where was the fun in that?

Big Mac was undeterred. As we approached Ms. Regina's house, Mom whispered aloud a prayer. Her whispering triggered in my memory one of several Bible verses that I learned in Sabbath school. I repeated it to myself. It was from the psalmist David. "Though I walk through the valley of the shadow of death, I will fear no evil."

We continued a steady but relatively silent approach toward Myson. He was waiting on the road slightly above his mother's house. My steady progress forward was encouraged by the firm grip Big Mac had on my hand. Mom's steps slowed along with Conroy and Kenny. As we approached, a small crowd gathered. Myson was enraged. He apparently had a posse of about six, whose unifying marks were bloodshot eyes and a faint smell of ganja (marijuana). Apparently, they had an early group session of "passing the chalice" (smoking weed).

I didn't recognize two of Myson's friends. I surmised they were from the nearby Accompong or Maroon Town. Accompong Town is one of a few areas in Jamaica where runaway slaves (maroons) lived freely—years before slavery ended. The British had colonized the island, but after several brutal and failed attempts to retake the town resulted in several dead British soldiers, they made a treaty to leave this proud band of warriors alone. After all, British soldiers in bright red coats, climbing green lush forestry, became easy targets for the Maroons.

Myson and his friends blocked the path. Big Mac stopped in front of Myson and explained that he was on his way to church and that he didn't think the animals that damaged Myson's crop were his. Big Mac tried diplomacy, suggesting that he would gladly talk on his way back. That explanation seemed reasonable to everyone except Myson. He instead insisted that he should be paid now, or we would not be allowed to pass. Big Mac asked him to step aside. Myson responded by removing a small towel from his back pocket to reveal a ratchet knife.

The right-handed Big Mac had both hands occupied. In his right was a brown leather book bag filled with his favorite books: *The Bible, Patriarchs and Prophets, Daniel and the Revelations,* and other religious writings from the church prophetess, Ellen G. White. I was led firmly by his left hand. His grip on my hand eased, followed by a gentle shove forcing me behind him. Clothed in his best suit and tie, Big Mac took a step forward, and Myson reached for the knife. With lightning speed, Big Mac unleashed a quick uppercut, and Myson toppled over backward. The back of his head collided with the limestone gravel, changing the white gravel to crimson as blood oozed from an unconscious Myson.

The posse scattered. There was a lot of yelling. Mom yelled for water, and Ms. Regina, Myson's mother, rushed out of her house and scooped a basin of water from one of the barrels on the side of the house, and dumped it on the face of her son.

Myson regained consciousness and limped his way back to his house with a rag covering the back of his head. Big Mac breathed a sigh of relief after seeing him regain consciousness. I stood speechless and was yanked back to reality as my father took my hand and we continued to church.

"That man's hand is loaded," someone said, which meant Big Mac's fist had supernatural powers from the spirit of the ancestors. That assertion was followed by indistinguishable arguing and murmurs of disagreement as we left the scene. The same voice repeated the statement, louder and with more authority, "I am telling you, it's loaded."

We spent the whole day at church, which was not unusual. It was Big Mac's belief that we should stay in church to keep the Sabbath holy. I was terrified as news kept arriving about what had happened and how an ambush was being planned for us on our way home.

Big Mac appeared unconcerned. His amen that followed the scripture reading of the same Shepherd's Psalm I had earlier recalled, "Though I walk through the valley of the shadow of death, I will fear no evil," suggested to me that Big Mac felt justified in defending himself and his family. I did not know this at the time, but during lunch, some of the leaders walked to Ms. Regina's house and spoke with her and Myson, none of whom where members of the church we attended. Violence was uncommon in these rural parts of the country, and the leaders successfully pleaded that there be no more violence. I was relieved when we walked home that evening without incident.

CHAPTER 3: **JOHNSON**

i.

For me, Seven Eleven meant that we had moved seven times by the time I was eleven years old. What prompted Big Mac's impulses to move remains a mystery. Was he seeking a change of scenery, looking for new opportunities, seeking to avoid confrontation with people like Myson? Whatever the reasons were, we were on our way to the neighboring parish of St. James to a small village called Johnson.

The ride to Johnson was slow, mountainous, and winding. As we passed through the villages of Jointwood, Elderslie, and Niagara, and into Johnson, we noticed that the crops people planted were mostly bananas interspersed with coffee, as compared to pimento and sugarcane in Cedar Springs. The highlight of the trip was Elderslie. We passed the primary government school that Conroy would be attending, the post office, and a boxing station for banana shipments. East of the Elderslie square was the Elderslie Cave, which was being marketed as a new tourist attraction.

We settled in the small village of Johnson, which had access to modern amenities. However, the house we rented was not wired for electricity or fitted for running water. The house was rented from our next-door neighbor to our left, the Hansons. They had built a new house next door, complete with modern amenities. Mrs. Gwen Hanson would become my kindergarten teacher at the one-room dirt-floor school located near the center of the village and opposite our new church. Her husband, Ralph, was the leader of our church, located next to their new house.

Our house sat on a slope above the main road at a lower elevation than the church and the Hanson's residence. It was more spacious than what we had lived in previously. One of its rooms was reserved for the Hansons' son, who was affectionately known as Banner. He worked out of town and came home occasionally. To the right and south of us were the Browns. They lived on the edge of the main road in a concrete house complete with modern amenities.

Across the main road below us were two additional houses, completely hidden from view by the acreage of banana and coffee in the fertile valley. In the center of the village, left of the Hansons, were two small grocery shops. Adjoining these shops were the homes of the owners. In one of these homes was the only operational television set in the village, at the time. As children we invited ourselves in to watch the only available channel, the Jamaica Broadcasting Corporation (JBC). We did not care that all we saw was news in the early part of the five hours of broadcast that started at 6:00 p.m.

The pastors of our churches were usually not from the districts in which they operated, and even though we moved, we had the same pastor until he was rotated. The central governing body of the church, the conference, had a policy of rotating pastors every three to five years. Pastors were the only paid church officials and ours was responsible for nine churches. Sometimes weeks would go by before the pastor visited. For the churches to function and perform their weekly activities, they relied on local leaders who were not college-trained theologians like the pastors were. These leaders supported the pastors' mission to grow the church and win more souls for Christ. The pastors were more visible at churches where there was a targeted crusade to grow church membership.

Johnson church pitched a large tent in the nearby district of Niagara with a mission to increase membership. On a Saturday afternoon, during one of the many Adventist Youth programs, my teacher, unknown to me, selected my name to do a presentation. I was surprised to hear my name bellowed over the public address system, tasked to recite all sixty-six books of the Bible.

I got up nervously, and I took the microphone. "The books of the Bible starting with the Old Testament are Genesis, Exodus, Leviticus, and Numbers . . ." I continued through the New Testament starting with Matthew, and when I ended with Revelation, I was again surprised by a loud "amen" and a standing ovation. My teacher and parents beamed. From then on, in every church we visited, my name would mysteriously appear on the program, and I would recite the books of the Bible.

ii.

During another uneventful afternoon after school, I walked to the back of the house to see the familiar sight of my mom bent over a tub of clothes and lathering away on a scrubbing board. She murmured under her breath, "That man . . . how did he manage to get stains on this shirt? Look at this," she continued. "How in God's name did he manage to get so much dirt and stains on this shirt?" As I walked over to look, she seemed startled by my presence. She was not inviting me to look, but was talking to herself. She dried her hands in her apron and looked at her fingernails, discolored and disfigured from repeated scrubbing and harsh detergents. "Where is your brother?" she asked. Before I could respond, she ordered me to go find him.

I knew she was talking about my younger brother Kenny. Conroy was the only other sibling living with us, and he was away at school in Elderslie, miles away. I walked around the house to see if Kenny was in sight. If he was not at home, he would be next door with the Browns. As I circled the house, I arrived at the window next to Banner's room.

"I didn't know Banner was home," I whispered to myself. The curtains were open, but the transparent louver windows were still shut. I peered in to get a closer look and thought the four eyes that stared back at me were my distorted reflection in the windowpanes. As I tried to refocus my eyes on the reflection, the outline became clear. Kenny's hiding place was revealed. Not only was he in Banner's bed, naked, but so was the neighbor's daughter.

"What are you doing naked in Banner's room?" I asked. I did not wait for an answer but summoned my mom, who got the girl dressed and walked her to her house.

"What were you doing?" I continued to ask Kenny who wore nothing but a sheepish grin on his face.

The thought of my younger brother in bed with a girl before I had contemplated any such move was pushed from thought as the sound of a vehicle approached. I watched the police jeep as it turned the corner and hummed its way up the hill.

The jeep passed my house and stopped in front of a small grocery shop in the town square. Police officers emerged from the vehicle and went inside the shop. Moments later, they got back into the jeep and drove back in the direction from which they had come. They rounded the corner and were almost out of sight when Natty B, a regular in the town, emerged from the banana plantation, below our house, with a machete in hand and shouted, "Babylon!" The term *Babylon* is a derogatory term used primarily by Rastafarians to describe the police as a corrupt system. Natty B was a mentally ill man whom people paid little attention to. He kept to himself, but carried a machete—typical of farmers. "Babylon," Natty B shouted again, and started running.

The jeep stopped and one officer got out. Natty B ran to the side of the road, picked up two rocks the size of baseballs, and tossed them at the officer. The officer pulled his gun and fired two shots, apparently to deter him. Natty B immediately gained supernatural strength and scaled the slopes between our house and the Browns' toward the thick woods. He continued running until he was out of sight. Moments later, curious onlookers gathered and retold their versions of the incidents. The police had not pursued Natty B in the bushes, but got back in the jeep and continued on their journey.

"What if he had shot any of the children?" someone asked.

"Well, thank the Lord no blood was shed," another said. "It could have been worse."

A gunshot in Johnson was still a topic of discussion when we attended Christmas service. Big Mac was acting as King Herod in one of the Christmas plays. King Herod gave an order to find and kill the newborn King of the Jews, Jesus, and moments later, Herod had a heart attack and fell to the ground. Four soldiers struggled to pick up the dead Herod. This was too much for Kenny, sitting in the front row next to Mom. He was not sure what was happening to his dad. Kenny jumped out of his seat and raced to rescue Big Mac. "Daddy," he cried repeatedly while kicking and biting each soldier until the dead Herod regained life and reassured Kenny he was okay. The audience erupted in laughter and spontaneous applause. "This is the best Christmas play I have seen," someone said, chuckling and patting Mom on the shoulder.

"I can't believe it," I whispered to Conroy. This is the same Kenny who was in bed with the neighbor's daughter, who didn't seem to know that Big Mac was acting in a play.

iii.

Weeks after Christmas, we were still playing Herod and teasing Kenny. While it rained, the household theater was in full swing.

"Stop the noise and playing in the house," Big Mac bellowed. The romping continued, and Big Mac became poetic. "If I lick you, you'll think a cow kicked you." Minutes later, he came into the room to carry out the licking. Conroy was first. With a leather belt, he fired a few lashes across Conroy's back. Mother intervened to tell Big Mac that Conroy had had enough, and was surprised when she found herself receiving lashes also. Mom became red with anger and left the house barefooted. Her bare feet left prints on the wet ground. It would be the first and last time that Big Mac would lay a hand on mother.

Mom left, unsure of where she was going. I was still in a daze. It was not unusual for us to be spanked. But striking Mom was a complete shock. Minutes later, Mom returned and Big Mac immediately left the house. I could feel the anger boiling inside me as I watched Conroy apply ointment to the swelling and bruises on Mom's back. Her soft skin highlighted the bruises and swelling. Conroy and Mom shared a special bond—not only because they share the same light complexion, but also because Conroy never met his father and Mom felt the extra need to protect him. I couldn't help feeling somewhat responsible for what had happened. After all, Conroy was playing with Kenny and me.

Days later, things were back to normal. I was not privy to how things were handled, but later learned that the church board had called a meeting and counseled my dad that men of God don't beat their wives. Apparently, children could suffer the beatings, as it is written "spare not the rod and spoil the child," but not the wives.

iv.

Every time my mom went away for a few days to visit other members of the family, Big Mac rearranged the house. It became a recurring theme. The changes he made could be slight or severe. They ranged from changing the direction of a bed, moving a cabinet to another corner, moving a picture on the wall, or all of the above. Mom did not seem to mind these changes. Initially, we were not sure if she had privately requested them. However, when she grumbled that Big Mac was looking for something, it became clear that the moving of furniture was Big Mac's initiative. Whatever Big Mac was looking for was found during Mom's visit to Kingston to see her sister. The evidence was so incriminating that he started packing his suitcase the morning after Mom's return.

It was early in the morning. He was dressed and ready to "catch" Confidence, the bus that traveled from Montego Bay to Mandeville daily. Catching the morning bus was not unusual, as he had recently obtained a job laying pipes at Revere, a bauxite processing plant some twenty miles away. However, this morning he had a suitcase, and Mom's fingers were latched onto the handle while she tried to appeal to him. The commotion signalled the help of the neighbors. Moments later, the church leader, Brother Ralph, and his wife, Sister Gwen, were both on the scene.

Big Mac let go and went back to the bedroom. Mom took the opportunity to hide the suitcase. Moments later, Big Mac returned and produced a copy of a deposit book for a savings account. He had found evidence of the secret savings account during his furniture rearranging. It was a joint savings account. The first name in the book was Mom's. The other name was not Big Mac's, but my brother Conroy's. The neighbors who had gathered seem to agree that having a savings account in a name other than the natural partner (wife and husband) was a concern. That agreement from the neighbors helped Big Mac regain some moral victory, and he calmed down.

In retrospect, it is clear that the neighbors were not just being nosy. Widows and other single mothers, old folks, and other destitutes were helped by the community. Neighbors gave money, food, vegetables, and other provisions from their modest farms. Reducing the likelihood of another destitute situation was a good strategy. Ralph, the church elder, pressed the case.

"Brother Mac, I understand where you are coming from. But if you leave, what will happen to the children?" Big Mac took a deep breath and did not respond. He needed that moral victory; he was still bruised from the scolding he received from striking his wife. Moments later, the horn of the Confidence sounded, and Big Mac left the house to catch it. No suitcase was in hand, an indication that he would return home that evening to his family.

V.

The wailings echoed across the hills and valleys: "Whoa, whoa, Lord, whoa."

"What happened?" someone asked. There were no residential telephones in these parts of rural Jamaica and shouting to each other was not uncommon.

"They found the little girl near the mouth of the river near Niagara . . . Laud Puppa Jesus."

The little girl in question was the twelve-year-old Metchess. She and her younger sister lived with their grandfather in Niagara, the adjoining district. Metchess's house was perched on the bank of the river, some distance from the main road. The family's nearest neighbor was some distance away but within shouting distance.

Three weeks prior, an intruder forced his way into their house, in the night during a rainstorm. The grandpa, who was almost fully blind, put up a gallant fight before he was pushed out of the house and down a ten-foot drop only a few feet from the river. Unable to see, the old man hugged a banana tree on the edge of the river, where he remained.

At daybreak, the old man was rescued by neighbors and led back to the house. He had shouted for help until he was hoarse. The pounding of the raindrops on the banana leaves and on the zinc roof drowned out his frail voice.

This story was recounted to several people (including my family) who visited Metchess's house after she was missing. It was speculated that a loner, Seril, had abducted her. Everyone loved Metchess; she was brilliant and sweet. It was rumored that on her way to school, she and her friends made a joke about Seril as they passed him.

Seril remarked, "I will give her something to laugh about." On a rainy night, he allegedly forced open the door of the house and pushed Metchess's grandpa down the ten-foot drop behind the house. Seril then went into the girls' room, and first picked up the little sister hiding under the bed. He realized his mistake and remarked, "I don't want you; I want your sister."

He then yanked Metchess out from under her bed while threatening to chop her with his machete if she made any noise. Next, he ripped the sheet from the bed and gagged her. He rolled her up in the remaining piece of bed linen and tossed her over his shoulder, and like a sack he carried her away.

Metchess kicked frantically and tried to scream. Nobody, apart from her terrified sister and half-blind grandfather, heard her screams.

After the neighbors learned what had happened, a search party was formed. Metchess was missing for several days before her body was discovered five miles upstream near the mouth of the river. It was rumored that Seril lived in a cave near the mouth of the river. After learning of the gruesome discovery, many villagers visited the site.

The journey to the site was off-road and accessible only by foot. I had not ventured that far in the woods before that day. There were a lot of people making their way toward the site. Parents ran ahead not realizing that the children would follow. We were dismissed from schools just minutes before the wailing began, and our teacher was ahead on the path.

The path was slippery, steep, and dangerous; the fact that it had rained the night before made the path more treacherous. Adults passed us and insisted that we (children) go back home. Each time, some students adhered, but others like me made a U-turn after the adults were out of sight. By the time I got to the site, a large crowd had gathered. The body was washed up on the bank of the river several feet below. The waterfall in the distance added to the whimpering and waling. The police had not yet arrived. I was more than fifty feet away, but could see that banana leaves were used to cover the body from the noonday sun.

The body appeared whitened and dismembered. Someone started a fire nearby and added green leaves to generate smoke that drove the flies away. Women wailed in unison, in what seemed like an effort to display who felt the most grief. I was working my way through the crowd to get a closer look when my mom grabbed me—her face was wet from perspiration and tears. She pulled me away from the site. Someone in the crowd started praying while the crying continued. Young men mumbled about what should happen to Seril when he was caught. The consensus was this was a very evil act, and it had touched the nerves of every member of the village.

We would leave Johnson before the murder was solved, but not before I had formed an opinion on the need for the death penalty.

CHAPTER 4:
TRINAIL

i.

Our next move was to Trinail, and as usual, the reasons were unclear. Was it Big Mac's desire to move closer to work? Did he want to move away from Johnson where his pride was still bruised after counseling from the elders? Was it Mom's desire to move closer to her mother and other siblings? Whatever the reason(s) were, we were moving again.

Living in Trinail had several advantages. The small two-room board house was situated on one hundred acres of land. Big Mac agreed to be the overseer of that property in lieu of paying rent. As an overseer, Big

Mac's major role was to help with the general upkeep of the property and prevent squatting and capturing. Capturing occurred if people laid claim to property that they did not own. With the passage of time, they could legally take ownership of a property if allowed to cultivate or live on the land for a long time without interference or reprimand from the actual landowner.

The property was mostly forest and mountains. However, some of the land was arable and sported fruit trees like breadfruit, mangoes, jackfruit, oranges, rose apples, and a lot of coconut trees. Since Mac was a big guy, he would not need to repeat himself if someone had to be asked to move.

Our new home had the advantage of being minutes from Maggotty and Revere Bauxite Company, where Big Mac worked. My sister Jenny and her husband, Patrick, also lived in Maggotty. They were now proud owners of their new baking and catering business. One of Jenny's biggest contracts was preparing meals for the workers at Revere Bauxite factory. In addition, Mom accepted a job and worked for her daughter, providing domestic help and child care.

Our dog Dash also loved it in Trinail. The proud terrier hunted and killed mongoose that preyed on young chickens. Chickens were reared organically before the practice became cool, and were often let out of their coops to go scratching for insects and other food sources. Natural corn and dinner leftovers, yams, bananas, and breadfruits were their main rations. After several days sitting on eggs and waiting for them to hatch, the hens did not rely solely on us for food. Each hen would teach her chicks how to hunt and be self-sufficient. It was fun watching the little chickens wobble as they learned how to scratch.

As the chickens scratched further and further away from the house, they would provide the mongoose an opportunity for a tender, sumptuous meal. We were usually alerted to danger by the sound of the mother hen fighting and pecking while complaining frantically with her clucking and crying. The sound would summon Dash into action, and he became the hen's hero. He loved the chase, and he was often very successful. Sometimes, the chase led Dash deep into the woods and out of sight. To prove his success, Dash often brought back his kill for me to see.

Years later when we obtained a second dog, I discovered something unusual. The hens were pecking at Dash when the dogs got near to them and the chickens. It took me days to find out the reason for this change in the hens' behavior. The new puppy had stolen eggs from the nesting hens and had broken their trust. From then on, the hens defended their chicks against dogs and mongooses. The egg-stealing retriever, not only broke the trust of the hens, but also earned herself a new name—Tricksty.

Despite the presence of other siblings, Dash became known as my dog. Since Big Mac's method of discipline was not confined to discussions or appeals to reason, Dash became fiercely protective of me. I loved him even more.

Big Mac's leather belt used to "instil discipline" did not get activated for "legitimate" reasons. Dash's defense, however, was more predictable. One evening, the dog sprang into action to defend me against Big Mac's belt. Big Mac retaliated, but Dash was too quick. He dodged the lashes from Big Mac's belt and kept attacking until Big Mac was exhausted and gave up the beating.

Compared to my other siblings, my beatings were infrequent. Many believed that my father favored me. The fact that many of my other siblings were not his offspring provided more credibility to that argument. Apart from Conroy, none of the others stayed with us permanently. Those who were not already adults stayed with their fathers' side of the family, usually with a grandmother.

In our two-bedroom house, all the children would pile into the same bed. This could range from three to six of us depending on how many other half siblings were visiting. Mom was forced to patch the sheets torn from being pulled in several directions, and thus our special quilted sheets were developed for protection against the bites of hungry mosquitoes, and for warmth.

Mikey and Collin visited often and sometimes stayed for months during the summer. Collin and Conroy were very athletic and quite helpful around the farm. Mikey was fragile, a chronic asthmatic. He was always wheezing. Mikey was liked by many. He had good verbal skills and was a great debater. Big Mac got along well with Mikey for many reasons. Mikey engaged him in theological discussion and was very respectful, and I am sure Big Mac felt sorry for him.

With all these brothers, I started to feel a certain kinship with the biblical Joseph. I never focused on the fact that Joseph was hated by his brothers because of the favoritism and love shown by his father, Jacob. I became more loyal to Big Mac, not only because I was fearful of his leather belt, but also because I wanted to honor my father and please God. I took to heart the scripture that reads, "Children, obey your parents in the Lord for this is right. Honor thy father and mother that *thy days may be long upon the land* which the Lord thy God giveth thee." It was clear to me that if I wanted to live long and avoid being beaten, I should obey.

My loyalty was not appreciated by my siblings, who got in trouble each time I made a report of the day's proceedings to Big Mac. To make matters worse, I did not do this in secrecy, but with my siblings present. This brutal honesty was not only disarming, but unsettling to them.

My parents, of course, used the younger children as their private eyes. When our sisters visited, for example, we would get commands such as, "Go find your sister and tell her to come and help me prepare dinner."

If I found Marlene with a boy, the boy would ask us to lie that we didn't find them. Since I didn't believe in lying, this would present a dilemma. After all, the Bible said, "Lying lips were an abomination to the Lord." To overcome this dilemma, I would tell Mom, "Paul (a name of one of the boys) said that I should tell you that I didn't find them." Many times, Mom did not catch the play on words since the "Paul said" part of the statement would be said under my breath, followed by a more amplified, "I didn't find them."

I noticed that Kenny and I were being sent on several fruitless errands, sometimes by our male siblings, but mostly by our sisters' boyfriends. The intent of these errands was to save the chatterbox from himself. If I was not around, then I would have nothing to report. The boyfriends mostly hang around when my sisters Marlene and

Beverly visited. These men were extremely nice to Kenny and me. We often got spare change to buy sweets and candy at the nearby shop. Surprisingly, if we returned from the shops too quickly, we would be given money and asked to go shopping again. Even though my single sisters, Marlene and Bev, had their first children away from home, I often wondered if my shopping experiences bore any responsibility for their pregnancies.

ii.

The mule and the donkey were also part of the family in Trinail. Dad rode the mule to work and used the donkey, Lizy, to carry farm produce and other heavy items. Lizy in heat was a situation that generated a lot of interest, not only to us, but also to boys around the district. We were on a farm and had seen mating between the cocks and hens, the ram and the ewe, the goats, and other animals. The size and power of the donkeys and larger animals engaged in sexual acts provided our version of pornography. Kids gathered to watch. All that was missing was popcorn, but that was substituted with Brown Draws. Brown Draws is corn parched and then pounded to powder, then sieved and mixed with sugar.

Lizy became pregnant and gave birth to a spirited cub. Days after the birth, Conroy decided it was time to ride the cub. He chased it all over the property and succeeded in jumping on its back. The cub ran and kicked frantically until Conroy was dislodged. No matter how many times he was thrown, Conroy landed on his feet. As soon as Dad got home from work, he got the report from Joseph the chatterbox with stories of many colors. "Daddy, Conroy rode Lizy's cub today."

In the eyes of his younger brothers, Conroy was superman. He outraced the other boys, and showed skills not only in running, but also in mud skating and climbing. He could climb his way up a sixty- to one hundred–foot coconut tree without much effort.

I somehow did not possess that athletic ability. I didn't climb or run very well. My need to learn to climb was reinforced when we found a prized fruit, the jackfruit, on the property. We could never get enough of the jackfruit. The fruit's sweet, succulent flesh was a delight to eat. The smell was not so delightful; it smelled of very ripe bananas with a tinge of rotten garlic that remained with you for hours, advertising to all who came close what you had just eaten. On a few occasions, Mom cooked or roasted the seeds, which were also edible. The gut that held the edible flesh could also be cooked to make a tasty meal, but most times it was discarded.

Conroy found the ripe jackfruit and we chased him to get a piece. He climbed up an orange tree and told Kenny and me that if we wanted a piece, we would have to climb for it. He tossed the gut down from time to time in mocking response as we begged. He smacked his lips to emphasize the tastiness of the fruit as he ate. Later, Collin joined him, and they shared the fruit. I tried with all I had to climb the tree. I finally succeeded, and by the time I got to the second limb, the Jackfruit feast had ended. "I bet you are going to tell your daddy about this?" Conroy said.

"No, I am not," I replied. In reality, I didn't need to. I had lost interest in being the chatterbox; my younger brother had now assumed that role in providing Dad with thc updatc of thc day.

While I was not yet a good climber, Conroy noticed my aptitude to trap birds. There were several methods used to trap birds. We could shoot them with a sling-shot (catapult) made from sticks and tubes from old tires. A calabash (a basket) was also used to trap the ground doves.

My most successful method was the "Broke Neck." A half of a fruit, such as an orange, would be tied to the limb of a tree twenty feet from the ground. Inches from the open side of the fruit was a noose made from a vine that extended all the way to the ground. I would hold the end of the vine and wait. As birds came to eat, they would peck at the fruit through the loop. My timing was almost perfect. Our division of labor strategy proved successful for several months; Conroy climbed and set the traps, and I executed. We feasted on a variety of roasted birds until mangoes were in season.

From an early age eating plants and birds, and milking cows and goats, I learned how to survive on the land.

iii.

There are several stories and folk songs that describe mango season in Jamaica. One of the most famous is "Mango Time."

> Mi nuh drink coffee tea mango time
> Care how nice it may be mango time
> In the heat of the mango crop

When di fruit dem a ripe an drop
Wash your pot turn dem down mango time

De terpentine large an fine, mango time
Robin mango so sweet, mango time
Number eleven an hairy skin
Pack di bankra an ram dem in
For di bankra mus' full, mango time

Mek wi go a mango walk, mango time
For is only di talk mango time
Mek wi jump pon di big jackass
Ride im dung an no tap a pass
Mek di best a di crop, mango time

The song essentially suggests that during mango season, all cooking and drinking of coffee and tea ceases. Everyone instead feasts on several varieties of mangoes.

The mango season had ended, yet we found a tree with a number of the prized fruits still attached. In lieu of climbing, we sometimes tossed stones at the mangoes. This was not an efficient method, as we succeeded in getting mature ripe mangoes as well as those not ready for harvesting. We decided this would be a perfect tree to trap the birds. Conroy, as usual, climbed up and picked a few mangoes and tossed them down. I caught each of them and stored them at the root.

Before I could position myself for the next catch, Conroy had made it down by swinging from branch to branch and uttering expletives. He was followed by a swarm of angry wasps. We ran away leaving the loot, and I was sure I could hear the birds in the nearby tree laughing and relating the stories to one another about what had just happened to the boys who roasted so many of their friends.

I was not stung, but Conroy's face was swelling fast. His right eye was almost closed and his lips looked like a piece of beef liver. The sting was the least of his humiliation. He was later teased by his siblings and friends that he had been kissed by Red Gals (wasps). There would be no visit to the clinic or medications. When you were kissed by Red Gals, you just waited for the swelling to go down. If it really hurt, you could rub some alcohol or kerosene oil on the sting.

iv.

It had rained all night. At daybreak, we discovered that the path that led to Big Mac's callaloo garden was blocked by a breadfruit tree that fell during the rainstorm. Callaloo is a green leafy vegetable, and like spinach, it is cooked and eaten. Dad left for work early, and Mom was home washing and mending. I picked up a machete and started chopping to clear away the branches that blocked the path.

Kenny came by and tried to help. He tried to remove the chips from the large branch that I was chopping. I was committed to the next chop with the machete above my head. My eyes received the signal, and my brain sent the message to stop or divert. The only problem was force and gravity. The machete caught the back of Kenny's hand. First, he was silent as we recovered from the state of shock, and then the wailing followed. I was successful in slowing down the force, but not enough to prevent a two-inch cut on the back of his hand. Mom came running and dressed and bandaged the wound. That evening, Dad barely made it up the hill on his mule before Kenny reported the day's activity. "Daddy, Joe chopped me with the big machete." For the first time, I felt empathy for my older siblings and retribution for the many reports that I conveyed about them to my father. I also understood that truth is not just a repetition of facts, but how those facts are shaped. My only consolation was that Big Mac just cautioned me to be careful with the machete. He knew I was trying to help.

V.

It was my first day attending Ms. Emmer's basic school in Harmony Hall. As we walked home, one of the boys came up with a game called "Touch Cars." We attempted to touch the cars as they passed by. Not many cars frequented the area. We had just turned off the paved road onto a graveled road that would complete our walk home, and on this road, there were few or no cars. Suddenly, a car sounded on the road that we had just left, and I ran down the hill to touch the car.

But I didn't check my speed, and slammed into the side of the car. The driver, Mr. Butcher, simultaneously slammed on his brakes, and then got out of his car and started cursing. He knew what we were doing and the danger involved. He was livid. I was not a sprinter, but on that day, I realized my marathon skills; I ran two miles—nonstop—all the way home.

Schooling at Ms. Emmer's did not last long. Dad wanted us to get a Christian education, so he sent us to Jointwood SDA School—seven miles away. There were no school buses. We got on the regular passenger bus whose timing was anything but regular. It made several stops along the way to Montego Bay. If we missed the bus or did not have enough fare, we would walk or "beg a ride" from passing vehicles. Oftentimes, we jumped on the back of a passing dump truck filled with sand or marl used in road repairs or construction of houses. Conroy would almost always catch the trucks, but would have to get off in disgust because I couldn't run fast enough to catch them. Since we were stealing a ride, we couldn't rely on the driver to stop when it was time to get off.

The area where we lived was mountainous, and a loaded truck would ascend the hills slowly. When it navigated a corner, it would travel more slowly. Getting on was easy! Getting off was the challenging part. I learned the art of getting off only after several times tripping and bruising my knees and chin. As painful as those bruises were, you kept them to yourself if no one saw. Showing your cuts and bruises and skin peeled off your knees inspired laughter, not sympathy. The laughing came from brothers and friends alike. Someone would call out your name followed by ". . . peel up" and a chorus of laughter. Since you were not supposed to be hopping onto a truck, you kept the bruises from your parents, also. Telling Mom or Dad would win a spanking—just in case the bruises had not provided enough of a lesson. Since we would be punished if we got to school late, we would often make the trade-off.

My most dramatic hopping lesson would come not on my way to school, but on my way from the grocery shop. I was in the company of Conroy and Kenny, and as the empty truck came up, I made a run for it. I was proud of myself since I caught it and Conroy didn't. It didn't occur to me that Conroy was not giving it his best effort since he knew Kenny, the youngest, would not be able to catch it.

The driver also sped up to elude boys trying to hop on. I hung on for a quarter of a mile and realized that I did not have the upper body strength to pull myself up to the back of the truck where I could stand or rest my feet to reduce the load on my arms. Since the truck was empty, the driver increased speed. I was swaying until gravity got the best of me, and I let go.

My feet hit the ground, but physics was not on my side. For every action there is an equal and opposite reaction. I made a couple summersaults before coming to rest on my knees and chin. I sprang up quickly and looked around to determine if anyone had seen me. No one had. I sat on a stone on the side of the road and spat on the area of my knee where my pants and skin were missing. I waited for the pain to ease and to give Conroy and Kenny an opportunity to catch up. I tried on my best poker face as they approached, and I joined them walking. Conroy's face had a look of respect until he saw the gingerly way that I was walking.

"You peel up?" he asked. Before I had the chance to answer, they started laughing. The laughter stopped only when he rolled up my pants and saw the condition of my knee.

Ripped jeans became a world fashion statement in the 80s and 90s as brand names fetched millions. As part of the designs, holes were deliberately punched and then sewn over with a different color cloth. I suspect that these fashion ideas were inspired by kids like us, whose moms tried hard to keep us clothed as our clothes unraveled from our extreme activities. The difference with the fashions of ripped jeans and other styled clothes is that they are worn for style. We wore rips out of necessity, and the zigzag darns and designs were exclusively by the designer, Adora (Mom).

I still remember being laughed at after my mom apparently tossed on a red patch onto blue crimplene pants that I wore. There were already several patches. This one stood out because it was bright red and almost covered the right side of my behind. A bunch of boys tried to outdo each other in comedy. They ran behind me and in unison let out a screeching braking sound. They were dying for me to ask, so I indulged them. "Why are you running behind me and braking?"

"Well, your break light is on, and we don't want a rear-end collision," they replied.

Today, I still cannot get over the irony that we spent so much time and energy trying to keep our backsides covered, while it is now hip to wear your pants loosely, so they fall down and expose your underwear.

vi.

We continued to attend Cedar Spring church some distance away, even though the Adventist church in Maggotty was closer. Dad was now one of the leaders and made sure we followed the principles of the church. "Remember the Sabbath day to keep it holy, six days shall thou labor and do all thy work, but the seventh day is the Sabbath of the Lord thy God, in it thou shall not do any work." When my other siblings visited, they discovered that these rules also applied to them. Since the fourth commandment was the basic Judeo-Christian difference between our denomination and other protestant churches, it triggered a number of debates about which church was the true church.

In addition, we did not eat pork or any other unclean meat. A number of our neighbors reared pigs, and they were not highly regarded by Big Mac. However, given the size of the land we were on, we had ample space, and the pigs were not a problem, except for the neighbors to the east, the Clarks.

The Clarks maintained a sty of pigs that was fenced off and fed organic material. One Sunday afternoon after a heavy downpour of rain, the soil was soft, and one of the hogs dug its way out of the sty and made its way several yards to Big Mac's callaloo garden.

Big Mac was consumed with righteous indignation as he grabbed the hog and held a kitchen knife to its throat. The hog squealed, and the neighbor, Ms. Clarice, called out in a vain attempt to get Big Mac's attention. There was no fence between the properties, but she obviously did not want to trespass. Her son, Audley, was also by her side. I was standing next to Dad and called out to him, but I was also ignored. When the squealing stopped, Ms. Clarice spoke in a clear but disdainful and distraught voice.

"Mr. Mac, from where I am standing, I could hear your own son calling out to you. Yet, you ignored us and killed my pig. You call yourself a Christian, and yet this is how you treat your neighbor." This last statement stung my dad. His facial expression betrayed his realization that he again had acted on impulse, but he was too proud to admit it, let alone apologize. Ms. Clarice walked away toward her house still complaining, "He always wants people to have Bible study with him; he believes swine is unclean and you shouldn't touch it; yet, he never had a problem grabbing it to kill it."

Ms. Clarice was referring to Dad's many requests to have Bible study with her or anyone who would agree. (In one of his Bible studies, Dad had pointed out why pig meat was unclean. In Leviticus chapter 11, God had given Moses guidelines to let the people of God know what animals should or should not be eaten. Only animals that chewed their cud and had parted hooves should be eaten. Pig was unclean because pigs did not chew the cud, even though their hooves were parted).

Mom learned of the pig killing and fought hard to control her tongue. Ms. Clarice was a widow with five children. She was not destitute. Her two boys, Desmond and Audley, were grown, and they and their mother took care of the girls. They lived in a better house than we did and were building a brick house next to it.

The hog was still on the ground at nightfall. No one had come to remove it. We children started a theological discussion. If the Bible was to be taken literally, how were we supposed to get rid of the pig? The Bible said we shouldn't touch it. Was the ground on which the blood drained now unclean? Could we still eat the callaloo?

At daybreak, we went about our chores taking the "clean" animals, the goats, out to pasture. My brother and I walked by the garden and noticed that the pig had gotten very stiff. Apparently, Big Mac had heard our theological discussion. On our way back from setting the goats on a fresh patch of grass, we saw Big Mac with a long pole, rolling the pig into Ms. Clarice's yard. The unclean beast was now Desmond or Audley's problem.

Needless to say, our relationship with this neighbor was strained for months.

The incident provided me an early glimpse into how people with religious zeal and good intentions and the desire to live a pure life in heaven can be intolerant and unsympathetic to their neighbors here on earth.

CHAPTER 5: **HARMONY HALL**

i.

"Are we moving again? Where are we going to now?" Kenny asked.

"Harmony Hall" was the answer. It was not unusual for Big Mac to act impulsively. However, no one expected him to purchase a house without telling Mom. The house that Dad bought was still under construction, and the roof was not yet added. Like many rural buildings in Jamaica, it was owner-constructed.

This kind of construction can take years, even a lifetime. The plan was to move into a rented house near the new construction site and work on building our house. We packed everything into the rented Leyland truck and moved.

Riding on the rear of dump trucks was not unusual for us boys. This time, however, it was legitimate, since we were not hopping on for a ride. Dash did not like being thrown in the back of the truck and protested. Once he was onboard, he calmed down.

The new house was made of concrete blocks and was more spacious. It boasted a veranda, a dining room, three bedrooms, and a barbeque platform, primarily used to dry pimento or coffee. Like the house in Trinail, this house had no electricity, no indoor plumbing, and of course no telephone. Unlike Trinail, we had to pay rent.

If Mom was upset with the decision to move or buy the new place, she didn't show it. I guess when coming from a two-room board house, anything was better. We would be only three miles from Trinail, and Dad continued to oversee the property.

It was while at the rented house in Harmony Hal, that I was told I would have a birthday party for my seventh birthday. The party actually coincided with a housewarming party at our new house, but I had no problem claiming it as a birthday party when it was presented as such. I couldn't recall having a birthday party before. Neither did my other siblings or children we knew. It was my first celebration as a child and also my last. We never felt deprived since we didn't know what we were missing.

In preparation for the party, my parents cooked curried goat, rice and peas, chicken, ackee and salt fish (codfish), and other Jamaican culinary delights. Dad roasted corn, yams, and sweet potatoes. Mom baked cakes, and sweet potato pudding, and toeto (a heavier version of a cake). The method used for baking was described locally as "Hell a Bottom, Hell a Top, and Hallelujah inna de middle." A large iron pot was the oven. Fire was made, and the pot placed on the fire. The pudding mixture was put into the pot and covered, and fire coals were put onto the cover of the pot. The fire at the bottom and the hot coals on the pot cover were considered hell. The sumptuous-tasting pudding in the middle was the hallelujah.

Relatives and friends from church brought other Jamaican dishes, such as fritters and tie leaf. For drinks, we had ginger beer, lemonade, and sorrel. The sorrel was out of season, but it was dried and preserved and then steeped when it was ready to be used. We also had ice cream. Since there was no electricity in the area, a manual hand-cranked bucket was solicited to make the ice cream.

Because we were indoctrinated to avoid "worldly music," I was very surprised when Big Mac provided secular music from his record player. We were aware of contemporary hits since we were regular radio listeners. The battery-powered radio that we listened to daily was our source for news, information, and sports, specifically the country's favorite pastime, cricket. The pulsating reggae, calypso, and other contemporary music that made up the weekly top ten was a necessary sacrifice to obtain news and information. Among the music played were all the finalists for that year's festival completion, including the winner, the number one singer with the number one song, Tinga Stewart's "Play De Music" of 1974.

Uncle Bengy ina de yard
Sit down pon a stone
Wife and pickney gone abroad
left him all alone

When the chorus came, all my pent-up dancing released. I danced, watching my shadow on the wall cast by the light of the kerosene Coleman lantern that we lit only on special occasions. If Dad was playing, I certainly could dance. God wouldn't mind since it was my birthday; "play the music."

ii.

Some of the boys that we played with were Enzert, Frankie, and Lynval. We discovered a special type of grass on a slope behind our newly rented house. We had not seen this type of grass before, and we called it oily grass. The name for the grass emerged after we discovered the speed that we were able to travel when we sat astride the bow from the coconut tree (like a snowboard), and slid down the hill. Some sections of the bow were too narrow to seat us properly and comfortably. Comfort of course was not the objective. As we climbed up the hill after each slide, we felt the fresh air circulating in our pants from the new holes that were created. Mom's patching and darning skills would always be in great demand.

One afternoon, Frankie and I decided to go bird hunting and exploring. Our mission took us deeper and deeper into cockpit country, areas of inland Jamaica known for their rugged terrain. As we made our way deeper and deeper into the woods, we shouted each other's names and listened to the echoes bouncing across the hills and valleys. Of course this was not a good hunting technique, as the birds stayed clear of our immediate vicinity. We became aware of this counterproductive effort as the climb got steeper and the wood thicker.

We came upon a cave, or rather, a sinkhole. We tossed several pebbles into the cave and listened to each stone hit the walls for several seconds as it descended deep into the bowels of the earth.

"Wow! That has to be over five-hundred feet?" I said.

"Yea, mon!" Frankie responded. "That is much deeper than our toilet." Frankie's father had utilized one of the sinkholes near his house for an outhouse.

We shouted in the hole and heard prized birds scampering from one of the trees that formed a thick cluster directly above our heads. "That was a baldpate," Frankie said. "You shouldn't make so much noise," he continued.

"You were making noise also," I protested. We peered through a small opening above trying to get the general direction of where the birds went. They stopped some distance away, and we followed. We had a general agreement that we would both be quiet.

We continued the hike for what seemed like hours and whispered when we spoke. As we progressed, we stooped and walked on hands and knees as we navigated our way through the thick and steep forest. We ended up in an opening where there were suddenly no trees above our heads. As we looked around, it was obvious that this football field–sized clearing in the woods did not occur naturally. The plants in this opening were all the same size, approximately our height.

The smell of something burning was in the air, and we looked around to find the source. The occasional coils of smoke seemed to be coming from one of the trees at the opposite side of the opening. We inched closer, and the outline of a hammock came into view. Above the hammock came the occasionally burst of smoke. Frankie froze, and we looked at each other.

We had smelled that pungent smell before. We surveyed the plants around us, only this time, more closely. I had seen the leaves of the plant before, but never the entire plant. It was unmistakable; we were standing in the middle of someone's marijuana plantation. Anyone who had made such an effort to carve out this area in the middle of the woods to conceal this crop was not going to be welcoming.

With our eyes fixed on the hammock, we started walking backwards until a dry branch cracked beneath the barefooted Frankie. The sound was deafening. We froze simultaneously as the outline of the Rastafarian in the hammock sprang into view like a zombie from a scene from *Tales from the Crypt.*

"Who that?" he bellowed as his head and locks swirled from side to side in an attempt to ascertain the direction from which the sound came. We did not wait around to introduce ourselves, but made a hasty retreat, knocking over a few plants as we exited the area. Frankie was the older of the two of us and was usually quicker and a better athlete. On this day, however, I was in front, and I did not surrender the lead. My state of mind was also a motivator in my effort to flee. I was not sure if the footsteps behind me were Frankie's or our pursuer's.

I visualized a huge machete above my head trying to catch up with me to dislodge my head from my body, or a gun trying to get a proper aim. I recalled Metchess's dismembered body near the river. The more I imagined, the less attention I paid to the bruises and scratches on my feet. Frankie's house came up first, and he was panting as he ran into his yard. Normally, I would stop; but today, home was my only refuge.

CHAPTER 6: **TRINAIL AND JOINTWOOD PRIMARY**

i.

Our time in Harmony Hall was short lived. Big Mac lost his job when the bauxite factory started cutting back and eventually closed. Hundreds lost their jobs. We moved back to Trinail. The house he had bought would not be finished anytime soon. Big Mac resumed sawing wood and Mom increased the number of days she worked with her daughter.

I had developed an interest in reading. *The Hardy Boys* became my favorite. I got these books from a Library on Wheels that visited the district every two weeks. Dad noticed my interest in reading, and while he was not opposed to it, he wanted me to read more spiritual books. He bought me the *Story of Jesus*. I was not opposed to reading this book, but since I already knew how the story ended, I was not in a hurry. I was active in church, and I had read and heard several sermons about Jesus. In fact, a group of us had decided to read the Bible in a year. I had discovered that Matthew, Mark, Luke, and John all contained a different vantage point of the same story.

Big Mac was not pleased when he asked me why I was not reading some of Ellen G. White's books. I tried explaining that those books were for adults, but he was not having it. He suggested Ellen G. White's *Messages to Young People* was applicable to me. Those books were for young adults, but at the time, I didn't find them interesting. Before long, my library card went missing, and I confronted my dad about hiding my library card. It was several weeks later before I found it. Someone had forced it between the space in the floorboard, and it landed beneath the house.

Exploring beyond my immediate vicinity had risk, as my trip deep into the woods had proven. However, I didn't anticipate that exploring the world through the pages of books would encounter resistance. This incident, however, would only be a temporary setback in my desire to explore.

ii.

I was excited, traveling with Grandma to visit her daughter Eunice (Nicey) in the big city, Kingston, the capital. I slept very little the night before the trip. We got to Maggotty early that morning and went with Mom up to Jenny's house (where she worked) and waited for the train. We were sipping a cup of homemade "chocolate tea" when the horn of the train sounded. (Many Jamaicans refer to hot beverages as tea. It is not uncommon to hear request for coffee tea, chocolate tea, cocoa tea, and fish tea).

Grandma dropped the cup, and we scampered to the station. Grandma's son Johnny was pushing Grandma, trying to get her to hurry. He cursed all the way, wondering why we had sat for tea instead of going directly to the station. The conductor held the train for grandma and she collapsed into a seat, breathing heavily. I looked around for the bags and noticed that two pieces were not on board. The bunch of banana and other food provisions that we were taking for aunt Nicey had made it, but not all the bags. How are we going to make it without clothes? I wondered. I told Grandma, and she was now very concerned. I then told her not to worry, that God would take care of it, and I whispered a prayer that God would get our bags on the train.

We approached Appleton station—near the Appleton estate sugar factory and home of the Appleton Rum. God had to answer my prayer, I thought. After all, I had heard several sermons about how God had answered prayers. As we pulled slowly into the station, a fast-moving blue car caught my attention. It was a blue Ford Capri that looked like the one Jenny drove. As it came closer, I could see her outline, and in the seat next to her was Mom. Jenny was honking the horn, and I waved at them through the widow. We met them at the door and took our bags, as the train pulled off. I went to Grandma and proudly announced that the reason they had come was because I had prayed. She smiled and started dancing to the sound of the rhythm of the train on the track. When I looked at her, she stopped; and when I looked away, she started again. She put a handkerchief over her mouth and laughed when our eyes met. "Grandma Mary and Joseph off to Kingston," she said as she tapped me on the head.

iii.

While we were away from Trinail, the mice did play. When I returned from Kingston, I was greeted with the news that Collin and Conroy had discovered a plantation of marijuana on the property, deep in the woods. Audley, a neighbor, was believed to be responsible. Big Mac was not amused.

The relationship with our nearest neighbor had not fully healed since the slaughter of the pig, and it was about to take another bad turn. Conroy, Collin, and I were playing in Audley's yard. Audley was smoking a cigarette, and Conroy and Collin took a puff. They puffed and puffed, and I asked to join the experiment. No sooner had I taken a puff than someone shouted, "Big Mac is coming." Audley grabbed the cigarette and continued smoking. I could not conceal the evidence however. The smoke poured from my nose and mouth with each cough and breath exhaled, in plain sight for Big Mac to see.

"Are you smoking?" Big Mac asked. Without waiting for me to answer, he turned to Audley and threatened to knock every tooth from his mouth if he gave his son another cigarette.

I knew then that I wouldn't smoke again for a number of reasons. Firstly, I didn't like the taste of the cigarette. Secondly, I was concerned for the safety of Audley and my siblings. I did not want them to have a meeting with Big Mac's fist of fury. Thirdly, I believed in a Bible verse constantly paraphrased by Big Mac: "Your body is the temple of God and you should not put impurities in it (like cigarettes, ganja, and alcohol) to defile it." Of course, you could take a little drink for the stomach's sake like the rum and lime that was given to me when I had the flu; the stout mixed eggs, milk, and carrot juice or raw oats that my brother told me could strengthen my back and improve virility; sorrel tempered with a little spirit at Christmas. Whatever the motivation, I never had the desire to continue the smoking experiment. As far as marijuana was concerned, second-hand smoke provided enough knowledge to satisfy any inclination to experiment.

iv.

Four of us walked home for the last four miles of the six-mile journey. The posse was John, his brother Horatio, my brother Conroy, and I. I was the youngest in the group. We played several games to pass the time and cover the distance. These games usually involved throwing stones. One of our favorites was "Ten Twenty."

Each member of the group chose a stone. After it was decided who would throw first, that first stone was thrown several feet ahead on the road. With our individual stones, we then each took turns trying to hit the stone, and then the furthest stone ahead. Each hit equaled a score of ten points. The first person to get to one hundred points won the game.

After we had gotten tired of the game, I was almost always provoked into a fight with Horatio. Horatio almost always won. He won not because I was afraid of him. Yes he was older, and thicker, but he won because I didn't believe in fighting. After all, Jesus didn't believe in fighting.

John and Conroy got tired of breaking us up, and they told me that I needed to kick Horatio's ass, so that he would stop pestering me. John emphasized the point: "As Horatio's older brother, I am telling you that is the only way to get him to stop bothering you!"

One evening as we played the game "Ten Twenty," Horatio set his books down to take aim at my rock. His book slipped into the ravine and fell some fifty feet below. Everyone laughed except me. While I found it amusing, and poetic justice, I declared that this is not what Jesus would do; and as much as Horatio would pick on me, I should not "render evil for evil." Such statements angered Conroy who thought I was taking this religious thing too far. If I didn't kick Horatio's ass, he would never stop picking on me. Before long, the ridicule shifted from Horatio to me.

"Who are you?" they asked, "God's Son?" Ironically, I had always wanted to be known as a child of God, but I did not find the nickname "God's Son" flattering. Even Horatio forgot his humiliation of losing all his books and joined in the ridicule. He slapped my face to see if, like Jesus, I would turn the other cheek.

Conroy looked away. He would not defend me anymore. I prayed silently for God to stop Horatio from bothering me, but the teasing continued.

V.

The year 1974 was a pivotal year. That year, the Michael Manley government declared that it was pursuing a policy of democratic socialism. Prime Minister Manley strengthened ties with Cuba, and many feared a communist outcome. Despite the denial of any communist intentions, the migration of the wealthy and highly skilled began, and many wondered if this was the same government that was swept into power on a landslide only two years earlier.

Manley pursued several grassroots programs that benefitted the poor. However, money was needed to fund these programs. The government targeted the main foreign exchange earner and doubled the levy charged on bauxite mining companies. In addition, there was a tax charged for a percentage of aluminium exported. All the bauxite companies in Jamaica protested and tried to negotiate with the Jamaican government. The Michael Manley government held firm, and the companies paid the taxes under protest. The companies also feared nationalization because the government was criticized for being too cozy with Castro.

The bauxite levy, coupled with increasing oil prices, fueled the exodus of bauxite mining companies and other foreign investors from Jamaica to other countries like Australia, and dealt a blow on the country's main industry and foreign exchange earner. One of the first companies to fold was Revere, the plant where Big Mac worked. The plant was smaller than the others and did not have the economies of scale to handle the increased cost. In addition, it was inefficient and suffered from numerous disruptions caused by poor design and union-induced sabotage. I met Bumpy, one of these saboteurs, several years later, who boastfully admitted acts of sabotage at the behest of union bosses and aspiring political leaders.

Bumpy told stories how he and others knocked out motors that disrupted conveyor belts that kicked production offline for days while the workers continued to receive pay. Bumpy was called bumpy because of the numerous bumps and blows he received to his head in one of his failed efforts to carry out his bosses' wishes at the cement company in Kingston. He was chased and beaten by groups of men opposing the behavior. He barely escaped with his life. It was lost on men like Bumpy how their actions disrupted the lives, including their own. Unions' representation helped to bolster the middle class in Jamaica. However, when leaders seeking power utilized unions as proxies in political fights, those efforts could be destructive.

In 1974, Ali and George Foreman rumbled in the jungle. I, like the rest of the world, was swept up in the brilliant marketing effort of the boxing promoters. We did not have television or electricity, so I went to a neighbor's house to see the fight. After watching the Saturday night's regular, *Little House and the Prairie*, the fight started. Like many, I supported the charismatic Ali over Foreman. I was inspired by the way Ali danced around and taunted his opponent.

That Monday after the fight, I went to school still celebrating Ali's win. At break, I went outside to play; and as usual, Horatio started harassing me. I bobbed, weaved, and he laughed.

"Who do you think you are, Ali?" He charged, and I sent him back with two left jabs to his face in quick succession. A crowd gathered and started cheering. From the corners of my eyes, I saw Conroy, my brother, and he was loving this. Horatio was humiliated, but was not a quitter. He moved in before an uppercut sent him staggering back. He was charging again before I decided punches would not be sufficient. I employed Bruce Lee's flying kick, which sent him on his back. As I rushed toward him, I was grabbed from behind by some older boys who had decided it was time to break up the fight. But the effort was enough to restore self-respect.

"Did you see that?" someone asked. "God's Son was fighting back, fist of fury." Several days passed, and I noticed that the harassment from Horatio ceased. My prayer had been answered not the way I expected, with the angels coming down and defending me. I didn't like fighting, but the lesson was clear: some things are worth fighting for. Standing up to bullies is not always just about self-respect, it is also about survival.

While Big Mac was fearless, he and others who worked at Revere often wondered how different their lives and the lives of their families would have been if they had acted against the agenda that people like Bumpy tried to enforce.

<u>Lesson 1:</u> Some things are worth fighting for.

vi.

The decision was made that we would start attending the government school, Retirement Primary. It was a bigger school than the religious school we attended in Jointwood. Unlike Jointwood, there was no requirement to pay a school fee. Conroy was now attending the Maggotty Secondary School.

I dreaded attending Retirement. I had heard stories of teachers feared because of the way they beat their students. Ms. Hazel, though petite, was larger than life and the talk around town. I felt lucky to have skipped her class because I was older than the grade she taught, grade one.

Some parents believed that the more a teacher beat students, the better they learned. Thus, beatings, for some parents, provided evidence of a good teacher. One story told about Ms. Hazel was how she taught her students to spell the word *more*. As students sang and spelled the word M-O-R-E, she would inquire if they wanted more, and applied more licks. I was generally well behaved and did not receive frequent spankings. However, when attending school, I was terrified of most of my teachers and had difficulty focusing while I was in class.

The schoolhouse at Retirement was a giant room, and each class was separated by chalkboards and other dividers. These dividers could be pushed back at anytime to create an auditorium for general meetings. On any given day, my terror was increased by the amplified screams of children getting spanked.

Some boys were pretty tough and refused to cry or be broken. Of course, that behavior only invited more lashes. I was not one of those tough guys. I cried at the sight of the belt. I remember not completing an assignment and having one teacher remark, "Why are you crying when I haven't touched you yet?"

I generally liked school; however, while at Retirement Primary, the high point of my day was going home. Usually I would leave class with a splitting headache. At my previous school in Jointwood, there were beatings, also. In fact, one teacher had a raw leather belt called the "Knuckle Duster." However, because Jointwood was a religious private school, there was a smaller teacher-to-student ratio, and teachers exercised better control. At Retirement, it was all business, and students had to be prepared for the common entrance examination, which determined the direction life would take.

Retirement Primary had its perks. One was powdered milk. The government received food aid, and distributed it to students to take home to their parents. This effort not only had the effect of reducing malnutrition in students, but also encouraged attendance. For some parents, this provided immediate tangible benefits for sending their children to school. Ironically, it could also mean that the more children you had the more powdered milk and other subsidies your child would take home.

It was easy to tell when it was free milk day, even if the three- to five-pound plastic bags of milk did not survive the journey home. The white trail along the road, the dusting in our hair and uniforms, and the hardened white mustache provided the evidence.

The term *lactose intolerance* didn't make it into my vocabulary until long after I became an adult. I was observant as a child and usually noticed cause and effect.

One cause and effect experiment that I conducted at an early age was drinking from a gallon jug while urinating to see if I could keep a constant uninterrupted flow of urine. I noticed a strong correlation between eating the powered milk and the cutting feeling in my belly that would usher me home for a quick visit to the latrine. It never occurred to me, however, that avoiding milk and milk products was an option. After all, milk was good for you, and the belief was that if you kept at drinking it, your body would get used to it and eventually the negative reaction would cease. "You will outgrow it," people told me. I never did.

In my math class at Retirement Primary, I was happy to see Terry, or rather Ms. Terry. She was a substitute teacher. She attended one of the churches I had visited, and her parents lived nearby our Trinail home.

I was confident I was going to marry Ms. Terry when I grew up. I worked hard to impress her. When I got three of her long division problems incorrect and she chopped my fingers with the edge of her ruler, it hurt not only my fingers, but crushed my heart.

The school at Retirement, though meager in resources, had more than Jointwood. There were more books, and there was the 4-H club. While at Jointwood School, I was a member of the Pathfinders Club, but we had little or no supplies and wore our regular khaki school uniform to club meetings. Despite my discomfort at Retirement school, I gradually settled down and before I knew it, it was Christmas.

We practiced carols and took part in plays for the annual Christmas service. As we sang a carol, "Little Donkey," I heard a commotion and all the students started running and screaming. The teachers were running also. As they ran, they knocked over desks and chairs. I was not sure what we were running to or from, and so I stopped. I peered out from behind a blackboard and saw the reason for the terror.

A former student, Basil, was chasing the entire student body with a machete. He slapped the machete on the desk and terrified us even more. He caught up with a female teacher and slapped her rear with the blade. He ran away as quickly as he had come, and everyone was sent home or left for home in the panic. Luckily, no one was actually chopped with the blade, though many had bruises from falling over desks and chairs. We wondered what would have happened if instead of a machete, Basil had had a gun. People said Basil had lost his mind, and some speculated that he wanted to hurt the teachers who had hurt him.

When the new term started in January, Kenny and I returned to Jointwood. One evening, as I walked home, I saw Basil and engaged him in conversation to see if he remembered the incident. He denied remembering, but he also wanted the details. I provided some, and he appeared proud of the fear he had caused. He was especially pleased with himself to learn that he had slapped Blanche—the teacher. I was aware of the risk I was taking in talking to Basil; however, I had started to develop the trait of asking the questions that most people only thought about, but never asked.

vii.

The turnover rate of teachers was high at Jointwood. More and more people migrated, as violence and uncertainty in Jamaica increased. My new teacher, Ms. Grizzle, announced that next term we would be taken to visit the zoo in the capital, Kingston. I had been to Kingston only a few times and looked forward to the opportunity to go. We would take the four-hour journey by a chartered bus and would need ten dollars for the fare. I wanted to go and I mentioned it to my parents, but I didn't ask them for the fare. I knew they wouldn't be able to afford it. I hadn't been to the zoo before, and in addition to seeing the strange animals, I also wanted to drive the bumper cars that would be in the same days' activity. How would I get the money?

I came up with the idea to sell produce. I found some mangoes and took them with me to a store and pharmacy run by Dr. Rhoden, who was a member of the church that operated our school. I was pleasantly surprised when Mrs. Rhoden bought them all and gave me $1.50. I just needed to find some more mangoes. The problem was that the season was ending and the mangoes I had sold were a special variety, a variety that even during season was not always easy to find. I kept the $1.50 and determined that I had no more hopes of finding more mangoes before the date of the trip. I needed another plan to earn $8.50.

I visited my eldest sister, Jenny, in Maggoty. Mom was already working at Jenny's house cleaning and helping to take care of her grandchildren. Jenny's house had all the modern amenities—except for telephones. There were two houses next to each other, which we called the Top House and Bottom House. Jenny and her immediate family lived in the top house. Extended families and workers who stayed over slept in the bottom house.

At the foot of the hill were two other buildings owned and operated by my sister: a bakery and a grocery store. In the yard between the bakery and the store were parking spaces for the trucks used to transport supplies and a van used to transport breads and bullas to supermarkets and shops on established routes.

I told Jenny of my desire to attend the zoo with my class. She inferred that I was getting ready to ask her for money and was dismissive. This was the kind of dismissiveness that developed from responding to the needs of too many needy relatives. Some of these relatives had an entitlement mentality that suggested that she should share her success simply because they were family.

I was undeterred, and Jenny was later impressed to learn that I was not asking to be given money to go to the zoo. Instead, I was offering to work for it. This would begin a long working relationship with my sister.

At the end of my Easter break, I had earned my fare and joined my class on our visit to the zoo. I even had money left over for several helpings of ice cream. To make this possible, I had packed store shelves, packaged baked goods, swept and mopped floors, washed vehicles, bathed dogs, and other chores. I also learned a valuable lesson: that you were more likely to get support when you try to help yourself than when you beg. In addition, I had left a lasting impression in my sister's mind as one who was ambitious, hardworking, and reliable.

viii.

I was definitely growing up. Back on the farm, my climbing had gotten better, but I was still not among the best. My personal best on the coconut tree was still only forty feet. This height was two times the height of the dwarf coconut trees. Fortunately or unfortunately, no one was around to witness this accomplishment. I picked several coconuts to take home to share, but mostly as proof that I had done it.

Descending the tree was also a challenge. There was the quick way and the slow way. The slow way was reversing the order of your climb. The quick way was sliding down the tree in seconds. I was to learn that while it looked easy, the quick way required technique and skill. I looped my arms the way I had seen others do it, and got to the ground in less than five agonizing seconds. My belly, arms, and legs were on fire from bruises sustained in the quick descent. There were new holes in my pants and the skin had disappeared around areas of my leg. It hurt like hell, but I felt good about the accomplishment.

ix.

The bruises did not deter my playing of some of the games at Jointwood School. Cricket, soccer flags, and volleyball were among the games we played. For most of these sports, we had little or no equipment.

School felt different now. Conroy and all the other boys now attended other schools. Many of the students had migrated with their parents, and the school population dwindled. A declining sugar cane, banana, and bauxite industry, coupled with fears of going communist, were among the reasons. Many evenings, after my best friend Rod exited the main road for his house, I continued the lonely journey home.

Rod was an outstanding athlete, and outran many boys his age. When his nephew, Lyndon, visited from the US and attended school with Rod, he became the center of attention. We loved listening to Lyndon's American accent, and the stories he told did not disappoint. Rod, however, would cringe when Lyndon spoke, because he talked about everything, including the length of his uncle's private. I realized then that talking to people from different cultures intrigued me, and I dreamed of traveling someday.

The road that led to the school from the main road was unpaved. And from time to time, the younger boys would organize teams and play stone wars. The objective of the game was not to hit each other, but to have the stones collide in midair, or to have the other team run if there were too many stones raining down.

Lyndon joined the stone war and within minutes, he took one on the forehead. Not only was I concerned about the gash on his forehead, but I was also worried about Rod having to explain the injury to his parents.

Within weeks after the incident, the boys were playing stone wars again. Some stones landed on the cricket pitch where the older boys (me included) were playing. It disrupted our cricket game and we got angry.

There were about ten boys playing the stone war game. They were divided in two teams (five on each team). The team closest to us was retreating from the hail of stones and was unaware that they had backed up onto the cricket pitch.

The cricket players picked up the stones that had fallen on the pitch and tossed them back in the direction of the stone-throwing team furthest away, urging them to move away or stop the silly game. The retreating team instead was buoyed by our action, believing that we were providing them reinforcement. I again shouted for them to "move away," but my shout was now drowned out by a sound of agony, and the sight of blood coming from Charles' head.

As soon as the stone connected, Courtney, a member of the cricket players, pointed a finger at me.

"You did it," Courtney said. This was the same Courtney who was throwing stones moments earlier.

"How can he be so sure since there were several stones flying in the air?" I said. But within minutes, there was unanimity that I was the one who had hit Charles. Even the teacher who emerged to take Charles to the nearby doctor agreed. Charles would receive several stitches. The sympathy I felt for his condition dampened my less than forceful protest that any of the boys flinging stones could have hit him. This experience taught me about mob mentality and scapegoating.

***Lesson 2:* Mob mentality is not rational. Be careful.**

***Lesson 3:* A scapegoat may be needed to accept responsibility for a group's action. When there is less than perfect information, you may become "The Fall Guy."**

The story did not end there. That evening, my teacher gave me a letter to take to my father. Usually, I delivered messages faithfully, but I had a sick feeling in my stomach and decided I wanted to see the letter. As I read the letter, I realized how the rest of the boys (in an aim to protect themselves) convinced the teacher that I was singularly responsible for what had happed. I had a dilemma. If I delivered the letter, Big Mac would be upset and would certainly beat me for my poor judgment. I tossed the letter, and the next day, I lied to the teacher when asked if I had delivered it. I figured that since my Big Mac attended a different church, it was unlikely that he would find out. A few days after carrying the lie, I became very sick. I had not had an asthma attack in years, but I was now wheezing.

In my deception, I did not consider that Charles' grandfather would meet my best friend's dad at a leadership conference, who would then inform Big Mac about the incident.

Big Mac was livid. Not only was he appalled by the incident, but he was also disappointed that I had not "come clean." I appealed for mercy, especially since I was wheezing, but my appeal or Dash's barks did not hold sway as the licks came. My time for explanation had long passed.

Big Mac asked me to write a letter of apology to Charles' family. Charles lived at his grandparents' house. In addition, Big Mac gave me money that could be used to help defray medical costs. Sunday evening, I was tasked with a long walk that went past my school in search of Charles' house. It was a long journey. As I walked, I wondered how I would approach Charles' family. Would they be angry at me? What had Charles said to them?

Finally, I got to Charles' house and saw his grandparents sitting comfortably on their veranda. They lived in a neatly designed house on the edge of the main road. The yard was nicely kept and so were the hedges and flowers. They invited me onto the veranda and offered me a seat. Charles was nowhere in sight.

Granma Bulgin took the envelope with the cash and my short apology and read it aloud for Grandpa Bulgin to hear. Then, in a kind voice, she asked, "Would you like to explain what happened?" This was the start of my redemption.

Grandpa Bulgin rocked back and forth slowly in his rocking chair while his wife, Grandma Bulgin, sat on the edge of her chair. Both listened attentively as I related my version of what had happened. They looked at each other, and both agreed that in light of my version of events, they would accept only half of the money I had brought to them. Grandma Bulgin made the ruling.

"I think all of you boys were careless," she said. "However, I don't think it is fair that you alone be held responsible. The stone could have come from anyone." Her husband nodded his head in agreement.

I thanked them and again apologized for the pain to her family. It was ironic; the only people who listened to me were from the aggrieved family.

I returned the money to Big Mac and explained what had happened. He sensed that I was feeling bruised and somewhat resentful of his refusal to listen to my side of the story. Big Mac repeated a familiar poem that I had heard several times read in Kindergarten school. This was his way of explaining why he had punished me.

Lesson 4:

"Speak the truth and speak it ever,

Cost it what it will,

He who hides the wrong he did,

Does the wrong thing still." (Author unknown)

X.

The house Big Mac had bought in Harmony Hall was nearing completion. Completion meant that it had a zinc roof. In addition, the ceiling was in place to reduce the heat from the hot sun hitting the zinc. The outside would remain untreated.

A professional contractor was not employed to take on this project. The construction crew was made up mostly of friends and family whose expertise came from working on their own houses or other friends' houses. Big Mac thought he could save some money by doing some of the projects himself. When it was time to put in the concrete floor, he decided, against Mom's request, to do just that.

After Dad lost his job, Mom had become the major earner with her job at Jenny's business. Her earnings now provided the financing to buy material to complete the project. This meant that she could not supervise the day-to-day operation, and only saw the work progress on weekends. When the floor was laid, Mom was not too eager to see it. Her instincts were right. Even an untrained eye could spot several problems. The floor was uneven, and some areas revealed palm prints where Big Mac had tried to smooth the surface before the concrete dried. Mom swallowed hard, and then told Big Mac what a ridiculous decision he had made. Big Mac stood quietly as Mom vented. They both knew that despite how the floor looked, they did not have the money to redo it, and they would live with it for the rest of their lives.

Several days before the house was finished, I went to the site to help. It was a weekday and school was out. I ran errands and started the cooking, among other chores. I saw a few empty dishes on top of an old oil drum that stored water used to mix the concrete. I picked up the dishes with the intent of washing them, but they fell into the drum of water. Big Mac saw the plates disappearing into the water and, without warning or an explanation, slapped me across my face with the palm of his hand. I was stunned.

All voices and sound seem distant compared to the ringing in my ear. Despite the agony of my face, I couldn't cry. I walked away. I couldn't hear and didn't care what Big Mac was saying. I didn't want to stick around. I surmised that I was moments away from turning green and busting up my clothes, and it would not be a pretty sight if Big Mac met the Incredible Hulk.

A wave of mixed emotion followed. I felt scared, not of Big Mac, but of myself because of my incredible calm despite my boiling anger. It was the kind of calm that could result in remorseless actions. I responded to the distant inner voice that prompted me to leave the area. I did not know where I was going when I left, but ended up at my grandmother Mary's (Meme). Meme always joked about the special bond between Mary and Joseph. This made me feel really special. She cried with me as I related what had transpired. And after I confided in Meme, she related some of her deeply held secrets.

Meme's first child, Mom, had a different last name than all her other children. Meme related a story that sounded like *Little Red Riding Hood.* In place of the bad wolf was a man who took her against her will and impregnated her as she walked the woods by herself. The pain was still evident as she related her story.

Big Mac believed in a verse that is paraphrased "spare the rod and spoil the child." On this day, my grandmother introduced another verse to me that provided some comfort. "Fathers provoke not your children to anger." I left my grandmother's house and continued walking until I reached my sister's place of business. On my walk, I did some thinking. I recalled another experience I had some years before that had led me to stockpile stones, bottles, and anything I could find, with the intention of throwing them at Big Mac when he walked up the hill to our house. Something had occurred at a neighbor's house that led to that decision.

I was playing in a neighbor's yard with several boys. Big Mac came by and made a fuss about something, and then lifted me in the air and failed to catch me, causing me to fall on my face. I was humiliated as all the boys laughed. I ran away from the scene to my house and stockpiled the rocks at the root of a banana tree, waiting for Big Mac to climb the hill that led to the house. As fate would have it, he never showed; and after waiting for what seemed like hours, I was driven into the house by a thunderstorm. As it rained, it occurred to me that he probably was playing, and my fall was accidental since he had tossed Kenny and me in the air and caught us several times. As I looked at my pile of rocks, I felt ashamed. That experience had taught me a vital lesson, and I vowed to avoid acting in anger.

I continued my mental conversation and concluded that the slap in my face today was in no way accidental. I could not understand how this man who played with every child he passed on the road and who was a leader in the church could be so cruel. It was another painful lesson that I was to learn. There is good and bad in everyone. I vowed not to be like my father.

I reached my sister's place of business and was questioned by her and her employees. "What happened to your face?" I did not realize it, but my face was swollen. I explained what had happened; I felt no loyalty or desire to protect Big Mac. They looked closer and concluded that they could see the palm print along the side of my face. Later, one of my siblings joked that my father's fingerprints were everywhere—on the floor that he had cemented, and now on my face.

***Lesson 5:* Avoid reacting or making decisions in anger.**

CHAPTER 7: HARMONY HALL AGAIN

i.

When we moved to the new house, it didn't feel like home. It was more spacious with three bedrooms, a dining area, and a veranda. There was no electricity or indoor plumbing, and the amateur workmanship showed. I told myself that it wouldn't be long before I left, and I drew check marks on the wall of each night I spent there.

The neighborhood felt different from the first time we were there. Innocence was lost, not just because I was growing up, but also because of the change in the political climate. There was scarcity everywhere, from basic groceries to raw materials. In addition, we heard several news reports of political violence. The violence was primarily concentrated in Kingston, but the news reports created the feeling that it was on our doorsteps.

The middle-class exodus was in high gear following Manley's re-election as prime minister two years earlier in 1976. It was reported that he had remarked that he and Fidel Castro would walk hand in hand to the top of the mountain. Several highly skilled professionals felt empty as they uprooted their families and migrated, leaving behind the place they had once called home.

Hopes that Revere Bauxite Company would be reopened were dashed, as efforts were underway to dismantle the plant. Areas that were mined for bauxite were left unclaimed. Coconut and other fruit trees were dying, and the cause was not known but was speculated to be the effect of chemical exhaust from the bauxite plant.

Since jobs and foreign exchange were scarce, many turned to the most lucrative cash crop—marijuana—as a source of income. The banana and sugarcane industries were already in decline. Ganja was now planted in conspicuous places in rural Jamaica. No longer did people bother to hide the plant in the hills; it was now interspersed with regular crops. You could help some neighbors pick gungo peas, but you had to be careful not to step on the ganja.

One of the boys that I played with the first time I lived in Harmony Hall, Enzert, now did not recognize or acknowledge me when I called him. Not only did he not recognize me, but also he was no longer bathing. It was rumored that he had smoked too much ganja, but I suspect that the migration of members of his family was a contributing factor. Seeing people develop unsound minds with the association with ganja removed any desire to experiment. Ironically, my only experimentation came one morning before I attended church.

My chronic asthmatic brother, Mikey, took the advice of someone to steep the cannabis as a tea and drink it for his cold and asthma. Mickey completed the brew with condensed milk and sugar, sweetened to taste. I was curious about the taste and was offered a half a cup. After consuming the brew, I walked to church.

I recalled two activities at church that day. First, there was the opening hymn. Next, there was a slap followed by violent shaking, awaking me from my deep sleep in time for the benediction.

Big Mac, of course, would not plant any ganja. He could not be persuaded to plant coffee, let alone marijuana. He believed in the writings of Ellen G. White that said "coffee is harmful to one's health."

I tried to engage Big Mac on these topics. I understood that ganja was still illegal, but why not coffee? Blue mountain coffee was now fetching a high price on the international market. Big Mac explained that since sister (fellow member) White said it was harmful to people's health, we would not help the production. I made sure I created some distance so I could run when I asked the next rhetorical question: Why did God create the plant if it did not have some valid use?

ii.

Students in Jamaica preparing for the dreaded common entrance examination (CEE) experienced symptoms of depression, nightmares, anxiety, vomiting, irritability, and psychosomatic illnesses. For several decades, this exam was administered to students between the ages of ten to twelve who wanted to attend high school. There was a limited supply of high schools relative to the number of students available. Less than 20 percent of all students would get that opportunity to attend high school, and only three in ten students taking the exam would get that chance.

Those who were not successful were relegated to schools deemed inferior, or completely denied the opportunity of a high school education. Poor families put added pressure on students since they saw education as a way out of poverty. Many families did not understand failure to be a problem of supply and demand, and a number of students considered this a personal failing for the rest of their lives.

The path for students who were not successful in this exam depended on the resources of their parents. There were a few opportunities, as well as vocational training. If families could afford it, students could go to a private high school. Other students could attend an all-age and secondary (vocational) school, or a technical high school.

All-age school would allow for additional preparation, after which you could take an achievement test and be sent to a technical high school. Secondary school was where everyone else ended up. Technical high schools were on par with most high schools, except that a skill such as surveying, welding, or agriculture was taught in addition to the academic focus.

None of my siblings attended high school or college, and I did not have a clearly established path to success. People generally thought I was respectful to my elders and concluded that I would do well. At that time, I was not sure what path would lead to doing well. I wanted to become a pastor because that was the most influential person with whom I interacted.

Because of the number of times I had moved, there was a lack of continuity in my educational progress. Jointwood School was an all-age school that prepared students for the next religious (private) high school. Retirement Primary was the only school I attended that prepared students for the CEE.

When I changed schools and re-attended Jointwood, I thought my opportunity to take the exam had ended. Unknown to me, my teachers had registered me for the exam. The term had ended, and I was home from Jointwood School early and was asked to pick up some groceries at the stores. It was also the afternoon of the exam. I walked two miles to a shop operated by the husband of a teacher who taught at the Retirement Primary School. Mrs. Collie was a well-respected teacher who knew me, even though I was never in her class. There were other stores I could have gone to, but I ended up at the Collies'. Mrs. Collie was tending the store and I was surprised at the way she greeted me.

"What are you doing here?" she asked.

"I came to buy flour, cornmeal, condensed milk, and chicken," was my reply.

"Today is the day for the common entrance exam. Why are you not at the exam?" I tried to explain that since I had changed schools, I didn't realize I could take the exam. She was visibly disappointed with me and mumbled something about parents who did not understand how the system worked.

Her disappointment stung me because for the first time, I realized that a teacher believed in me. Mrs. Collie actually believed that I could have passed the exam, a belief that I, at that time, didn't share. My last opportunity to take the exam had passed. I also realized that I should start taking more interest in my education. My parents didn't understand how things worked.

On the day the results of the exam were released, circulation and sale of newspapers would more than double. In my case, I knew what the result would be. I never sat for the exam, and it was impossible for my name to show up as passing. I got a paper from someone and looked at the long list of names printed. I looked under where my name would have appeared, and of course it wasn't there.

iii.

I was not yet a successful student, but would be a successful Bible student. During the summer, my church conducted a crusade to win more souls for Christ. I was heavily involved in the operation. The church pastor would attend every night to preach. Big Mac was one of the leaders. I conducted song service and got children and adults involved as a prelude to each night's proceedings. A friend, Devon, and I competed to see who would be the best song service conductor. The best was the one who got greater involvement from the crowd. I chose songs that involved actions, not just singing. Action songs were clear winners with the audience.

One night during my song service, I spotted a new face. She was the sister of one of the new members, but she lived in the Cayman Islands. The electric light gleamed from her soft velvet black skin, and I was sure it created a halo. When she smiled at me, she revealed the whitest teeth I had seen. I fought hard to stay focused. At the end of the service, I sought her out and chatted. Her name sounded similar to the name of Scottish ale—McKewan—and I was already drunk.

We chatted for a few moments and I learned some interesting facts, including the fact that she was two years older than me. I was disappointed when her eldest sister called her away, but I now had a new reason to look forward to the next night's service. For the next two nights after the service ended, I left my parents and walked with McKewan's group as they walked home. My parents couldn't understand why I had become so impatient to leave after the service. They stayed back to help rearrange chairs, clean up, and count offerings.

I did not leave immediately every night, because I was careful to avoid starting a rumor. But I was content to be in McKewan's presence. On our way home one night, I was in a group of twelve. Some older boys were in the group and made a play for her. One remarked loudly that he would like to keep her hands warm, and started walking next to her. She shot back that she had someone she was walking with and came over and held my hand, sending shivers up my spine.

I felt so proud and was convinced that I had grown two inches taller. McKewan did not care that others teased that she was after the son of the preacher, Big Mac. The jeers and taunts grew distant as we floated in the cloud, hand in hand. Our routine continued for several weeks until the crusade ended. On weekends,

I found more reasons to visit my uncle Soldier's house, since he lived a short distance from where my angel now lived. When my mother asked where I was going, uncle Soldier became the convenient answer.

One Sunday afternoon, I found myself at McKewan's house just as it started to rain. She and another sister were home babysitting for their eldest sister with whom they lived. I was relieved that her eldest sister was not home. The pounding of the rain on the zinc roof was not enough to cover the throbbing of my heart as we stole a kiss for the first time. Her sister in the other room pretended to be asleep.

I started to relax in her judgment; she had a better grip on timing. While I lost my head, she maintained her poise and could pull a stoic look or poker face, the meaning of which would only be clear to me when company appeared, and it was too late. After a long day of church, McKewan told me that they (her sisters) would be going to the main road later that evening. This meant that they would pass by my house.

It was already dark, and I went to check on the goats that we kept. The goats were tied to trees or shrubs. As they ate the nearby grass, they sometimes became entangled in thickets. It was important to free them because as they slept, hungry packs of dogs bothered them or tried to get an easy meal of goat meat. If the goats were entangled, they could jump and strangle themselves.

My timing to check on the goats was matched perfectly with McKewan and her family walking to the main road. McKewan had laughed loud enough for me to hear, and I am pretty sure her siblings must have wondered what they had said that was suddenly so funny. I walked with them for a couple miles and then ran back home. I was not aware how long I was gone.

When I returned, I was surprised to see a search party of my parents and siblings with flashlights and bottle lamps looking for me. They had yelled out my name, and none of the neighbors had seen me. They found the goats Joseph had gone to see, but no Joseph. Since I was miles away in the company of my love, I did not hear them.

My parents were concerned because it was unusual for me to disappear. In addition, there were several stories about young boys who had become disoriented in the woods and were found several days later, miles away from where they were supposed to be. The feeling was that duppy (ghosts) were responsible for this.

Our elders told several stories of ghosts and rolling calves (a ghost cow with a chain around its neck). After listening to stories like these, the imagination could run wild. Unknown sounds in the dark would send kids running. As twigs entangled the feet of someone with a highly imaginative mind, it created the belief that chains of a rolling calf were tying one up. The fight to free oneself could sometimes prove deadly. I had heard the story of a boy who was found with thorns and cuts in his flesh; in his effort to escape the duppy, he ran into thickets of thorns.

There was also a prevailing belief that neighbors who did not like to see another child progress would go to the Obeah man to work witchcraft and prevent another's child from being more successful than theirs.

I found the idea that my parents were looking for me somewhat amusing because they had taught us not to believe in ghosts or witchcraft. My parents were not amused. I saw relief on their faces, and I tried not to encourage additional questions about my whereabouts.

I eventually told them where I was, and my dad complained that I thought I was now a man. As I laughed at the absurd idea of ghosts taking me away, I recalled an incident in Trinail when I had gone to watch TV next door. I stayed later than expected and watched the latest horror movie, *Dark Shadow*. As I walked home, I sang to prove that I was not afraid.

As I approached the hill leading up to my house, I heard chains moving, followed by a sound like a dragon blowing its nostrils. I ran back to the neighbors' house and they made me a bottle torch and sent two of the boys to follow me part of the way home. They laughed as I sailed up the hill, sending the flames from a vertical to a horizontal direction.

The next morning, I went to the area to find a fierce bull. The bull was loaned to Big Mac to mate with our heifer, Betty. I was not at home when the bull arrived, and I felt silly at the sight of my perceived rolling calf. I concluded then that there were no ghosts and things always had a logical explanation.

<u>Lesson 6:</u> Duppy know who fi frighten. (Ghosts know who to scare)

Several days later, Big Mac had a social at our house and invited friends from church. The men played dominoes and told stories. I became upset when Big Mac kept inquiring about my whereabouts every few minutes. McKewan was in attendance and my annoyance at Big Mac's constant inquiry was evident. We sat at the side of the house talking, and he came by and ordered us inside with the others.

A week later, after another night of church, Big Mac was looking for me. He suddenly needed help organizing. I was not responsive and was chased with a belt. He made his signature threat overheard by many in the congregation who had not yet left for home.

"If I lick you, you'll think a cow kicked you." He continued, "Ever since that new McKewan girl moved here, you now believe that you are a man."

Our public humiliation was too much for my love to bear. She became cold and distant and avoided me like the plague. One night as we walked home, she made no effort to walk beside me. I stood in her path and as she turned in the direction of her home. I apologized for the silliness of my father. "I know what my father did was painful, but that was not me. Nothing will change the way I feel about you."

Her eldest sister remarked that it seemed like I had something on my mind that would drive me crazy if I didn't get a chance to say it. As McKewan laughed at her sister's joke, I felt a gulf between us grow wider and wider, and I was sure now that I had to move.

iv.

It was Friday evening, and we were preparing for the Sabbath. For me, this meant cleaning up the yard and shining Big Mac's shoes until I could see my reflection in them. Big Mac was at home. Mom was out working at Jenney's house. The son of my sister Bev was now living with us. Horace was now the youngest child living with us, and he now had the role of the reporter. Like all of us, Horace called Big Mac Daddy.

"Daddy, Tricksty stole another egg." It was only a month before that Big Mac decided that he would teach the dog that stealing eggs was wrong. In order to accomplish this lesson, Big Mac boiled an egg and shoved the hot egg into the dog's mouth and held it shut. This dissuaded the dog from stealing, but later, hunger had revived the urge.

Learning of this theft, Big Mac felt defeated and opted to teach the puppy another lesson. He grabbed the closest thing he could find—a piece of board—and slapped the puppy across its back. I screamed as the puppy's hind legs became limp, and they dragged on the ground as Tricksty tried to escape.

I rushed to the puppy's aid, biting my lips to hold back the tears. Big Mac was subdued. He realized that he had again succumbed to his tendency to act impulsively.

I tried to convince myself that this man was not my father. I counted all my siblings and their associated fathers as evidence to support this belief. At the same time, I could not hide the truth that the man truly loved me and would do anything to protect his family. He loved his church and God. How then could he be so cruel to God's creatures?

I reiterated a pledge to myself after the one and only time he had hit Mom. I will not hit my wife when I am married, and I will not act impulsively. There was a passage in the Bible that drove fear into my heart each time I heard it, and I prayed that I would be spared. "The sins of the father visit the children unto the third and fourth generation." I was not sure what it meant, or if my dad's father was the same way. One thing was certain: I did not have to be that way. I reaffirmed my vow to become the opposite of him.

V.

After the re-election of the Michael Manley's government in 1976, US interest in Jamaica increased. Manley was too close to Fidel Castro and there was no way the US was going to allow another communist country on its doorstep. This set off a long silent proxy war in Jamaica with deadly political, economic, and physical consequences. The acronym CIA was as popular as the acronym for the two major political parties—PNP and JLP. Manley's People National Party (PNP) blamed the Jamaica Labour Party (JLP) and the CIA for production sabotage, scarcity, and violence.

Seaga's close alliance to the US was, not only the result of his free-market philosophy, but also the fact that he was born in Massachusetts. He was described as a strong technocrat and held a finance degree from Harvard University. When the violence and the election ended in 1980, the Jamaican people had decided on a change, and Edward Seaga would lead Jamaica as the new prime minister.

Jamaica was a different country, and I was a different thirteen-year-old. People had lost confidence in their leaders as I had lost confidence in my father. It was hard to believe how rapidly the country had declined. It was only twelve years before that the Jamaican dollar was as strong, or stronger, than the US dollar. In addition, Singapore had sent a delegation to Jamaica to study the country's model. Little did many know that Jamaica would never be the same again.

Seaga set out to repair the damage done to the economy. He borrowed extensively to create demand and to fill the gap left by the collapse of the bauxite industry. He sought to diversify the economy. However, new industries would take time to grow and creditors would not wait to knock at the door and demand payment on the huge debt. Just like Uncle Sam, Uncle Bengy had shaken off slavery and British colonization. But now there was a new master. This master was faceless but eloquently identified by the words of King Solomon in the book of Proverbs, "The borrower is a servant of the lender."

CHAPTER 8: MAGGOTTY

i.

I spent all summer working in my sister's business. With respect to school, I was unsure of the next move. One thing was certain: Something had to change soon. As usual, I worked very hard at the bakery and grocery store. Sister again repeated that I should help her supervise. In essence, that meant that I should let her know if the workers where stealing or goofing off. However, I took it to heart and started instructing the men on what to do. Some resented me, but all eventually responded to my instructions. The concern for pilferage was not unfounded. The effort some workers put into stealing can simply be described as unbelievable. If it was not nailed down, it was at risk.

After the summer break, I returned to Jointwood School. I was still locked in a mental debate regarding where my next school should be. I consulted with my teacher to find out how to register for an exam that would get me into St. Elizabeth Technical High School (STETHS). She was not sure how, so I traveled to Santa Cruz, where STETHS is located, only to discover that the exam was already in progress. I had a feeling that my opportunities were slipping away.

To rectify my educational situation, I wrote to the newly elected prime minister. I congratulated him and explained why it was imperative that I get into a high school. My parents were unaware of my decision, and I was pleasantly surprised when they brought a letter in my name from the office of the prime minister. As delighted as I was with the response, there were three problems I was not sure how to overcome.

First, the prime minister's office had asked that I go to the office of a member of parliament on a date that turned out to be a Saturday—the Sabbath. That was a day that Big Mac, according to the Bible, insisted that no business be done. Second, the letter was late and that date had already passed. Third, the recommended member of parliament was not from our constituency, but from the constituency in which the school was located. From an adult retrospective, the choices seem easy. I should have impressed on my parents the need to take me to the representative's office on the next business day or solicit the help of my sister. I did not follow through on either of these options, and the opportunity was wasted.

The new Prime Minister Edward Seaga got off to a highly publicized start. He was the first foreign leader to visit the newly elected President Ronald Reagan. Two years later, Reagan made history by being the first sitting US president to visit Jamaica.

A large drug eradication program followed Reagan's visit. The eradication was the joint effort of US/Jamaica military operation. The locals were not happy, as tons of ganja was burned, and some was removed by helicopter, supposedly to be dumped at sea. Skeptical locals joked that either there would be an increase in the appetite of hungry sharks and other fish at sea or an increase in the financial status of Jamaican and American security leaders.

Joseph – Student at Maggoty High

At the start of the new year, I transferred from Jointwood School and registered at Maggotty Secondary

School. The numbers of available secondary schools were not adequate to house the numbers of students attending. To alleviate this problem, a two-shift system (morning and afternoon) was developed for the secondary schools. Students alternated shifts each school year. My routine would be set for the next four years. I would live with my sister, work, and attend school in Maggotty. The shifts system fit perfectly with my work schedule at the bakery.

While attending school on the morning shift, my workday started with the responsibility of opening the bakery gates, usually between 4:30 a.m. and 6:00 a.m., to allow the vans to leave and deliver breads to grocery stores and shops. Usually, these vans were loaded overnight, but some were also loaded early in the morning. To complete these duties as quickly as possible before rushing off to school, which ran from 7:30 a.m. to noon, was imperative. After school, I returned to the bakery and worked from 1:00 p.m. to closing time (usually after 8:00 p.m.). When on the school's afternoon shift, I woke up, opened the gate, and worked in the bakery until 11:30 a.m. I then got dressed and attended school from 12:30 p.m. to 5:00 p.m. After returning home, I worked in the bakery until it closed. Homework would follow and occasional television.

My religious resolve was strengthened by the necessity of having a day to rest. On Saturdays, I was so tired that I welcomed the Sabbath day of rest. After I returned from church, I spent the afternoons sleeping. On Sundays, I helped with general cleaning and maintenance work at the bakery and around the house. These days were not as structured as workdays, but since I had had my rest on Saturday, I was expected to play a vital role.

I got paid in cash, and after I deducted 10 percent for tithe and an additional amount for offering, I left the balance at my parents' house hidden from all eyes. I had opened a savings account, but decided it was not possible to travel twenty-five miles to the nearest bank each week. The cost of such travel would eat into my meager pay.

I didn't want to keep money around with me when I stayed and worked at my sister's place. I was handling a lot of her money, and I did not want my integrity questioned. On several occasions, I came across notes or stock of money on the floor of her house and returned it. After coming across money in some fairly unusual yet visible places in my sister's house, I concluded that I was being tested. I theorized that while my sister and her husband were busy people, they were certainly not that careless with money.

One weekend after I arrived at my parents' house, I noticed that the hiding place that stored my weekly wages had been raided. I started an investigation, and almost instantly, Mom had the answer. The culprit was one of her granddaughters who was now living with her. For more than a week, Mom was puzzled why each evening her granddaughter did not seem to have an appetite for her dinner. "The girl barely touched her dinner," Mom remarked. In addition, she had become very popular with her friends at school, as she purchased goodies for her friends. My hard-earned cash was the source of her new lifestyle of the rich and famous.

iii.

Life was challenging with my new extended family. The immediate members of Jenny's family were her husband, Patrick (Mr. P), and her three children, Ken, Chris, and Mark. Other extended family members were Sandra, my brothers Conroy and Collin, and Patrick's brothers, Winston, Vincent, Andrew, and Fuzzy.

Patrick's parents and family had fled China to avoid communism. Patrick struggled with English and the Jamaican dialect. Since I was becoming exposed to Chinese culture, I was fascinated to learn the Chinese words for eat, rice, money, and a special cooking utensil called the wok. In one of my early encounters with Patrick, I was in the kitchen as he searched for his favorite cooking utensil. I tried to help, but I was not sure what he was looking for. What is a "flying pan?" I wondered. Only a few seconds would pass before it dawned on me that my brother-in-law was looking for a frying pan.

Patrick (Mr. P) was usually very calm, patient, and pleasant. People who pushed him would be surprised when his tough interior was exposed. I liked him from the start. He avoided drama, but would be unmovable when he found the right cause to fight. He had found the right cause with my sister Jenny. His family initially was not very supportive of his choice for an interracial bride. However, Patrick was captivated by her beauty, and he would be unmovable.

His decision turned out to be a great choice, not only for their relationship, but also for the business. When they launched out on their own, Jenny's business acumen and determination were responsible for moving the business beyond any level they had imagined. Patrick was analytical and had an aptitude for fixing things. He had been a truck driver at the bauxite plant before he and Jenny started their own business.

On Sundays, Patrick fixed all that needed fixing at the bakery. As he repaired machines, vehicles, and electrical fixtures, I stayed nearby to hand him a screwdriver or pliers. Although I did not necessarily like to spend all my time working, I came to appreciate Patrick's work ethic and concluded if you wanted to be successful, then you had to work hard.

Jenny was outgoing, determined, and someone who got things done. She had no formal education, but was smart, a leader, and a fierce protector of her immediate family. Her beauty and smile were disarming, and if that was not enough, her tough interior and persistence vanquished stumbling blocks that got in her way.

Jenny had a hard life growing up. She felt abandoned by Mom, and after living with her stepmother from hell, she found refuge with her paternal grandmother, with whom she developed a strong bond. At a young age, Jenny vowed not to have any children if she couldn't take care of them the way she wanted to. They would not endure the life she had had as a child.

As a little girl, Jenny attended school in Maggotty. At lunchtime, she visited her dad at the bakery where he worked, and he would come outside to see her since she was initially not allowed in. He would provide her with lunch, usually baked products. Only Jenny knew then, by the vow she had made to herself, that one day she would own the bakery she was initially restricted from entering.

Kenloy was Jenny and Patrick's first child. He is two years younger than I am. When I met him, his vocabulary consisted mostly of words that my dad expressly forbade. Kenloy was also a month older than my youngest brother—also by the same name. Since Jenny and my mother didn't get along, I have often inquired into my mom's psychological state that led her to name her last son the same name as her eldest daughter first. (Kenny's original name is also Kenloy, but we all call him Kenny.) Christine, Mark, and Shalane would complete Jenny and Patrick's lot.

I noticed with interest how Patrick and Jenny treated their children. I did not witness any beating or slaps when those children asked questions that were considered off base or when they "talked back." Like many children, they challenged inconsistencies, yet they remained well-mannered children. I concluded that this is how I would treat my children and how I would have liked to be treated. This "don't spare the rod and spoil the child" thing was overrated and overused.

Kenloy successfully passed his common entrance exam and attended a boys' boarding school, Monro College. As soon as Mark and Christine were school aged, they were sent to boarding school and would come home on weekends. Another member of the family was Sandra, Jenny's cousin. Jenny felt some kinship with Sandra as they both grew up without mothers. Both were left with their grandmothers and fathers while their young, beautiful, free-spirited mothers tried to find themselves. Sandra stayed in the top house, and her early interest in cosmetology emerged as she became Jenny's personal hairstylist.

Not all of Patrick's siblings had the business acumen he had. Some kept having false starts and would return to live and work with him. Mr. P's eldest brother, Vernon, was depressed, and the workers nicknamed him Fuzzy." He had not seen his daughters since they left China. However, it was rumored that the girls were now in the US. He barely spoke the language and had given up on life. Their mother was also present. She cursed everything and everyone in sight. I remained respectful to her, and very soon we were having what little conversation we could.

As the years progressed, I found out that staying at Jenny's house to rest on Saturdays was not a good idea. She had a philosophy that says that there is always something to do, and usually I was among those to do it. She constantly found reasons to request my help. She would explain that she was short staffed because a worker was absent. I would always argue that worker shortage was never a problem in Jamaica. The fact that I had claimed the Saturday as a religious day was little deterrence to her asking. She and her family were Catholics, and they attended mass on Sundays.

Kenloy, Christine, and Mark were usually home from school on weekends or during breaks. They did not like boarding school initially and spent time catching up with each other. Rarely would I have time to play with them except for when I was babysitting Mark. While they were home from school, they were allowed to be children; they were not expected to work every available waking hour in the business. I concluded that I was an employee and couldn't expect equal treatment with Jenny's children.

My weekly payments ceased, and I inquired about it. Jenny told me that the business was mine, also. Therefore, I should not think of myself as a regular employee. This seemed reasonable. I concluded that I was learning more than the average worker, and my weekly paycheck did not reflect my true contribution. However, I couldn't help but notice that the weekly payments had ceased after she learned that I had a savings account. The frequency of my visits to the bank to make a deposit increased after my savings were raided. Jenny was curious, and one morning as I prepared for church, she visited my room and chatted briefly, before asking to see the passbook for my bank account.

I was surprised by the request, but recovered quickly with the conclusion that I had nothing to hide. I also theorized that the request was not unreasonable since I sometimes tallied her daily cash sales. Even at this early age, I could tell that because this was a family business, there was little focus on proper internal controls. In addition, nearly all transactions were in cash.

Jenny inspected the entries made by the teller in my savings account book. The entries were not unusual, given my weekly payment. However, it was clear that I was a saver. My feelings were bruised since she had demonstrated that her trust had to be verified. Given the loss of my own savings, I understood the need for her action, but I still felt betrayed and concluded that I too should do some verification of my own.

I had liked the idea of being considered a partner in the business and felt motivated by that approach. However, my bruised feelings prompted me to ask some lingering questions. One was why her children, who had natural claims to her assets, did not play the same role I played when they were home from school. In addition, why was I asked sometimes to clean their shoes as they prepared to return to school? Couldn't they clean their own shoes?

Patrick and Jenny built a spacious villa on the beach Black River, forty miles away. In addition, there was a smaller one-bedroom board house for the person taking care of the property. Some Sundays after Sis and her family returned from church, we jumped in the back of a pickup and traveled to the beach. As a devout Catholic, Jenny invited me several times to her church. I went occasionally but I held fast to my protestant beliefs.

This beach was not among the best beaches in Jamaica. It was near the swamp, and when it rained, it was impossible to lie quietly on the beach and relax without being attacked by hungry mosquitoes. Inside the house or in the water were the only refuges from these bloodsuckers. I quipped that if someone wanted to torture you, then they could simply tie you up and take your shirt off. I did not realize that my joke would be proven true. Several years later, after I had left, mosquitoes was one of the reasons given for the disposition of the property. A Doberman was left overnight to guard the property and could not get any refuge from the bloodsucking insects, and died after they swarmed him. Luckily for the new owners, there is now better control over mosquitoes in that area.

While we were at the beach house one Sunday, Jenny announced that she was going into one of the rooms to rest. She continued, "I am always on my feet working! If I am not careful, it is only a matter of time before I collapse, leaving all of you to fight about who would get my property." It was an innocent statement said in jest. My response—equally innocent—caught her off guard.

"You mean Ken, Chris, and Mark (Shelly was not yet born) squabbling over what they would get!"

"What do you mean?" she asked.

"Well, they are your natural heirs," I replied. My response was an expression of the obvious. The name of the beach house was Kenchrismar villa, a shortened version of the names of her three children: Kenloy, Christine, and Mark. But it was an awkward way to explain that I had no rights to join in any squabble for Jenny's property. However, the response had hit a nerve, and Sis delayed her rest until my response was thoroughly explored. Was I harboring any kind of jealously of her children? Did I really love them the way she thought I did? Was someone—our mother?—putting ideas in my head?

The truth was I loved her children. However, it was clear that I was living out an absent childhood vicariously through them. I was protective—especially of Mark (the youngest at the time). I viewed them as siblings rather than as niece and nephews. They were not brats, but well-adjusted kids, liked by everyone. Ironically, Mark and Christine did not like being boarded and would have preferred to be home, like Sandra and I were. That would be another valuable life lesson of perspective.

Lesson 7: ***The grass is always greener on the other side.***

The extended family working at the bakery included not only Patrick's siblings but also Jenny's siblings (Collin,

Conroy, and I). Collin purchased a bicycle and enjoyed riding almost everywhere he went. Unfortunately, his outfit did not include a helmet. On his way back from running an errand for Patrick, he collided with two students running across the road and toppled over the handlebars, and, after defying gravity for a few moments, his head and body came to rest on the asphalt.

Collin got up and walked back to work. It was several days afterward when Mon visited that she noticed he was in pain and insisted on taking him to the hospital. He was then flown by a helicopter to a hospital in Kingston where brain surgery was performed. Collin would never be the same again. The accident resulted in slurred speech and loss of mobility on his right side. Through physical therapy and his own determination, he learned to walk with a limp and trained his left arm to do what his right arm previously did.

This accident did not stop Collin from riding, and he was upset when his bicycle was stolen. Years after the accident, Collin was performing light duties at Kenchrismar villa, providing general maintenance, gardening, and security.

Occasionally, Collin came to the bakery and collected groceries and other items before returning to the villa. One day, he returned to the bakery with a bicycle. Surprisingly, when he left for the villa, he left the bicycle at the bakery. I thought it odd since he spent most of his time several miles away in Black River at the villa. However, I didn't mind since I had started to ride it.

Before we left for the beach one Sunday, I decided to take the bicycle with us. I thought Collin could probably use it in Black River. No telephones were available to contact him. I also decided that if he didn't want to keep it, we would take it back with us after riding it at the beach.

As we drove through Black River Town, I saw one guy taking an interest, not in Sandra who was now a knockout, and scantily clad sitting in the chair in the back of the truck, but in the bicycle. Jenny, her usual outgoing self, requested that Patrick, who was driving, stop, so she could say hello to her friends at another villa. It would be a quick stop before we proceeded to our beach house.

I saw one of the guys I had seen earlier in town gaining speed on his bicycle. As he came closer, I encouraged him on, as we were moving again. He was saying something, but I couldn't hear him, nor did I think it was important. We turned into the driveway to our villa, and I got out and opened the gate. Patrick drove in, and I waited and closed the gate. I turned to walk down the driveway when the rider on the bicycle came up and stopped. He smiled, then asked, "Whose bicycle is that in the back of the truck?"

"My brother's," I replied.

"Where did he get it?"

"I don't know," I replied as I walked away.

Moments later, the police arrived. This was not unusual as my sister was generally friendly with law enforcement officers and took an interest in knowing them. Several became close family friends, including Mr. Clarke who had an infectious laugh. They were not in uniform and would have a beer and eat with us on some occasions.

I let in the officers, and they spoke with Jenny. Moments later Collin was called, and he had a sheepish look on his face. It didn't take me long to realize that this was all about the bicycle that I had put in the truck. Collin's original bicycle was stolen, and Collin had decided it was unfair for him to lose a bicycle, so he had simply stolen someone else's. The police were beseeched not to press charges, and the aggrieved boy just wanted his bicycle back. The argument not to make an arrest was persuasive, given the fact that Collin would not fully heal from his accident. Collin's ability to learn the right lesson may have been impeded. He complained that I almost got him arrested. I was adamant when I told him, "You almost got yourself arrested. You are the one who stole the bike."

"You have a lot to learn," he told me. "You think the world is black and white."

<u>Lesson 8:</u> Two wrongs will not equal a right.

CHAPTER 9: **MAGGOTTY HIGH**

i.

A feeling of loneliness and isolation crept over me. I didn't feel connected to any family and I started to think that all I did was work. Even friendships seem to come at a cost. A number of students, including those who attended my school, often came to the bakery to buy lunch. The lunch purchased was primarily patty, coco bread, and drinks. A number of these students recognized me and always sought favors. "Can you give us lunch?" they would ask. I would smile and decline the requests, but it was happening too often. One day, I asked, "Why, why should I give you free lunch? Who would pay for it?"

"Nobody, nobody has to know, besides, we don't have any money," was the response. I had thought long and hard about this before and had made a decision, which made it easy for me every time I was asked.

"What is the relationship of the owner to me?" I asked.

"Your sister!"

"And what is your relationship to me?"

"Your friend?" was the response, which was more a question.

"Okay, my friend—whose name I don't know—what is your name?"

"Omar!"

"Omar, if the owners are my family and you are my friend, why would I steal from them and give it to you?"

I had made my point, but making the point would win me few friends. It is not that I didn't understand need. I grew up poor. However, I had already analyzed the situation and concluded that if I gave a patty and coco bread to everyone who asked, we would not make a profit, and very soon, we would all be poor and begging. My sister grew up poor, and she was determined not to go back.

I certainly did not consider myself rich—since I was not banking on her wealth. I was learning how to avoid poverty, and I certainly was not going to be a drag on her. If I gave one person a coco bread, not only would they be back tomorrow, but they would also tell their friends about how good I was to them, and then their friends too would want to call in favors. And if I didn't, they would threaten to tell since they had not benefitted. I continued my mental analysis: If I gave away things, what kind of example would I be setting for the workers that I was supervising? The answer to all would always be no.

The afternoon shift had already started and as I hurried off to school, I could not shake my feeling of loneliness and isolation. I lamented that all I did was work: I prepared my uniform to attend school; cleaned my own room; and I worked in the bakery. I continued my repine citing the example of the last Sports Day. There were no classes and I was excited to watch the competitions. As soon as I had settled in a comfortable spot to view the track meets, I received a message from a student that my sister said the bakery was busy, and she needed my help. I have no time to enjoy life I moaned; all I do is work and attend classes.

I continued my hurried pace to school and I walked through the shortcut that bypasses the square and ran next to the Maggotty River. The road was unpaved and had several holes, craters, and potholes filled with puddles of water. A group of boys from my school was coming in my direction. I said hi and continued walking when the oldest boy blocked my path.

"I am late," I said. "I don't have time for this."

"Well, you are going to make time!" he retorted. When I attempted to push past him, he grabbed my book bag, ripping the handle off and sending books and bag into a muddy puddle. My fist instinct was to push him in the water. But there were five of them and one of me.

"Why are you bothering me? I didn't trouble you," I said. With the dripping bag, I attempted to pass but was again blocked. "Wait right here," I said. "I will be back."

I was angry as I hurried back to the bakery. Were they among the many that I had "insulted" by not giving free lunch, patty and coco bread? I couldn't recall.

I went to the bakery and picked up a knife and shoved it in my pocket and headed back in the direction of school. Student leader or not, I was going to teach these assholes a lesson. As fate would have it, Jenny caught sight of me as I made my way through the gate. She noticed my ragged look, shirt not tucked in pants, torn shirt pocket, torn bag strap, and my hurried movements. She rushed outside to find out what had happened.

I told her I was fine, but she wasn't buying it. Collin came behind me and asked if I was in a fight with somebody. I gave a shortened explanation of what had happened, and then I retorted that those boys were fucking with the wrong guy.

Expletives were not regulars in my vocabulary, and hearing them signaled to Jenny and Collin that this was serious. I pushed on, only now realizing that the boys had followed me to the bakery. I was rushing toward them—knife concealed in my pocket—when Jenny grabbed my shoulder and asked me to wait. Collin read my body language and went for the older boy and grabbed him around the waist with his left functioning hand (the right was still not fully active from the accident). Collin shifted his grip to the right hand and was about to deliver a blow with his more agile left when Jenny called out for him to stop. She then walked up to the boy, released Collin's grip, and grabbed him by the shirt collar.

"Why are you bullying my brother?" she asked. She listened to them trying to tell her that I did not want to serve them when they came to buy. She said, "I can't believe that is what happened. However, if you ever lay your hands on him again, you will have to answer to me."

I cleaned up and left for school. I was now more than an hour late. However, the loneliness and isolation I felt were gone, knowing that my family cared. My sister actually came to my defense. That meant a great deal to me. Despite all the arguments we had, she really cared. For her to be successful, she had to be a tough, no-nonsense woman, but the knowledge that she actually cared mattered. That feeling that someone had your back was better than any therapy could have provided. Big Mac had always provided that. Now Big Sis had assumed the role.

After the incident, I took a more active role in handling production in the bakery behind the scenes. The decision could be my sister's genius. She may have realized that I would not win popularity by constantly being asked to give away her stuff and refusing. My role in production planning resulted in me finding several ways to improve and shorten production processes.

I was not worried, but I told Jenny that I didn't think the workers liked me. They didn't like me ordering them around. The response was that if my workers liked me, it was an indication that I was not doing a good job. That was her philosophy, and she actually believed that.

ii.

In tenth grade, I was nominated to run for deputy head boy, the second highest elected office for a male student. Teachers were responsible for fielding nominees for this position, the most visible student leadership positions.

Nominations for Head Boy/Girl were from grade eleven, the final class before graduation. After teachers selected the nominees, they were presented to the students who elected their choice by popular vote.

At the time I was nominated, I was not sure what the duties were, but teachers assured me that I would do just fine. We were asked to give speeches. I was nervous, even though I had some familiarity with public speaking, primarily at church. We all felt nervous. It was not discernable in all the voices, but from the vantage point of the platform, you could see the vibrating pants and skirts that were hidden from the view of the general public by the lectern.

The speech was the extent of my campaigning. I didn't stick around to meet members of the other shift. I participated in very few other extracurricular activities. After the speech, some students wanted to talk—not about any specific issues, but to gain a comfort level with their prospective representative. This concept was lost on me as I brushed them aside and went to take care of my duties at the bakery. A friend, nicknamed Prekay, quipped that I needed to start giving away a lot of coco bread and patties. I made it known that I didn't think it was funny.

The results of the election were not told to me ahead of time; I sat with the student body as the results were read a day later. The new deputy head boy had won decisively even though he had recently moved to the area and attended school only a few months. In such a short time, he built relationship with teachers and students alike and had made enough friends to help him win a decisive victory.

I congratulated him and the other winners. I was not at all concerned with popularity, nor was I image conscious. However, I had come to the strange realization that perception guided reality. Fairly or unfairly, I was perceived as all business. A few of my classmates had mimicked me looking at my watch and quickening my steps. This was a signal that I did not spend enough time around them except in class.

Ironically, I was starting to see similarities leveled at the prime minister, Edward Seaga. He was known to be a hard worker and a performer, but he alienated friends and colleagues alike with his autocratic and brash leadership style. His more charismatic opponent, Michael Manley, was more liked and had better people skills. Despite a devastating defeat in 1980, when people thought his career was finished, Michael Manley was engineering a comeback.

I couldn't help but take object lesson from the lives of these men and from my sister. She was tough with her workers but friendly with customers and suppliers. This would be a lesson for me to learn. There was no guarantee that I would be nominated for head boy the following year, but I would be the best student I could be.

Over the next year, I would not find more time, but I could be more efficient with the time I had. I occasionally took my lunch to school and ate with classmates. I also became the emcee for student programs. I was still not popular, but I gained respect, and people developed a comfort level with me, knowing that I was reliable and could get things done. When it was time again for the election for head boy, I was nominated to run against the popular deputy head boy. The only campaign event would be speeches at the general assembly before the vote. To pull this off, I would need to involve the students in my speech, and that was not going to be easy. The acoustics were not good, and that meant maybe 50 percent of the speech would be heard.

I began by formally addressing the principal VP, members of the academic and administrative staff, my worthy opponent, and my fellow students. I borrowed a memorable quote—modified to my situation—that I had heard given by Edward Seaga in 1980. "And now, fellow students, I am feeling like an expectant mother counting down the days to delivery. After seven days, six days, after six days . . . " By the time I go to five days, the entire student body was with me. "After two days, one day, and after one day, Election Day." When the speech ended, staff and students alike were on their feet laughing and clapping. A day after the election the results were announced, and I had won the hearts of the staff and students of Maggotty Secondary (now Maggotty High).

iii.

There was great anticipation in the air for the annual Sports Day, and preparations were in high gear. To facilitate preparations, regular classes were missed or interrupted. For many teachers, it was a welcome divergence, not only from classes, but also from the intense salary negotiations between the national teachers' union and the government. During this long process, the teachers conducted themselves overtly with professionalism. Among colleagues, however, they were frustrated with the pace of negotiations, and patience was wearing thin.

All was going well with Sports Day preparations until a student, who was a senior, had an altercation with a female teacher. The student was verbally abusive and concluded the conversation by "telling the teacher, 'go fuck yourself.'" This incident became the catalyst that brought unrelated issues to a boiling point.

The irate teacher left the field where the incident had occurred and bemoaned her frustration to a sympathetic staff. The staff then decided that there would be no Sports Day, and the principal reluctantly went along with the decision. The teachers were frustrated that the extra time they were putting into extracurricular activities, beyond the requirements of their jobs, were not rewarded by the government nor respected or appreciated by the ungrateful students.

Naturally, when the announcement was made, it angered the students, and a tense situation boiled even hotter. I was made aware of the situation as I walked from the bakery to the campus. Students stopped me on the street to get information, oblivious to the fact that I was not aware of this new development. In many students' minds, this was collective punishment, and it was unfair. Why didn't they just suspend the boy? Why cancel Sports Day and punish everybody? Within minutes, the solidarity that students had for their teachers' collective bargaining effort evaporated.

The fuse was already set, and only a spark was needed for the campus to erupt. With this level of intensity, any student's protest would almost certainly involve rioting and destruction of property. Athletes talked among themselves about how they had prepared and now would not have a chance to compete. Competing could set the stage for these students to get scholarships or set the stage for completion at a higher level. Vendors who had stalls near the entrance of the school, as well as businesses in the community, were gearing up for increased demand for an event only days away.

I walked in the corridor in the direction of my class. A voice called out to me, "Head Boy, what kind of fucking nonsense is that?" I knew the voice. Ordinarily, I would have reprimanded that kind of talk, especially coming from a student leader, Kenroy, but this was no ordinary day, and this boy was representing the feeling of the students. My role was not so clear-cut. My role was an extension of the staff, but the students had elected me. I did not want to encourage Kenroy since he was already in a militant mood. Ignoring him, however, could be at our peril.

"We are going to find out what happened," I said. "Where is Paulette?" I asked. (Paulette was the head girl.)

"She is upstairs," came the reply. "And there is nothing to find out. They cancelled Sports Day!"

Paulette was one of my classmates. Another classmate was her best friend Herma—sister of the now-militant Kenroy. As I walked to find Paulette, I asked Kenroy to delay any protest action, but I was not convinced that he would listen. I entered the classroom, and found Paulette talking with other members of the class. She had come to the same conclusion. Something had to be done. More importantly, we had to do something.

"Let us go see the principal," I suggested. "Also, could you ask Herma to talk to her brother, so he doesn't start any protest?" Paulette was from the same town as Herma and Kenroy, and she volunteered to talk to him.

We met with the principal and made sure we did not cross him. Previously, he had appeared visibly annoyed if students came and sat in his office, especially if he did not offer a seat. Paulette and I made sure we did not commit any of those errors. We made our case and Principal Thompson listened respectfully before retorting.

"The teachers had made their decision which I support." He was taken aback when I asked if we could speak directly to the staff. But then he smiled and agreed. The meeting was set up. Paulette went to encourage Kenroy to keep things calm.

I went in search of Clive—the boy who was involved in the incident. I knew him. He had acted up a few times, but was not a bad kid. He was also feeling ostracized as the cancellation of Sports Day had not won him any friends. Before the meeting with the teachers, Paulette and I spoke with Clive and confirmed that he was sorry for his role in what had transpired.

We told him of our plan and assured him that he would not be beaten. We could not guarantee this, but beating students at the senior level was unusual. After all, size does matter. Occasionally, however, students would get collared and even slapped as teachers proved that they still had it. I too, had suffered this fate in an earlier grade, despite the fact that I was a student leader at the time. As a prefect, I had tried with little success to keep a group of students quiet during a general meeting. The principal was walking through the crowd and saw the group talking and disrupting the proceeding and started hitting all involved, including me. I protested and explained my role, and he promptly apologized and shook my hand. I accepted his apology, but the hit would ache for another two days.

We took turns addressing the teachers and apologizing for what had happened. We continued to explain why this collective punishment would not only be a miscarriage of justice but would send the wrong signal about personal responsibility. We explained that even Clive was sorry for his role in this.

Finally, the aggrieved teacher interrupted. "Why are you apologizing, and you didn't do anything? Clive should be the one apologizing!" she continued.

I agreed and excused myself and called Clive whom we had asked stay close. He came into the classroom, somewhat sheepish and remorseful for what had happened. Before anyone spoke, the aggrieved teacher addressed him.

"You have a nerve coming in here." She moved toward him, and a male teacher stood guard. I held up my hand and asked them to stand back. I didn't want him spooked. The aggrieved teacher took him by the shirt and complained. Clive avoided eye contact and was genuinely remorseful. The teacher let go of his shirt, and he stood his ground and apologized. I was proud of him.

We thanked the staff for meeting with us, and moments later we left. We went outside to curious students trying to read our faces for new developments. There were none. The staff was meeting, and we had to give them time. We would meet the principal later for a follow-up.

We met with the principal reinforcing our request to avoid the collective punishment. We were in the middle of our discussion when a group of approximately a dozen students were heard banging on the rail and desks. "We want to see Mr. Thompson right now," Kenroy shouted. I wondered if it was a tactical error not to include him (the student councilor) in the discussion, but then decided that it was the best decision. He was an unguided missile and could have angered the teachers with his rhetoric.

The charming and always elegantly dressed Ms. Anderson, our math teacher, implored the principal not to go outside, as she feared for his safety. Principal Thompson stepped outside, ignoring her advice, and addressed Kenroy. I looked at Paulette, and she was furious. Kenroy had not listened. Mr. Thompson explained that the students' concerns were being represented by the leaders of the students now in his office. He returned to the office and expressed satisfaction with the way we had handled ourselves as student leaders. We talked for a little while longer, and I met the glances and smiles of Ms. Anderson.

I couldn't help recalling some of my earlier days when I had a crush on her. Her soft, dark skin, and a slightly darker shade of stocking that covered her long legs. She had an air of sophistication, poise, and elegance that was reflected in the way she dressed, spoke, and walked.

I was brought back to reality as the principal had his administrative assistant ring the bell for a meeting with all students. After students gathered, he explained that no one should touch Clive on his way home. He said something complimentary about how Clive faced the issue he had caused. Then, he commended the students for their selection of a head girl and head boy. We made it clear that our effort was responsible for a change in the decision that would reinstitute Sports Day. The students erupted in applause and jubilant celebration and danger was averted.

iv.

My sister Jasmine visited Jamaica for the second time since she immigrated to London. She and brother Valentine were from Big Mac's previous union. Since her initial visit, she made plans with Big Mac to purchase property in Jamaica with the intentions of retiring in Jamaica and providing her children an opportunity to reconnect with their roots.

Big Mac was on cloud nine. Not only had he reconnected with his daughter, but he was also in charge of helping her locate a property and build her house. Even though Jasmine was not Mom's daughter, they had a relationship that allowed Mom to warn her, in a not so subtle way, that her dad was not good with money.

Big Mac went into action and Jasmine purchased a property in rural Trinail. Mom tried to convince him that, for a woman who had lived most of her life in a city where modern amenities were taken for granted, she would find it difficult to live there. Her recommendation was ignored.

Three years after the purchase, Dad started building, and by the time I was head boy, Big Mac was spending most of his time on the property. He stayed at a small two- bedroom house that was on the property. Big Mac's building ended with the construction of a tank made from stones, marl, and cement. Jasmine's resources would later be depleted, and her house never got built.

However, she can take solace in the fact that her investment in a water tank now served members of the community who sought water when the public supply ran low.

Big Mac felt a sense of empowerment from his daughter's assets. His ego was boosted and so was his libido. He started a relationship with a young woman and fathered a new daughter.

Mom was not going to take this lying down, so she set out to win back her husband. I was still working at the bakery and attending school and didn't have the time to process what had happened. On weekends, Kenny would fill me in. He dramatized and made fun of the situation, and it took the sting out of it as we laughed at the latest detail. Mom, of course, was humiliated by all of this, but kept fighting to get her husband back.

I was at the bakery when there was breaking news from Maggotty Square. Less than a quarter of a mile from the bakery, Big Mac, the preacher, my father, his girlfriend, and his wife, my mother, were involved in a fight in the town's market. The employees at the bakery repeated their own version of the story as I grimaced. Seeing Big Mac and the girl together was too much for Mom. She slapped the "concubine" and issued an order to leave her husband alone. Big Mac tried to break it up as the crowd gathered for what became a spectacle in an otherwise sleepy town.

As the day ended, it occurred to me that this could be the beginning of my humiliation. I had attained the most visible student leadership position at Maggotty Secondary School, and my parents were in a fight in the town's square. A statement I have always heard my grandmother use now had meaning. "The higher the monkey climbs, the more he is exposed." After much careful thought, I vowed that I would not let my parents' behavior define mine. I would face the music and hold my head up high. I could not be held responsible for their actions. Little did I know that the music was about to get louder.

On my way to class several months later, I noticed a group of students sitting in an area not designated for classes. I walked over to find out what was going on. Some of the students noticed my approach and smiled, waved, and hurried off to their classes. One remained, and I sensed a challenge to my authority as head boy.

"What's going on?" I inquired. "Don't you have class?"

"Leave me alone, you rasshole (Jamaican expletive) fucking Big Mac boy. You think you are all that, and your father is a bombow claut (more Jamaican expletives) convict."

I was stung, but did not show it. "Well, that does not explain why you are not in class," I said.

"Leave me the fuck alone," he continued. I couldn't. I knew if I did, I would slowly lose respect and become a public laughingstock. I implored him to go to class, but he was not moving. I left him and reported the incident to the vice principal, who seemed upset and went in search of the boy. When the vice principal found him, he issued a strong reprimand seasoned with some lashes.

I felt relieved and nauseated at the same time. This was the first student who would receive lashes because of my inability to handle the situation. No doubt I was upset and impatient when confronted with the behavior of my parent.

For a while, I reflected on the incident and concluded that the student was no doubt disrespectful. However, he was simply stating a fact; and though it hurt, he was telling the truth. My father was now in prison. He had gotten into a fight with a trespasser on Jasmine's property. Mom attended the sentencing, and her jaw hit the floor as the judge read his criminal history prior to sentencing. Big Mac had fled his former life and had left a path of death and destruction.

Months later, I visited my father in Jamaica's most notorious prison. He was in survival mode and had nothing to tell me. He had lost weight and was now a smaller man, but he was not broken. He asked for money, and I gave him all I had except what I needed to travel home. We did not talk about anything in particular. When the sergeant proclaimed that visiting time had ended, I watched him walk away. I did not understand my emotions or what I expected of him. As I walked away to catch the bus, I covered my face with my hands in a losing battle to hold back my tears.

(After serving a year, Big Mac's sentence was reduced as he was paroled. His newfound relationship with God, his age of fifty-eight, and an overcrowded prison system could be thanked for his early release.)

<u>Lesson 9:</u> The higher the monkey climbs, the more he is exposed.

V.

As graduation approached, I wondered what would be next. I wanted to continue my education, but I did not have a clear path.

It was customary for the head boy to be asked to be the valedictorian. However, this year, my counterpart, the head girl, had other ideas. Paulette mentioned to our homeroom teacher that she was concerned that every year only the head boy became the valedictorian. I had a sense of fair play and did not disagree with her. Graduation went by smoothly, and Paulette was the first head girl to address her graduating class.

At the end of the summer following graduation, my sister took Sandra and I to see the principal of STETHS, Mr. Burton. He lived on the school campus, and we made an unannounced visit one evening. Jenny chatted with him for over an hour, and Sandra and I went back to our car as they continued the discussion.

Mr. Burton was learning something I already knew—that my sister was a determined and persuasive woman who never accepted no for an answer. When she exited the principal's residence and joined us in the car, she was partially disappointed with the compromise. I had gotten into STETHS on the basis of my leadership progress at Maggotty Secondary. Unfortunately, Sandra had not.

There would be no time to waste. Registration was over, and some classes had already begun; I was already at a disadvantage. I had gotten into STETHS through the persuasion of my sister and through precedents. Other student leaders and outstanding athletes from Maggoty High had gotten into STETHS in previous years. The principal had used his discretion after seeing how many students had returned to school for the new term. Some had migrated or accepted opportunities elsewhere. I got to work right away obtaining books. I sat with the guidance counselor who told me in no uncertain terms that I needed a study plan.

Throughout my entire life as a student up to that point, I had no meaningful study plan. Not only was I older than many of the students in my class, but also most of the subject matter that I would be taught would be new to me. I would have only two years at STETHS. Many of the other students viewed these grades as revision of the syllabus or extending their knowledge of concepts they had learned in earlier grades. This would end with preparation for the external exam in the eleventh grade.

Weeks later, my guidance counselor would give me more tough-love advice. She told me that I needed to delete the word *late* from my vocabulary. Working at the bakery and missing the bus to school was not going to be an acceptable excuse. This was invaluable advice, but it would be a difficult sell to Jenny, who had done very well despite the fact that she had less than a high school education, and who was conflicted. Her business would need someone she could trust and rely on. However, if I excelled, then it was possible that my future would not be in her business.

I realized that my sister had the same work expectations of me, but I had to decide that I could not make the bakery a priority. I was behind academically and had to make the most of this once-in-a-lifetime opportunity. This was the opportunity I had sought when I wrote to the prime minster years earlier. The opportunity had come in the unexpected way of Jenny appealing to the principal.

My new focus on school created tensions as my sister realized that I was laying off responsibilities at the bakery to focus on the rigors of school. My other sibling, Collin, who worked at the bakery, made it clear that life did not revolve around me. When I got home from school, he and other workers would leave, making it more difficult to end the day's operations at the bakery.

One evening, I pleaded with Collin to delay going to see his girlfriend and help finish up the wrapping and packing of baked products. After reminding me that I was not the boss of him, he repeated advice he had given years earlier. He reiterated that since I was given the opportunity to handle several thousands of dollars, I was a fool not to take small quantities and put it away for myself. "You are working very hard," he continued. "But you will not have any claims to any of what is around you. The children who will inherit this are not here, and you should think about that."

Collin meant well. I explained to him that because I didn't steal was the reason I was trusted to continue handling money in the first place. If I violated that trust, it would be next to impossible to regain it. Not only would I be breaking one of the Ten Commandments, but also I was grateful to Jenny who had fought to get me into a technical high school. "In addition," I continued. "She was the one who fought to keep you out of jail after you stole the bicycle. Now you are giving me advice to steal from her?"

I won the argument with Collin, but not his help, and I struggled to complete packaging the breads and buns for delivery. Collin was right about one thing. Jenny pushed her children to attain academic excellence. In addition, she made friends with a number of teachers who visited and tutored them during the breaks. With me, however, she was conflicted.

It was after 8:00 p.m. when my work at the bakery was done. I now had to complete several school assignments before bed. Minutes after I handed over the bakery keys to my sister, the lights went out. At first, I was angry with the utility company, before I made a strange observation. That's strange, I thought. The top house still has light, and so does the bakery, and the shops, and the streets. Apparently, someone had decided that we were wasting energy and turned off the electricity from the breaker controlled by the top house.

After futile calls and appeals to restore the lights, I decided that this was just one more challenge. I picked up my books and a chair and utilized the outside light from the bakery. Very soon this became a routine, and Ridgeback, the watchdog, became my study companion as he lay at my feet late into the night.

The relationship between Jenny and me was not improving. She made more demands on my time, and I pushed back. I solicited the help of one of her friends to explain to her the demands of school. Her friend, Mrs. Rowe, was a teacher who boarded Mark and Christine at her house. I thought she would be the ideal candidate.

Mrs. Rowe did the job, and the light stayed on. Less than a year later, their friendship ended, and I was forced to wonder if her intervention on my behalf had set in motion an irreconcilable strain.

My first report showed me doing well in accounting, agricultural science, and biology. However, I struggled with math, physics, and chemistry. I had decided on this mix of subjects to give me a mix of business and the sciences. I loved the sciences except for chemistry, which remained a mystery.

I knew what the problem was after my first and only lab session. Because of scarcity and lack of funding, most of what we learned was theory. I had no knowledge of what some of the basic chemicals were like. I was a visual person, and working with chemicals in the abstract was not my strong suit.

I solicited the help of my math and physics teacher, Mr. Levy, to diagnose why I was having such difficulty with math and physics. His diagnosis was very instructive.

"You grasped the larger concepts quickly, but you struggled with the math portion of the problem! You are highly logical, but you are missing some of the building blocks that would make you a proficient math student. Mathematics is very simple. All you do is add, subtract, divide, multiply, or a combination of adding, multiplying, dividing, or subtracting. Understanding the sequence is what is important."

His advice was very insightful, and I set a plan into motion. I resolved to learn basic math. I would start from kindergarten and work my way up. My tutor would be my mathematics textbook that catered to this approach. The only issue was time. Time was not on my side.

Before the school year ended, it was clear to me that I could not remain at the bakery. Jenny was increasingly agitated, and I could not understand why I made her that angry. I moved back to my parents' house, which extended my commute to school. Homework was now done by the light of a kerosene lamp.

I had new friends traveling to the same school from the same area: Roy, Wayne, and Andrea. They were hardworking, self-motivated students. The bus we took was always crowded. One morning, I found myself outside the bus, hanging from the door as it departed. If I missed that bus, I would be hours late for school.

While hanging from the bus steps, I had a sudden urge to fight my way inside. I fought the odor of barely deodorized armpits and made it to the second of three steps that led into the bus. Less than ten seconds had elapsed before the bus swerved to avoid collision with an oncoming truck, navigating the steep curve on the narrow road. On one side of the road were protruding rocks visible after the road construction. On the other side of the road was the downward slope continuing down for several hundred feet.

When the bus swerved, the rocks from the upper side of the road scraped off the passengers who hung from the back door. Three of those who were scraped off got up quickly, but one lay unconscious on the ground. Everyone got out of the bus to get a look at the boy lying on the ground. He was not a student. (These buses carried the general population and students alike.)

I looked up and saw a familiar van, a Ford Econoline approaching. It slowed at the sight of the crowd and stopped. I walked over and noticed Jenny and her driver. They were on their way to Montego Bay. I explained what had happened and she immediately ordered her driver to turn around, put the boy in the van, and take a forty-mile detour to the hospital. After less than a mile of travel, we knew he was dead.

vi.

I barely had time to contemplate my narrow escape from death before it was the summer after my first year at STETHS. I had left Jenny's house and would need a new source of income to continue to finance myself. Ideally, it would have been nice to spend the summer catching up on schoolwork. However, the reality was that I needed to work to be able continue school next term.

I went to work with another sister Beverly (Bev). Bev worked as an administrative assistant for an elevator servicing company in Kingston. The staff of the company was friendly and I fell in love with them immediately.

Bev had a great sense of humor, and everyone liked her. She was not the "go-getter" that Jenny was, but she would be the one to give a hug when one was needed. As the summer passed, I received word that Jenny had given birth to a beautiful baby girl, Shalane. I was shocked.

"I didn't know she was pregnant," I said.

Bev laughed. "You didn't know she was pregnant? You probably didn't even know that is why you guys were fighting all the time. There is a lot you have to learn about women," she continued. She was right!

At the start of my second and final year at STETHS, there was another surprise in store for me. The teachers nominated me to run for head boy. I was totally surprised. My grades for my first year were not exceptional, but most were better than average. Because I never took an entrance exam, I had always wondered if I really belonged. This doubt pushed me. I had worked hard to close the gap to prove to myself that I could measure up to the academic performance at this level.

What prompted the teachers to make such a decision to nominate me for head boy would remain a mystery. Did my repeated interventions and requests to students to minimize class disruptions have anything to do with it? My motive was known to my classmates. I had had to learn things in a much shorter time and could not afford clowning around. Obliviously, teachers took note of my efforts to help them maintain control of the classes. I was fully aware that some of the students were brilliant and their behavior in class were not always indicative of their abilities. Some were earlier introduced (in earlier grades) to some of the concepts I was now learning. For them, some class work was revision or extension of a concept previously learned. I would not have the luxury of learning this information more than once.

My defense of a neighbor's son about to be hazed or "grubbed," also created some waves with the teachers. The boy, like me, was new, but in a lower grade. He was walking his way around the campus when several seniors, many from my class, cornered him. I intervened, pushing them away and appealing to them, since he was my neighbor. Some classmates, some of whom had suffered this treatment in earlier grades, were not too happy with my interference and reminded me that even though I was in the senior grade, I was also a freshman and shouldn't assume that the pass I got was to be extended. I reminded them that I was as big as and older than many of them were. Therefore, I was not given a pass; after all, size does matter.

Nothing prepared me mentally for the possibility that I would receive consideration for student leadership. After all, it was only a year before that I started. However, the campaign was in earnest, and the major event would again be speeches in the auditorium during general assembly.

After my speech, many students stopped me in the corridor to chat. I was told repeatedly that they would support my election. Surprisingly, when the election votes were tallied a week later, the victory was close, but conclusive. I would be the next head boy. I was humbled. I recalled earlier the words of my grandmother and paraphrased them. The monkey had climbed a little higher and was now even more exposed. This was added motivation. As a visible leader, I had to succeed; failure was not an option.

***Lesson 10:* Size matters.**

With new responsibilities, my time would be even more limited. To shorten my commute and give me more study time, two of my classmates and I roomed together at a spacious house near the school. The couple with whom we boarded had no children. My roommates, Donovan and Darville, had developed good study habits, and I was pleased to be with them. Since our certificate would be in agricultural science, we were involved in several projects, including raising chickens for sale at the school. The proceeds from this venture would be used to celebrate our graduation.

Jenny and I had made up again. On weekends, I got the job of going to the beach house to clean up to prepare for guests. This worked out perfectly. Most of the time, it was unoccupied, and after I cobwebbed, mopped, and watered the plants, I would have the entire weekend to study.

The bag that I carried to the beach consisted mostly of books. I had not devised a good system to carry wet shorts and underwear with my books. At the end of each weekend before I left the beach house, I would wash the salt water from my shorts and hang them out to dry. Of course, that would present a dilemma if I wanted one last swim before I hit the road. To solve this problem, I would run to the back fence and look right and left, to make sure there was no one walking on the beach. Then, I would streak my way out to the rejuvenating waters of the Caribbean Sea, wearing only a broad smile. While in the water, people would walk or jog by. Clothed more than waist high in the refreshing water, I would wave politely, hoping they wouldn't stop for a chat. Luckily, the chats never lasted longer than an observation of how beautiful the day was, if it was likely to rain soon, and what effect the rain would have on the mosquitoes.

Final exams came and went, and it was time for graduation. The exams had lasted for a period of several weeks, and we were exhausted. The results of the external exams would not be known for weeks.

Graduation Day – STETHS

Addressing Graduation Class – STETHS

Graduation is a major event in the community. It is estimated that between five and seven thousand people were in attendance at my graduation ceremony. People attended for a number of reasons. Friends and family showed up to celebrate with their loved ones. Some used the event as a reunion. Some came to catch an early glimpse of track stars and other athletes destined for greatness. Others came to see dignitaries, and to be inspired by the speakers.

When it was time to deliver the valedictory address, I took the podium. I was nervous, but confident. I had personally written the speech with coaching from my English teacher, Mr. Ram, and acting principal, Mr. Lynton. Mr. Burton, my original principal, had taken another position at a private high school in Mandeville, Belair High.

In the audience were the faces of teachers, family and friends, and people who had had an influence on our lives as graduates. Those faces shone with pride and anticipation, and I addressed them on behalf of the graduating class.

When the speech ended, I knew that a new phase of our lives was about to start. Before it did, however, we would have to wait—wait to see how many O-level subjects we had passed. Depending on those results, I would determine which university and career path to choose.

After graduation, I plunged back into Jenny and Patrick's business. Our agreement was that I would work for a year, plus breaks and summers, in exchange for the payment of my college tuition. Jenny and Patrick had started to diversify and had developed an area in Maggotty called Apple Valley Park. It was a four-hundred-plus-acre property, seven miles from the world-renowned YS Falls, with an old five-bedroom great house. The great house was surrounded by a lush plantation and some mined-out areas left unclaimed by the demise of the Revere Bauxite Company. However, vegetation had now grown over most of the mined areas, and it all looked green. Since we were forty miles from the beach, we needed a new concept, and ecotourism became the driving force. The concept took off, and local and international tourists responded.

We took visitors on several guided tours, driving tractors to the edge of the river for visitors to see several of the twenty-four waterfalls on the property. Patrick put his creativity to work, and very soon there was a park with several pools for children to swim in, ponds for people to fish in and have their fish cleaned and cooked, merry-go-round rides, and other fun activities. Sugarcane was planted on the property and then sold to the nearby sugar and rum factory. Jenny also solicited help from the nearby maroon chief, who sent groups to perform ritualistic dances for the delighted guests.

Since tours to the area would usually include the nearby Appleton Estate rum factory, my sister added to her diversified business portfolio by catering authentic Jamaican meals for the visitors who rode by bus or train to the sugar estate. I never got tired of smelling the shavings from the pimento wood as it smoked the jerk chicken and other delights.

With all the growth, it was clear that one thing was needed: proper systems of internal controls. I thought I was the one to provide that, and I needed training. Old habits, however, would die hard; and trying to convince mom-and-pop entrepreneurs that systems were now required for growing operation was going to be difficult.

CHAPTER 10: NORTHERN CARIBBEAN UNIVERSITY

i.

The results of my external exams were back and I had passed all the subjects I had registered for, except chemistry. In accounting, I had scored exceptionally well. What a difference two years had made! My celebration was short lived. I had to make a choice about college. I worked at the bakery for a year while I evaluated my three local options for college: The University of the West Indies (UWI); The University of Technology (U-Tech)—formerly CAST; and Northern Caribbean University (NCU)—formerly West Indies College, operated by my church organization.

The University of the West Indies followed the British university system. However, the prospect of another two years for A-level preparation did not appeal to me. I applied to UTech and NCU, and after my acceptance to both, I visited each campus.

I liked UTech. They had a great business program and highly skilled professors, and their program would prove invaluable to the growing operation at Apple Valley Park and the bakery. (I had already settled on studying business administration.) In addition, the tuition was subsidized by the Jamaican government.

NCU catered to a wider audience. The student body was comprised of students from more than forty-four countries, including the United States, as well as some African countries. Up to this point, I had still not traveled outside Jamaica or traveled anywhere by airplane. The prospect of meeting students from all over the world was intriguing. I knew NCU would be my dad's preference, but since my parents were financially incapable of paying any of my bills, they would not be a factor in my decision. Besides, Big Mac's desire would be for me to study theology, and that was now no longer my passion.

It is difficult to quantify what led to my change of passion. Was it watching my sister wield influence? Was it my realization that while pastors, priests, and mother Teresas were forces of good in society, business leaders motivated by profit created jobs that gave people dignity and the ability to sustain their families. Whatever the reasons, I was now a business major.

I evaluated my options thoroughly, but my selection process was less analytical. I sat under a tree on NCU's campus and was swept away by the tranquil spring-like atmosphere. A gentle wind whistled through the leaves of the willow trees and brought with it the distant a-capella sound of a male quartet. The voices were from students in the men's dormitory, bellowing as they summoned the courage to take a cold shower in the heater-less bathroom. Their voices were melodious and reminded me of one of the things that this college had become famous for—good singing. The hymn they sang became one of my favorites.

> Come, Thou Fount of every blessing,
> Tune my heart to sing Thy grace;
> Streams of mercy, never ceasing,
> Call for songs of loudest praise.

When the singing faded, I realized I was lying on my back with my arms folded behind my head. I knew then that I had found a home for the next four years. Big Mac, I knew, would be pleased with my choice of a school, even though my choice of major was business administration.

ii.

What would you do if you lived on an island and when a hurricane threatened, there was nowhere to run? Three weeks after I started adjusting to life in the dorm at NCU, I was exposed to my first hurricane. Jamaica is surrounded by the Caribbean Sea, which together with the Gulf of Mexico and the North Atlantic Ocean, forms the Atlantic Basin. This basin, according to the weather service, is responsible for virtually all the hurricanes that directly affect the contiguous United States.

With this level of activity, Jamaica has had a number of threats and close misses. When a hurricane threatens an island that size, there is nowhere to run, and people prepare in different ways: Some people prepare by buttoning down; some move from low-lying areas; some pray; some drink; some do a combination of things; but all tell stories.

I had just convinced myself that nothing could be worse than my first college registration ordeal. We spent several hours in line to pay tuition, to register for a class, to speak to an advisor. The entire process seemed inefficient. Hurricane Gilbert was about to provide evidence that things could get worse. Despite several near misses, this would be my first experience with a storm that took direct aim at the island.

I opted to remain on campus during the storm. Being two thousand feet above sea level was somewhat more comforting than where I lived in Maggotty. As the storm approached, there were several stories circulating, stories about the previous storm to hit the island in 1951—hurricane Charlie. NCU's belief in self-sufficiency was evident even before then. When I attended, the college had a farm, which included livestock, despite the fact that a vegetarian diet was strictly enforced in the cafeteria. In addition, it produced its own cornflakes, boasted a bakery, a cannery, a printing press, and other enterprises.

As the stories go, in 1951 when the storm hit, the roads were impassable and no food supply was forthcoming from Kingston.

The college harvested a lot of corn that the wind had blown down. The chef at that time utilized corn for all meals that he prepared. For breakfast, lunch, and dinner, there was some version of corn: corn on the cob, cornbread, corn pudding, corn porridge, corn hominy, turn cornmeal, corn fritters, and corn casserole.

After a week of this diet, all the men in the dorm woke up before dawn and started crowing like roosters. After the second day of crowing, the college president visited and addressed them. "Gentlemen, I understand that you have had more than your acceptable ration of corn. And believe me, anyone who consumes that much corn deserves to crow. But please don't do it so early in the morning. Even the cocks don't start their crowing that early."

Of course, no hurricane stories session is complete until the Rastafarian (dread) or his impersonator speaks. Not only does the dread flash his locks and cause lightning, but we also get a lesson on how the different categories of hurricane are produced. The speed or the revolution of the flashing dreadlocks determines the hurricane category. Category 1 results from slow-flashing locks; category 2 indicates an increased revolution—increasing to category 5.

Humorous stories are Jamaica's way of saying that no matter how beaten up you are, no matter how humbled we are by Mother Nature's fury, the sun comes out and smiles, reminding us that life goes on.

Hurricane Gilbert caused severe destruction to homes, businesses, farms, and infrastructure on the Island. There was damage to some of the college buildings. We watched from the dorm as roofing materials peeled off the college chapel. Adrenaline rushed through each body, and some cheered at the prospect of no chapel. Others expressed disbelief at the cheering and the destruction. All were in awe at the power of Mother Nature.

The next day, I left the campus and went to check on my family and was pleased that all were fine, despite the fact that our bakery had sustained some damage. Although many methods of communication were disrupted, the radio gave several updates that reassured people about loved ones. I was inspired by the way everyone jumped into the cleanup effort. Neighbors used axes, saws, and machetes to clear public and private roads. With strong governmental leadership, a resilient local attitude, help from neighbors and friends from near and far, and with aid from abroad, the country was able to bounce back within weeks. Two weeks later the college resumed classes.

Resilience does not always demonstrate itself in ways that make everyone proud. News reports of men and women in certain parts of Kingston emptying electronics stores of refrigerators and televisions during the storm produced a popular refrain with many, including my father. "I wish they would stop calling them looters. That sounds too civil. They are "*damn thieves*."

iii.

After the hurricane, pundits speculated that an election would be called. Not only had I never voted before, but I also was not registered to vote. Jamaica adopted the British Westminster system of government, where a prime minister can call an election at any time during a five-year term. In 1983, a snap election was called only three years into

Edward Seaga's term. It was approaching five years since that election.

Mr. Seaga dismissed the idea of a snap election after the disastrous hurricane Gilbert. Instead, he focused on rebuilding the country's infrastructure. People were generally impressed with the pace of his administration's reconstruction efforts and Seaga's crisis management skills. Seaga expected to benefit from this goodwill, but he did not. Normalcy reminded people how much they disliked his autocratic management style. Months later, when the election was called, Manley was re-elected in a landslide.

Mr. Manley had done a major job rebranding his image after a devastating defeat to Seaga only eight years earlier. Manley was no longer close to Fidel Castro's regime, and with the Soviet Union poised for collapse, the USA was indifferent to the election outcome. Manley was now a vocal champion of the free market system and ran to the right of Seaga on some issues. For me, however, it was another election in which I had not voted because I was not registered to vote.

iv.

Graduation Day – NCU (Left to Right Joseph and classmates, Marva and Terrence

Even though my major was business administration with emphasis in accounting, my program included a number of subjects not business related. At first, I was apprehensive about the theological content of some of my subjects. While I was not opposed to these subjects, I questioned their utility, especially since they required tuition payment. I was reminded, however, of the college mission to produce well-rounded individuals for service for the here and hereafter. This holistic agenda focused on the physical, mental, social, and spiritual needs of students.

The physical aspect included regular exercise, gardening, manual labor, and the cafeteria that served only vegetarian meals. Almost instantly, I became a "campus vegetarian" feasting on menus that reminded me of my carnivorous diet. The soy-based mock chicken and beef prompted me to savor the taste of my sister's jerk chicken and beef patties when I went home or left campus.

Despite the fact that I agreed with the teachings of the church to maintain a healthy lifestyle and treat people with respect, I had made a decision not to accept dogmas without challenging them. It was one of these discussions with the professors that won me the friendship of Owen who along with two guys (both named Errols) became our study partners. I had challenged the good-natured professor on the biblical interpretation of something he had said. After class, Owen asked me why I had backed away from the challenge.

"Simple," I said. "I don't understand Greek or Hebrew." My instructor claimed that the King James Version's translation of the original text of the passage in question was not the best translation. Since I could not read the original text, there was no point in continuing the discussion. In addition, the mission of the church organization was to do good. I didn't need to accept all the theological teachings to support a mission of service to others.

After my second year in college, I applied for graduation for an associate degree. Jenny, who had succeeded without a formal education, decided that since I had graduated, I had had enough education. I reminded her that our agreement was for a four-year degree, but she declined to continue our financing arrangement. I was disappointed, but I thanked her and told her in no uncertain terms that I would continue school.

It was not going to be easy; I didn't have any savings. I spent a week looking back over the past two years. I had taken several steps to reduce the cost of college. After the first semester, I had reduced the meal plan from three to two and was pleased that Jenny and Patrick noticed my commitment to reducing cost. In year two, I moved off campus and gained additional savings. During breaks in the semester, I went home and worked. This apparently was not enough. I recalled a word of advice I had gotten from a friend and teacher of Maggotty Secondary—Mr. Brown. Mr. Brown cautioned me about attaching my dreams to someone else's dreams.

The fact that I now had an associate degree turned out to be a blessing when I went in search of a job. The job I needed would allow me to attend college in the afternoons and evenings.

Lesson 11: ***If you confuse the dreams of others as your own, you could wake up to a nightmare.***

V.

I had not known much about the Belair High School when I walked onto the campus. But it soon became evident that the lifestyle was a slice of Jamaica I had not seen enough of. Many students drove to school. Belair was a private school that catered primarily to the wealthy and middle classes. Generally speaking, the wealthy and middle classes preferred the public high schools since, by most indicators, they performed at the highest standards. Belair allowed the children of movers and shakers to network and form bonds with each other.

Expatriates from the USA working in Jamaica sent their children to schools like Belair since these schools catered to students preparing to attend US colleges and universities. In addition, many Jamaicans living in the US also sent their children to schools like Belair. These parents hoped to prevent their children from adopting the prevailing bad habits in some US public schools, whose pupils did not think it was cool to be smart.

I was pleasantly surprised when I met with the principal at Belair. He was my former principal from STETHS. As soon as we got through the preliminaries and I told him my desire, he told me that I might just be the person he was looking for. He needed a boarding master to oversee the boarding-house in which nearly forty boys stayed. I immediately raised an objection because I attended classes in the evenings. He assured me that I would not be the only boarding master, and I could work out my schedule with another boarding master. This would not be a paid position, but it provided room and board. I would also have a paid position as a teacher of business subjects such as accounting and principles of business and marketing.

I was thrilled at the prospect and ignored caution from several members of the staff who told me I might want to reconsider the boarding house option. I was single-minded. There would be no reconsideration. I would get my bachelor's degree, and this was going to be the vehicle with which to do it. I felt extremely lucky and set out to find another boarding master for my principal.

I found Emile, a theology student from Haiti, who was happy for the break. Our happiness was short lived as the summer ended and the boys started arriving. It took less than two days to realize why members of the teaching staff had advised against me taking on such an assignment.

My job brought many roles I had not anticipated. In addition to being a teacher and a boarding master, I was also a counselor, a big brother, and a father to some of the boys. Most were typical boys with bundles of energy. However, some were from broken homes and told stories verbally and behaviorally that required full-time attention, more than I could provide. Little did I know that if I didn't find time, they would demand my undivided attention.

Our job was to supervise the boys for study and make sure they left the dorm to attend class. A team of ladies cleaned the dorm and prepared meals for the boys. On weekends, some boys would go home. Those who stayed would play, do homework, and visit town.

At first, my approach was autocratic. My time was limited and I wanted quick results. This approach worked for only a short time. The younger boys responded, and things went well, but not with the older boys. Neil was the eldest of the boys, only three years younger than I was. He resented this treatment and rebelled. He also decided to build an effective opposition against me.

One afternoon while the boys played soccer, I rang the bell to announce the start of study hall. I could hear Neil, advising that they should keep playing and "ignore the bell." The younger boys who defied Neil's instructions could pay dearly. Neil's methods of encouraging conformity were not available to the teachers and employees.

This issue came to a head one Friday. It was nearly midnight and the boys were restless and not responding to lights out. In retrospect, since this was a weekend, I could have let the issue slide. However, I understood that my authority was being challenged and things were already getting out of hand. As I walked in the dorm, I picked up a piece of board thrown into the passage by one of the boys. The board kept the mattress in place on the bunk beds. The boys sometimes removed them from the beds as a prank and watched with delight as their fellow boarder and mattress fell to the ground or onto the bottom bunk.

I walked through the room while several boys dashed for cover, and some found refuge in the wrong beds. I slapped the board on the rail of those in the wrong bed, and some boys laughed at being discovered and ran for their own beds. After a few other similar incidents, an eerie calm took over. I walked back to my room, and very soon the entire dorm was in an uproar. Furniture was being overturned, and threats were being made to burn down the dorm. I did not consider it an idle threat, as one of the boarders had torched his parents' house.

When I re-emerged from my room, Neil and other boys confronted me, complaining that I was beating the boys with the bed board I was carrying. While he championed the cause of protecting the boys from physical abuse, he punched any boy who did not want to be part of any protest. I went to talk to Neil and found myself surrounded by five older boys.

I approached Neil and said in no uncertain terms that he was playing with fire. I suspect that they had planned to jump me, but were thrown off when I didn't flinch. I was soft-spoken, and they had calculated that I would run away when confronted. They were wrong. That night, the boys complained and chanted, and their protest escalated.

On Saturday, I called the principal, but did not speak with him directly. However, he was already apprised of the situation by the house matron, who also lived on campus next to the dorm with her daughter and son who attended another high school. Her version of the story was from the perspective of the older boys. She was very close to them, and it was not unusual for her to be seen cuddling them in a "motherly way" in her house and bed. This matron wore a tough exterior despite the passing of her husband.

The issue escalated as I told several boys that they could face suspension, and they called their parents. I was certain that after what had happened, suspension would be a solution for a few. However, I made a tactical error in mentioning "suspension" before updating the principal of the situation. It was his decision if a student was to be removed from the dorm. He also had to consider what would happen if a student was removed from the dorm, but not from school. I obviously had not thought about these issues or had my authority level defined.

The *suspension* word caught the attention of several parents who were shocked that their angels would do anything that was not perfectly appropriate. For my part, I had not used the proper chain of command, and when parents called the principal concerned about suspension, he quickly dismissed those ideas since they were not discussed with him. This was a valuable learning experience for me. I had the tendency to handle situations and resolve them myself.

However, it was important to respect the chain of command. I had a responsibility to protect my superiors from being blindsided, and clearly I had not done that. In addition, I had allowed the grapevine report to be a substitute for my report. This was clearly an error in judgment.

At Belair, I also learned about the clash of cultures—American and Jamaican. Several boys had grown up in America and started to assert rights that were not consistent with the Jamaican culture. They expected to be treated with respect. The Jamaican culture used threats, humiliation, and violence to encourage conformity, while American culture encouraged dialogue and respect in resolving disputes.

I recalled my experience with my father and had vowed not to be like him when I raised my own children. However, dealing with several boys, I found that the temptation was always there to take shortcuts, especially with time as a scarce commodity.

The situation remained tense as the weekend passed. None of the boys was suspended, and I was not resigning. The other boarding master, Emile, remained unscathed during this time. He was focused on his studies and spent most of his time on the college campus. He came home only to sleep and preside over his study hall.

Emile was in charge of study hall on Monday when a teacher from the school came by and interrupted study to address the students. I had an evening class, but I came home to see him there. He provided a forum for the students to vent, and when I walked in and stopped to listen, they had come to the conclusion that I was to leave.

<u>Lesson 12:</u> Not only is it important to do the right thing, but also to do the right thing in the right way.

I took the floor to speak, and at the time, I thought that this was our dorm, and he should have asked permission before addressing the students. However, since I was not sure what had transpired before, I did not address that issue. When I spoke, he realized that soft-spoken and wimpy were not synonymous. I made it clear that I was going nowhere. Anyone who wanted to leave was welcomed to do so. I would remain the boarding master unless asked by the principal to leave.

After that experience, there were several lessons learned. Neil understood that he had made a miscalculation. When Neil graduated, he boasted in the student yearbook that he was responsible for the departure of five boarding masters. At the time, I did not realize that this was a game to him, but I had escaped being one of his statistics. Mr. Burton—through his agent—learned that I was committed. I learned that I had a difficult job on my hands and needed a new approach in dealing with the boys. They were smart and intelligent young men, and I could not treat them all as little boys.

What followed was an amazing transition. I had a meeting with the other boarding master and some of the older boys, and I decided to put a few of them in charge of monitoring study hall and as dorm prefects. Emile was on duty the first time Neil was in charge of study hall. When I came home, I was amazed to see how quiet the place was. The session ended soon, and Emile told me the quietness had lasted during the study. Neil and the older boys had managed to keep order and control better than I or Emile could. It was not a fluke, and Sheldon, Chuck, and others also instituted strict discipline.

I started spending a few minutes each day chatting with the boys and learning their stories. Apart from the many broken homes, their stories were interesting. They spoke mostly of their parents. Some parents were very successful professionals, business people, and politicians. Some parents were just barely making it and hoped that by sending the children to private school, they would have a better life.

One father was imprisoned for drug dealing and other crimes. Some boys were expelled from other schools. Some had personal tragedies, the loss of a parent or a sibling. All the boys wore tough exteriors, but all sought acceptance and respect.

Our relationships continued to improve. I played volleyball, soccer, and arm wrestled with the boys. The relationship between Neil and me also improved. I provided tutoring to him, Sheldon, and others for my accounting class, and found that they also helped me to gain better control of my classes. It was a remarkable turnaround and a valued lesson on the benefits of shared responsibility.

I introduced a point system that rated the boys on how they kept their beds. Those with high scores were rewarded with longer free time. Competition was a good motivator, and even I was surprised at the remarkable improvement in how the boys began to keep their beds and dorm.

Despite improvements, everything was a juggling act. While my relationship with the boys improved, my own grades in college suffered. My days on the honor roll would not return despite my best effort. I also learned that systems do work, but life is constantly changing. When Emile left and a new boarding master was hired, things had to change.

vi.

Emile had had enough and did not return. He was replaced with another boarding master—Richard—who took control. I was happy for this, since I needed to refocus on college. He was also good with the boys, and since he was older, he gained their respect as a father figure.

As soon as we hit a stride, Richard got caught in a power struggle with the house matron. They both competed for Mr. Burton's ear to gain influence. I stayed neutral, and this greatly disappointed Richard. He requested a meeting with the principal and house matron, and he assumed I would jump in and take sides.

One evening, while I was on duty, Richard kept the only phone available for the boys' use in his room. The phone was mostly used to communicate with parents. Since study hall was in session, I didn't mind, but after study hall, the boys started making requests to speak to their parents as they had done repeatedly. I knocked on Richard's door and told him I was getting requests from the boys. Half an hour later, I tried again. He opened the door and then slammed the door in my face. This was a little too much for me to handle, and I ripped the line out that led into his room.

Richard was upset and came out with a baseball bat, threatening to take me out. He was threatening and vocal while I remained silent. All this occurred as the boys gathered around and watched the spectacle. The next day, he was gone, and I would remain the lone boarding master until the term ended.

During the fracas, Richard had said that the boys hated me, and that I should leave. I was not particularly bothered, but I was pleasantly surprised a week later when Neil publicly stated that Richard was not speaking on the behalf of the boys. "Sir, we don't always agree with you, but we respect you." I was heartened by Neil's attempt to be magnanimous, and I was convinced that, despite his antics, he was a leader. Neil's leadership was about to be upstaged by a returning boarder, Kimani.

vii.

The reputation of the returning boarder preceded him. Kimani was a brilliant boy, but very deceptive. Every member of the boarding staff dreaded him. Even Neil's influence was undercut significantly. Kimani lived in the

US. His parents were brilliant doctors. He was articulate and respectful; but at nights, things "just happened." The only TV would be turned on at a high volume, and no one could say who did it. The security guard who dozed off on the sofa would wake up to find toothpaste covering his face and his shoelace tied together. Of course, the guard could not complain because he should not have been sleeping in the first place. Water would mysteriously appear on the floor, and a host of other pranks were no longer off limits.

None of the boys crossed Kimani. He was more confident, smarter, and more calculating than any other boarder. He wore a pleasant and respectful demeanor. He was the kind of individual who could work wonders for the CIA. None of my methods worked with Kimani. Frankly, I did not have the worldview to handle him. Luckily, I didn't have to worry for long. Kimani left as quickly as he had come. He had moved away again with his parents.

As graduation approached, Neil worked hard to improve his grades. Many others made impressive efforts as well. I, too, was getting ready to complete my four-year term in college and had also signed up for the work and travel exchange program that was available to many college students.

From Jamaica, many students would travel to Europe and North America, where they would work and travel during the summer. I had attempted to do this earlier, but was unable to secure US sponsorship. A US sponsor was required to sign an affidavit, pledging support in case of need, and also to ensure that the student return to his or her country of origin. My aunt lived in Maryland and my effort to secure her help was unsuccessful. It was then that I asked Pam for her help.

I met my sponsor on NCU's campus. She worked as a member of the administrative staff while I was a student. NCU arranged a program called Campus Parent. This program ensured that students could form bonds with members of the faculty, staff, and other students. It was a successful program and particularly helpful to students from other countries who missed a family setting.

My first campus parents were the Francises. Mr. Francis was finance instructor. He and his family had relocated to Jamaica from Barbados. As the student population grew, Pam (my current sponsor) became a campus mother and coordinated activities with the Francises. Pam was slightly older than I was, but was a visual benchmark of qualities to seek when prospecting for a wife.

Before I contemplated any possibility of dating her, she was whisked off to live in the Bronx with her new husband. I contacted her through the school, and she gladly prepared the documents I required for sponsorship. She was pregnant with her first child, and I had no intention of encroaching on her family if and when I visited the US. She had signed my sponsorship letter as a favor, and that would be the extent of my request.

I prepared the necessary documents and took them to the American embassy in Kingston in an attempt to obtain a visa. At that time, the lines at the embassy were long and people waited several hours to make an application in person. (The system is now revamped, and a more efficient appointment system is used.) It was humbling to see rich and poor in line together. While I didn't like long lines, the symbolism of equality was appealing. In Jamaica, the well connected almost always circumvents existing systems. The line to obtain a visa to visit the US seemed to be a great system equalizer.

I completed the interview and was congratulated shortly after. I left my passport to allow for visa processing and returned to pick it up that afternoon. I thanked the US immigration officer again, and he interrupted me to explain his decision.

"Joseph," he said. "You shouldn't thank me. I wasn't doing you a favor. I was simply doing my job following guidelines and procedures. You have yourself to thank. It is your hard work that led you to this qualifying point." His words were far reaching. They captured the essence of America. The Jamaican culture discourages self-aggrandizement, stating that "self-praise is no recommendation."

However, the interviewing officer was right. I had worked hard to finish college. I often had to forgo instant gratification and opt instead for personal growth and development. I was recognized as a leader in high school and college because of my effort. America emphasized individuality and personal responsibility. By his words, my interviewer had crystallized the concept that "I write my own ticket." He was not granting me an opportunity to travel out of the goodness of his heart. I had earned it.

The advice continued: "My only suggestion to you is don't make the mistake others do and overstay your visa. Follow the direction of the immigration officer when you arrive in the USA." He handed me my passport with an envelope attached. I was instructed not to open the envelope. It should only be opened by a member of Immigration on my arrival in the USA. "Good luck," he said.

All was now clear for me to travel, for the first time, to the United States of America. Up to this point, I had not flown on a plane or traveled outside the confines of Jamaica. I was looking forward to this trip, and I quit my job in anticipation of my four months of work and travel experience in the USA.

***Lesson 13:* You can't influence where you came from, only where you are going.**

CHAPTER 11: NEW YORK

i.

I was now twenty-three years old and leaving Jamaica for the first time. Every aspect of maiden voyage would be absorbed: the scenery of the baggage handlers loading bags into the belly of the plane; the fuel truck refueling the plane; and most definitely the air hostesses giving instructions on how to fasten seatbelts and inflate life jackets. My fear of heights was superseded by my desire for the best view when I requested a window seat.

American Airlines taxied down the runway and took off. The force and seatbelt kept me in my seat. I felt giddy, more from being overwhelmed with the moment than from any lift force. My eyes took in a view of Jamaica that I had never seen before. The water near the shore appeared green. That green became blue as the depth of the Caribbean Sea increased with distance from the shore.

Almost immediately, Kingston Harbor and the famous Port Royal came into view. The history of Port Royal that I had learned in school was fresh in my memory. I visualized pirates staking out the city, drinking, singing, and, chasing women. I recalled stories about buccaneer Henry Morgan who pirated at the behest of the English-installed Governor Modyford. The eventual destruction of the city by the devastating earthquake of 1692 did not destroy the link between politics, violence, and criminality on the island.

The plane continued its elevation and course correction. Clouds and smog from the cement and other factories disrupted the silhouetted skyline of Kingston and rolling hills of St. Andrew. Further inland, I tried from my distance to distinguish among the banana, coffee, and sugarcane plantations below. Very soon the island disappeared and a smile crept across my face in response to my own mental joke.

I was comparing the speed of the plane to other modes of transportation, such as a bus traveling the countryside and stopping ever so often to pick up produce and people. Even if you were lucky to find a seat, it was not unusual to get off the bus with the scent of perfume, cologne, and body odors that were not yours. I recalled the surprise of a woman who was seated and had a baby dumped in her lap because she failed to notice and volunteer her seat to the mother standing there with a child in one hand, while the other hand held the rail for support.

I waited for the outline of Cuba to appear and was later to understand that the route would not be as clear-cut as I had envisioned it. Because of the US embargo on Cuba, direct flights over Cuba were not permitted for US aircrafts.

We were somewhere near the Florida and Georgia coastline when the flight attendants started serving dinner. The flight attendant serving me appeared preoccupied with her own thoughts and ignored my request. I was given the first thing in her hand. It turned out to be one of the meats my Leviticus diet prohibited, pork. She was annoyed that I had opened it before returning it. I assured her that I had no other way of knowing what was inside if I didn't open it. She inquired again why I couldn't or wouldn't have it. I patiently explained. I was disturbed by her tone, but I was not ready to allow anyone or anything to change my optimistic and anticipative mood.

Hours later, we descended and the outline of New York City was in view. The pace of vehicular traffic appeared quicker and more ordered than what I was accustomed to. Before this voyage, New York was an abstraction that I had seen on TV. I pinched myself with the realization that soon I would actually be in "the city that never sleeps."

When we landed, I went through customs without a hassle. I was scheduled to stay at the New York Student Hostel located on Amsterdam Avenue in Manhattan. I paid the shuttle and soon realized that New York would not be cheap.

While on the shuttle, I secretly counted my wealth—a whopping $111. My goal was to spend three to four months working and traveling in the USA on a student exchange program. At that moment, excitement gave way to reality: $111 would not go far in New York City. In addition, it would be difficult to find work during a recession. Suddenly I felt smaller, and native. Instead of taking a bite out of the big apple, I was on the verge of being eaten by the big monster city.

We arrived at the New York Student Hostel. That same night, I found a job working as a security guard at that hostel. Instead of money, I was rewarded with a place to stay, working sixteen hours per week. Luckily, an office for the exchange program was in the hostel, which meant that they understood that my visa allowed me to work.

I shared a room with seven other guests, and I had the bottom of a bunk bed. The room was mixed-gender, a new experience for me. My only other experience with a dorm situation was on my college campus, and girls were not allowed in the dorm. On one occasion, I entered the room and witnessed a European couple who had just checked in, trying to squeeze in a quickie on a top bunk. I was a security guard, and clearly it was against the rules, but I was not ready to be the morality police.

I felt comfortable among the guests and other staff members who shared the room. The lack of modesty of some of the ladies surprised me, however. One morning,

I awoke to see dangling legs from the bed above me. The legs belonged to a six-foot-tall female guest from the former East Germany. When she jumped off to make her way to the bathroom, I realized that she was decked in her glasses, T-shirt, and panties. As I thought about the need for modesty, I laughed at the irony. It was only two years earlier, when I lived on the college campus, that I argued that I was treated as a child when prevented from visiting the female dorm after-hours. Now I was in a mixed room and concerned about modesty.

Another guest, Ahmed, was also placed in a co-ed room, but was not so compromising. He was from Saudi Arabia and found the idea of sharing a room with women offensive, unsettling, or simply against the rules by which he lived his life. I recall our effort to calm him down as the front desk made an effort to accommodate his preference for a male-only room. Experiences like those reinforced my interest in different cultures and religions. It almost made me less dismissive of rules with which I disagree. I pledged that if I didn't like or agree with a rule, I would first try to find out the reason for it before amplifying my objection.

I made several friends easily. The first was the student I sat beside on the first night of orientation for a work and travel exchange program, Barbara. Barbara was from the former West Germany and was very kind. She invited me to join her in touring New York City, but my priority was to find a job as quickly as possible.

***Lesson 14:* "Seek first to understand, then to be understood." —Dr. Steven R. Covey.**

Looking for additional work in New York City, outside the hostel, emphasized the importance of the social security number (SSN). I got several job offers, but no one wanted to give me a job without that number. The exchange program and visa allowed for work, and the organizer encouraged quick application for SSNs. Three weeks passed after I had applied and my SSN had not yet arrived. I visited the Social Security office and was amazed at how a member of staff treated people seeking welfare assistance. The staff not only seemed overwhelmed, but also discourteous. I immediately concluded that it had to be a design to discourage people from getting too comfortable on government assistance.

My next interaction with government service was with the motor vehicle department. I stood for more than four hours in line only to get an appointment for a learner's permit. That permit was scheduled for three months in advance, about the time I would be leaving the US. I had an international driver's license, but working as a driver would be easier if I had a US license. I thought that a driving job would be a nice way to learn about the USA. I found a job with a piano moving company. The manager was not too impressed with my use of the clutch in the city during traffic.

After my second day with the company, I came under suspicion. I had taken a piece of furniture to the truck and ran up the flight of stairs to help the other movers. The piano was on the fifth floor, and I sailed past that floor in my zeal. I was between floors six and seven before I noticed that I had stupidly passed my floor. I walked slowly back, trying to conceal my overzealous run. The owner on the fifth floor saw me coming from upstairs and inquired aloud why I had gone up there. I explained, but it was evident from the silent treatment of the other movers that my story was not immediately believed.

I soon learned that as a black man, I was part of a demographic group that made it easier to believe I was scoping out the place rather than a naïve and overzealous employee running too fast up several flights and missing the floor.

After attempting to obtain my license, I started to form an opinion about the comparability of government service with so-called third world countries, like Jamaica. However, when Hans, a German student I had met on my arrival, returned from Maryland with a driver's license and four thousand miles on the car he had purchased, I realized that I had a lot to learn about America and its multiple states system of government. (Federal and state regulations have changed since, and foreign students have a different set of rules for obtaining SSNs and drivers licenses in the USA. After the arrival of my social security number, I started jobs at McDonald's and Pizza Hut).

I met students from several countries: Britain, France, German, the Netherlands, South Africa, Japan, and others. We exchanged addresses and promised to stay in touch. I realized that many of my new friends were from other counties, not the United States. That was understandable since most were tourists. The staff at the places I worked, however, was predominantly American, and many whites maintained cordiality during work, but avoided eye contact after work or off premises.

I surmised that some people just wanted to be left alone after work and didn't pay much attention to it. One evening, I took some pizza to the hostel and shared it with the staff. While they ate, I was taken aside and given a lesson in race relations. My teacher was Suzanne, an attractive African American journalism student from DC. She wanted me to be careful how and with whom I socialized. "People don't like seeing you with white women," she advised. I protested since I never considered any of my activities dates. She understood, but told me to be careful nonetheless.

"You are a friendly guy, but this is America."

I told her that I had seen some of the history of America and what transpired in the South, and that I would be careful, but that I did not plan to live my life in conformity to how others thought I should live. Besides, the majority of students in the hostel were white. Therefore, it made perfect sense that they would be the majority of my friends in this environment. I continued to illustrate the point by indicating that the majority of friends I had met were, like me, from other countries.

"Our friendships would be influenced partly by our environment," I continued. I suggested to her she shouldn't be surprised if she visited Jamaica, a predominantly black country, and discovered that the majority of my friends were black. Suzanne was very outgoing and did not need my advice about friendships. However, I suggested that she also open herself to new friendships.

Suzanne suggested that if I wanted to see America's conscience, I should visit some non-international churches. There, she said, I would see America—absent legislation for equality. It would be several years before I would understand this statement.

Meanwhile, Barbara had found a new apartment. She shared an apartment with a lawyer who worked in the city, but would be away most of the summer. She invited me to go see it. This would be the first time I would actually get to see the inside of an American home, and I looked forward to it. For the first time, however, after my conversation with Suzanne, I was self-conscious. As we walked from the subway to the suburb in Queens, navigating dog poop, some too soft to pick up, I felt stares from curious onlookers. By the time we reached the apartment, she noticed a difference in my body language and inquired if I was okay. Before we had left the hostel, she had also been discussing a passionate issue with her fellow German student. I was later to learn that some of the discussions revolved around her friendship with me.

I consider myself a freeman and did not want to live my life according to people's perceptions. At the same time, I did not want to overcompensate in my effort to prove my liberty and become provocative. This would become a dilemma that would follow me as I navigated the social strata of America.

ii.

Nadine was one of the front desk employees at the hostel, and in my estimation, the most attractive girl on staff. She wore the most elegant smile and was very focused. She was African American and hailed from Roanoke, Virginia. On her day off, I invited her out to see some of the city sights and was thrilled when she accepted. I tried to get her perspective on the race issue, but she did not want to have that conversation. She thought too many people were focused on a person's exterior rather than getting to know them inside. Her perspective reminded me to be slow to categorize and generalize views. I later learned from Nadine that she was biracial. She also had a son in Virginia and had left him with her mother, and was in New York to avoid an abusive relationship.

I found some of the concept of classifying mixed racial groups ridiculous and inadequate. Any white person with black blood could be classified as black, denying them of their mixed heritage. Sometimes, I couldn't tell who was black just by looking and had to rely on someone to self-indentify in a racial category.

I wanted to see the aquarium. Nadine insisted that I go, but she had no desire to. I suggested that I would pay for her just so we could remain together. She politely and firmly refused, but insisted that I go ahead.

"You'll be in this country for a short time, you should see all you can," she insisted. While I went to the aquarium, she found something to occupy her time. When I returned, she was waiting for me and inquired if I had had a good time. I respected Nadine's independence and selflessness. Little did I know that she would be my introduction to strong-willed American women.

That weekend, five of us visited a nightclub. The group consisted of three girls—Nadine, Sarah, Sarah's daughter—and two guys—Rafi and me. As we entered, Nadine disappeared. The other members of the group, particularly Sarah, were concerned. I didn't think it was a big deal, but decided to join the group to search for her. I was not accustomed to "clubbing" and did not know club protocol. I thought if Nadine wanted to go off by herself, it was her choice.

When Nadine reappeared, everyone pretended that they were all having a good time. I was not so diplomatic and told Nadine that we were all concerned and had been looking for her. She was not sure why everyone was concerned. But we all agreed that we would communicate if anyone wanted to wander off by themselves, since it was understood that New York was a dangerous city.

On our way back to the hostel, we stopped at a coffee shop. Several beggars and street people passed by. Sarah, a white North Carolinian, was in a discussion with one of the beggars, a black man. I kept an eye on the discussion while Rafi and I chatted. Before long, my suspicion and fear were realized. At two in the morning, Sarah's polite demeanor was mistaken for an invitation to invade her personal space.

I wanted to intervene, but was looking for a signal from Sarah that she was uncomfortable. What I did not realize was that she was terrified and did not want to offend the guy. Finally, she asked the guy, "Do you mind?" This was all I needed. I got up and walked toward him, pointed at his chest, and like a drill sergeant, I told him to back off and leave the lady alone. He protested, but complied.

Later, Nadine joked that she never realized I could be that stern. "You can be all our protector when we go out," she quipped. I realized her dual meaning. While she was grateful, she also was suggesting that I didn't need to be a knight in shining armor—they (women) could take care of themselves.

I found Suzanne's advice on race to be right in some respects, but she also took my suggestion to open up herself to non-traditional friendships. When I came home one night, she was sitting on the floor in the passage, giggling with Ivan from Boston. Ivan and I had talked previously about Bob Marley and Yellow Man, reggae singers.

The obsession with race was again on display as I returned from the grocery store with a gallon of milk. I met Fred from Ireland who joked with another member of the staff that I was drinking all this milk to become white. The comment placed Susanne's earlier warning into context. I quickly remarked that while I drank milk, it affected me. Also, I was happy and comfortable in my own skin.

As we chatted, Fred asked what I had that he didn't, since I was making so many friends. I quipped that maybe I'd get him some chocolate milk the next time. We laughed before I proceeded to explain that while I was sure that some people saw me as a novelty and were conducting their own social experiment, an individual had to be friendly to make friends. You had to get out of your comfort zone.

Later, I introduced him to Sarah and other ladies. Before long, they were hurrying to get away because of some of the jokes he made.

My friendship with Yolanda, a white Jewish girl and a literature student, became one of my most enlightening experiences in New York. We met as she attempted her best impression of Jamaican singer Buju Banton's "Bum Bi Bi Inna Batty *Boy* Head." The song (while without controversy in Jamaica) had become controversial internationally. The song in essence spoke of shooting gays and raping lesbians, and Yolanda wanted to know if that song was one of my favorites. It was not!

As we spoke, I learned that Yolanda (in addition to working at the hostel) volunteered at a hospice where she cared for people afflicted with AIDS. I commended her for such a noble act and asked why she chose an AIDS hospice. She educated me on the HIV virus and emphasized that while it was not a gay disease, she had a gay friend who was affected by the virus.

"Does that mean you are gay?" I asked reflexively.

"Yes!" she replied. I didn't believe her and surmised that she had responded in that way because of the forwardness of my question. Attempting to change the subject, I announced that my grandmother had told me that one of her grandfathers was Jewish. Yolanda zeroed in on a distinction that was worth explaining—the difference between Jews as a religion and Jews as Israeli, a nationality of Israel. Protestants with a Judeo-Christian belief system were usually identified with groups of Abraham's seeds, and I was no exception.

We resumed the discussion on homosexuality. I conceded that while my view was shaped by my religious belief, and I didn't support the lifestyle, I did not believe in violence against gays or any group. I had come from a culture where no one openly professed to be gay. I related two of my previous experiences with the gay question.

At age fifteen, I was propositioned by a carpenter who was working for my sister. I told him that I would use the hammer against the side of his head if he ever talked to me in those terms again. He didn't, and I spent the next few weeks lifting one-hundred-pound sacks of flour and sugar to prove my manliness. She laughed at my response to the carpenter, and I reminded her that I had been fifteen.

I recalled another incident where it was rumored that one of the vice principals of one of my schools was gay. Shortly before graduation, that vice principal saw me walking and offered me a ride, which I gladly accepted. When I was about to get out, I noticed that the door handle on my side of the car was missing. He apologized for not getting the door fixed, got out of the car from the driver's side, and walked to the passenger's side to open the door from the outside. I did not appreciate the chivalry of having my door opened. I felt embarrassed as I thanked him.

Silently, I vowed never to accept another ride in that car. When I told my schoolmate and deputy head girl of my experience, she laughed uncontrollably. This vice principal was highly credentialed and acted as principal. Years later when I met and spoke with him, he was sure that he had been passed over for the job of principal because of those rumors. The rumors persisted despite the fact that he was married with children.

Yolanda and I talked for hours and she invited me out with her friends on Saturday night. I got in the car with her two male friends, Jim, a bookstore manager, and Rob, a psychologist. They had a great sense of humor. Yolanda and I sat in the back as we drove down Broadway. I was paying attention to the scenery and thinking that a few weeks earlier I had only seen New York on TV, and now I was actually driving down Broadway. My attention shifted to the conversation between the two men in the front. My face betrayed my discomfort. Yolanda rightly concluded that their conversation was making a naïve Jamaican squeamish. She apologized and inquired if I wanted to get out. Not knowing where we were or where we were going, I told her I would be fine.

We went with them into a bar and since I didn't consume alcohol, I ordered non-fermented zero-aged orange juice on the rocks. I continued my conversation with Yolanda and suspected that she was carrying out her own social experiment with me. Glancing around the huge bar, I notice that the women seemed interested in other women, and men seemed interested in other men.

"Is this a gay bar?" I asked, even though I was sure of the answer. She nodded a response. What followed were some of the most intellectual discussions I'd ever had. We discussed sexuality, religion, and politics. Rob and Jim joined us at the table, and we continued the conversation. To my relief, no one propositioned me. However, Jim's first comment of the conversation is etched in my memory for life: "Free your mind, and your ass will follow." I didn't take the statement as a "come-on," but they clearly believed my mind was closed. I asked for enlightenment by asking a number of questions.

If *homosexual* means attraction to the same sex, why did some homosexual men dress like women? Also, if the behavior was genetic, not a choice or a learned behavior, why did some homosexuals proposition straights who expressed no interest in homosexuality? We talked about children raised in homosexual homes, and I put forward the hypothesis that those children would be more likely to engage or experiment with homosexuality based on what they had learned and not necessarily any genetic inclinations. I concluded that while I undoubtedly was a product of my cultural and religious upbringing, I didn't consider myself close-minded. Admittedly, I used my religion as a principle-centered governor of my thoughts and behavior.

It is this principle-centered governance that controlled my behavior when I was provoked and prevented me from striking the provoker. It was also this principle-centered governance that prevented me from making an advance or grabbing all the women I found attractive; this was something that the dominant ram goats in my village did to every ewe.

When we concluded our discussion on the subject, I had not changed the views of Ron or Jim, nor had they changed mine. However, I was no longer a homophobe. I was now comfortable in their friendship and a lot more relaxed in my heterosexuality. The same could not be said of Yolanda. She wasn't sure that she was or wanted to be a lesbian, or that she was not in an experimental phase of her life. I felt proud of myself and entertained the notion that I could possibly change the heart of a lesbian.

My views on politics were not so certain. Ron couldn't understand why I was arguing for George Bush's re-election against the Arkansas governor, Bill Clinton. As it turned out, I did not have an articulate answer. From my vantage point in Jamaica, I had seen how Bush 41 led a successful coalition against Saddam Hussein and had removed him from Kuwait, ensuring that the price of oil did not rise to a level that would damage economies like the US and Jamaica. (It was the action of OPEC to increase the price of oil in the 1970s that led to decision to levy a bauxite tax, which then led to the exodus of several plants from Jamaica and the layoffs of men like my dad.)

I was tremendously impressed with how knowledgeable Ron, Jim, and Yolanda were, and discussions with them heightened my thirst for knowledge. (During the campaign season, I took more interest in the US election. As a result, I asked my program director to extend my stay in the US for an additional month to give me a chance to observe the November presidential election in which Bill Clinton was elected to office.)

iii.

While I was grateful for a job flipping burgers at McDonald's, it was nauseating and emotionally draining to me. I was also not too keen to be reminded of my dad each time someone ordered a Big Mac. The job taught me the importance of standardization, while at the same time, it exhibited waste. The sequence of when the onions and mustard should be placed on the buns was made to be so important that the manager insisted on throwing out entire trays if it wasn't done correctly. However, I noticed how discriminating the tastes of the customers were as they walked away satisfied. They learned to rely on the taste of McDonald's being the same regardless of where they purchased a burger.

I was not particularly thrilled to say "thank you" each time my superiors, high school students, asked me to take out the garbage, and I figured that I would not last very long at this job. In addition, the waste greatly upset me because while buns and burgers were tossed out, beggars and homeless people were everywhere: on the subway, in Central Park, and less than a block from the restaurant. How could a country with so much ignore its own people with so little?

The fact that I understood the business concepts behind some of these decisions did not reconcile the issue. Instead, it brought my religious and business understandings into conflict. Self-reliance motivated people to act and produce for their own survival and self-interest. However, if the safety net was too broad or continued indefinitely for the able bodied, it could condition people to be helpless and dependent on the state.

The other evening job that I held was at Pizza Hut. I enjoyed riding around on my bicycle, making pizza deliveries in Manhattan. One of the owners and managers was Mr. Singh, a Sikh from New Delhi, India. Also, in his employ was Ihram Khan, a college student from Pakistan. When time allowed, Khan and I talked about cricket, especially since he had the name of a famous cricketer.

The bicycles used for pizza delivery were far from comfortable and were poorly maintained. The seat cushions were torn off, and the bolt on the seat drilled a hole in the pants that I wore as a uniform. As the hole got bigger, it revealed my underwear. This reminded me of jokes made about me years earlier, and I would use it as a punch line with the other riders. "The colors of our underwear can be a traffic signal. If we wore red, it was an indication to those behind that we were stopping. White meant we were backing up. For our safety, I would strongly advise against wearing green."

The other delivery guys roared with laughter. I continued to joke that when I was growing up, we were ashamed to show our backsides. Kids and young adults now wear their pants loosely and let them fall off their backsides, freely revealing their underwear.

I was learning the city very fast, and soon I started getting large orders. One evening, Mr. Sing kept me in the store. Since I was not making deliveries and earning tips, I inquired why I was being kept in the store.

"I like the way you clean the bathroom!" he said. "Very, very, very clean," he continued.

I thanked him, but I told him that since I made little money cleaning and no tips, then he was sending the wrong signal. Doing a good job cleaning meant being rewarded with lower salary and more time away from tips. If you didn't do a good cleaning job, you were sent out on delivery where you made significantly more money. The unintended message is "don't do a good job cleaning."

Following our discussion, he tried to make it up to me by sending me out with the big orders. One was my biggest order yet: five large pizzas. I hurried to the address on Second Street. A young man walked up to me and asked if the delivery was for the address I was looking for. I said yes, and he yanked the pizzas from the bike tray and walked off. I naively followed, thinking he was going to go into the house to give me money.

As he walked past the address, I realized that this would not be a regular transaction. The boy with the pizzas noticed I was still following and then shouted out an instruction to "get him!" It was then that I became aware of three other boys behind me. They were about to jump me, and I dropped the bike and grabbed the chain that I used to lock the bike. In quick action, I whirled the chain in the direction of their heads. They backed up and quickly realized that they had messed with the wrong Jamaican.

On an adrenaline high, I chased them like a madman with the chain in my hand and cussing "Bombo and Rass cloth" and other Jamaican expletives that I was never comfortable using. I quickly regained my sanity, stopped the chase, and went to secure the bike that I had left behind. My attackers made off with the five pizzas, failing to get the accompanying sodas or any money I was carrying.

Mr. Sing was disappointed and sent me to make a police report. The net result was that I lost again, since I spent most of my working time in the police station that evening—no tips or pay since I was off the clock.

Riding a bicycle was a great, yet dangerous way to learn the city, and I bought one for myself. My plan was to take on a job as a courier, delivering packages, in addition to my job at Pizza Hut, and instead of McDonalds.

iv.

After a few weeks in Manhattan, the feeling of claustrophobia that often enveloped me was easing. The Hudson River and Central Park had become my regular spots for therapeutic relief. Sometimes, I stopped near the river and gazed, avoiding anything that blocked my view. As the weeks passed, I had grown more comfortable in the city and ventured to other sites on my list of "must-see places" in New York: the World Trade Center, the Empire State Building, the United Nations, and others.

I frequently left the hostel and walked, unsure of where I was going. One afternoon, I found myself in a difficult area of Harlem. I was asked for the time, then a quarter, followed by requests for another quarter. The question that jolted me was a direct question of where one could score drugs. Of course, I didn't know, and I didn't hide my annoyance with such questions.

Within minutes after the drug question, I saw a man running from an apartment building and another chasing him. Moments later, shots rang out, someone screamed, and then there was a crash. I didn't wait around to learn the details, but set out for my next sightseeing at the United Nations.

At the UN, I was intrigued by the emphasis on communication and listening to different views. It was there that I renewed the idea of visiting another country. I would visit Canada. I had obtained a temporary Canadian visa before I left Jamaica, but it had expired. I thought it would be easy to renew and was surprised by the tone of the staff at the Canadian embassy in New York. Every question I was asked sounded like an accusation.

"Why do you want to go to Canada?"

"You are a teacher and a student?"

"Why, do you think because you are traveling in the US you can also travel to Canada?"

The interview officer threw my passport back at me, trying to provoke anger. I did not take the bait, and I restated my desire to travel. I mentioned that I had worked briefly in an industry that welcomed a number of visitors to Jamaica, including Canadians, and that I had treated all with respect and courtesy. He stopped his agitation and looked at me. Then, he picked up the passport and sternly said, "I will not give you more time than you were given previously."

"That is fine," I responded as he slammed the window that separated us and left.

I was still in shock at what I had just witnessed. The difference in professional courtesy shown to me at the Canadian embassy in New York and in Jamaica was the difference of night and day. My feelings were still bruised when I accepted my passport from the attendant and left with a visa for a three-week stay in Canada.

Nadine followed me to the bus station and helped with my bags and bike onto the bus. I gave her my address for Jamaica and suggested that we stay in touch.

Instead of three weeks in Canada, I spent three days. I took a bus to Toronto and checked into a student hostel. That night, I stepped into the lounge area of the hostel, which was also a bar. I struck up a conversation with Mark, the bartender, after a sip of my orange juice on the rocks. Soon, I met Dick. Dick had been in an accident and used crutches to get around.

I was starting to learn more about him when he said something that brought John and others in the bar to my defence. Being defended against a partially disabled man might have been funny, if the racist comment had gone over my head and Mark had not insisted that he would not allow that kind of talk in the lounge. I thanked Mark and said goodnight to everyone, including Dick.

As I left, I wondered what the meaning of the "coon" comment was that Dick had made. Why was someone in his state trying to be mean? Was he lashing out or trying to make himself feel better by trying to put someone (me) down? Did his injury have anything to do with a person of color? I was told that Canada did not have the kind of racial intolerance that the US did, yet this injured man had tried to use the issue, perhaps as therapy.

For the first time, it occurred to me that many racists are people with self-esteem problems. In order to feel good about themselves, they had to feel that they were better than someone else or a group. The cycle of racism fuelled circular reasoning and self-fulfilling prophecies. If you denied a group of people opportunities for advancement, you could then point to their lack of success as evidence of their inferiority.

I had taken my bicycle with me to Toronto, but decided against assembling it, because I had decided to head back to New York. I was not leaving because of any incident. I had not scratched the surface of the USA and would not have had the same opportunity to work and travel in Canada. I could also now proudly conclude that I had traveled to two countries outside of Jamaica. Before I left, I made some quick tours around Toronto and was impressed with how clean and wide the streets and sidewalks were.

On my third day in Canada, I boarded a bus and headed for New York City. When we got to the border, the customs official searched every inch of my luggage and clothes. They went through my wallet and even inspected a condom that had been in my wallet before I left Jamaica. I obviously didn't like the intrusion, but I remained calm and thanked the custom officers as they attempted to help me re-pack my things.

As I got back on the bus, all eyes were focused on me. It was apparent that no one else had endured my level of scrutiny and inspection. I was the last to get on the bus. I looked around and concluded that I was the only black person on the bus, but I was wary of jumping to conclusions.

I smiled at everyone and apologized aloud for the delay. They erupted with laughter and smiled warmly at me. The driver remarked that was what happened when you traveled heavy. I had a suitcase and my bicycle (in a box) with me. I continued conversations with some of the passengers and made several friends.

I thought my scrutiny was over, but I was again surprised when I got to Buffalo and we were asked to change buses. The bicycle that I had traveled with from New York to Toronto and from Toronto to Buffalo was now suddenly an issue for the bus company. They wanted me to pay to ship it or leave it in Buffalo. After refusing to pay additional money in the middle of the journey, I spoke with an attendant, an African American who could not understand what the fuss was about. He picked up the bicycle from underneath and moved it inside all the way to the back of the bus. I sat with it, trying to conceal it from the driver.

The leg of the journey back to New York was uneventful. I had a conversation with a lady sitting in the row across from me. She told me all about her life with an ease that initially caused me to doubt her story. As we chatted, I realized that since it was unlikely that we would meet again, she had no reason to lie. She was a working girl and worked the streets of many cities and strip joints. She made good money, but she did not want her kids in Ohio to know what she did. Her two children lived with their grandmother, and she went home once per month. Before she dozed off, she thanked me for being a good listener. I smiled, trying to remain nonjudgmental.

When I got back to the hostel, Nadine checked me in. She knew things had not gone according to plan. The next day, I sought to get my old jobs back and was glad I was extended that opportunity.

The next few weeks, I decided that I should save some money to take back with me to Jamaica. I worked and saved while I paid attention to the election campaign. Bill Clinton was now president elect, but my boss told me he had voted for Ross Perot.

The night before I left for Jamaica, Yolanda, Derriere from the Netherlands, and two French students chatted for most of the night. Yolanda was making plans to move to Alaska to work in the fishing industry. We exchanged addresses, hugged as she cried, and soon I was on my way.

I called the airline and was told that my bike would cost $130 to get to Jamaica. This would not be cost-effective and since I could not find a buyer, I left it at the hostel for people to use if needed. Little did I know that the next time I would own a bicycle would be ten years later.

I made my way to the subway, gathered all the pennies I had accumulated, and decided to get rid of them. They totaled more than thirty cents, and I added other coins and gave them to the elderly African American subway attendant to provide me a token. The man refused to accept the pennies. I inquired why, since pennies were still a legal tender in the US. I got no explanation except a stubborn, "I am not taking no damn pennies."

He raised his voice, which attracted the attention of two police officers nearby. To avoid any confusion, I walked over to the officers, greeted them, and explained what I was attempting to do.

They smiled at each other as if to say "Is that it?" I nodded and walked back and made another attempt to buy a token, but was again told, "I don't want no pennies." It was still early in the morning, and the station was not yet crowded. I paid from a dollar and said loudly, "I will keep my damn pennies."

The station was not full, and I wondered if there was a rule preventing the use of pennies to make the subway's process more efficient. If that was the case, why didn't the attendant say that, instead of making this about him? Weeks earlier, I had seen a little boy kicking and tossing pennies from his pockets.

"Why are you wasting money?" I had asked.

"Those are only pennies," came the confident reply. I stopped and picked them up to make a point. I was from a country where devaluation reduced the value of the local currency to a few pennies. Other countries had families living on less than a dollar a day. Here in America, a black kid tossed pennies away while begging for a quarter. How could I blame the kid if adults like the subway attendant said things like, "I don't want no damn pennies." Was the need to be efficient sending the wrong signal?

A couple weeks after I was back in Jamaica, I was pleased to receive letters and postcards from friends I had met. Suddenly, I had a desire to visit the Netherlands, France, Germany, South Africa, Miami, and all the places from which the postcards had come. I was most intrigued by the letter from Yolanda. She was getting ready to move to cold Alaska. Could a tropical boy survive in Alaska? I wondered. That was a question I would not have to answer, since that was the last of our contact.

V.

Mom's disappointment with me was palpable. She expected more from me. I had spent four months in the USA, and as far as she was concerned, I had nothing to show for it except the stories that I told. Sure, I had brought back some gifts, cheap cameras, handheld radios, socks, and clothes, but that was nothing in comparison with what the seasonal farmworkers brought back when they returned from working in the USA (the promised land). (Several Jamaicans worked seasonally in the USA as farmworkers and in the hospitality industry. After four to nine months in the US, they returned with barrels of clothes and electronics.)

My uncle Jonny was an example. Every year he traveled to the US to harvest sugarcanes and apples. He and his wife, Olive, were very conservative and managed to build a modest house for themselves and their four children. A number of farmworkers had similar success stories. Some houses would take years to complete. But when it was completed, they owned it, free of a mortgage.

Not all seasonal workers were success stories. Some blew their hard-earned dollars on electronics and exotic prostitutes. Some violated the terms of their visas and sought residency illegally in the USA. Many who took this option would later realize that living illegally in the USA was not only stressful and costly for them, but for the families they left at home. Since they were no longer able to travel freely, children grew up without fathers, and families were often broken up. Some would regain legal status and be able to reunite with their families. Then there was the unusual story of a farmworker who eventually became the owner of a US farm on which he had worked.

With the success and failure stories of seasonal workers, it was apparent to Mom that I had not made a good start. My explanation, that my main focus was to gain international exposure, was met with skepticism. Farmworkers, some unable to read, had returned from America with lots of goodies. I was the first in my family to go to college and had not done better than those workers.

I resumed working with Jenny and Patrick, but I was restless. After two weeks, I traveled with them to Kingston, and we had a long talk. It was apparent that some New York assertiveness had rubbed off on me because during our discussion, I heard myself explaining that if I was going to invest my life in their business, I should be paid a salary, or we should develop a written agreement. It did not go over well, and for a few days, I received the silent treatment. I believed in what I was doing. There was no doubt in my mind that the business could use my talent. I was process driven and customer focused and could be useful.

The silent treatment continued for a few days until we had another discussion that was somewhat more amicable, but no less purposeful. Jenny and Patrick were not surprised by my resolve. They respected it and relied on me in difficult situations. However, my resolve had not usually been directed in opposition to them, and it made us all uncomfortable.

We were not seeing eye-to-eye and it was time for me to move on. I would have jumped at the opportunity to invest my energy in the family business, but I was not sure how to leave my future entirely in someone else's hands. In addition, their oldest son, Kenloy, had just finished college in the USA. He returned and started to take control of his birthright.

Kenloy's passion was music, but he had studied business at the insistence of his parents. He was cordial and pleasant, generally a delight to be around. It was not long, however, before he started seeing me as a rival to his rightful inheritance. I suspect that the feeling was encouraged by the staff trying to cement their loyalty rather than Kenloy's genuine desire for rivalry.

My suspicion was realized when I learned about a meeting in which Jenny proposed organizing the business in divisions and giving me some responsibility. This proposal was met with opposition by Kenloy, who repeated some of the staff's claims that I was being placed above him. Soon after, the bakery, the farm, and the guesthouse were under Kenloy's stewardship. No discussion was made with me as to where I would fit in the business, and I left for Kingston to chart my own course.

CHAPTER 12: **KINGSTON**

i.

I stayed with my sister, Bev, and her husband, Len, in Portmore, considered a bedroom community for Kingston and Spanish Town. A few weeks later, I rented a room from an elderly couple in the same community. Many of the houses in Portmore were made with prefabricated slabs of concrete, including the roofs. Usually they had no air-conditioning, and the concrete kept the heat long into the night after sunset.

The first available job was a commissioned-paid door-to-door salesman with the promise of promotion to management, and I jumped at the opportunity. The company was new to Jamaica, its home office in Boston, Massachusetts. Since few owned cars, the sales staff utilized public transportation and foot to peddle small electronics, cookbooks, and utensils in sacks or boxes. The company insisted on professional attire notwithstanding year-round temperatures ranging from eighty to ninety-eighty degrees Fahrenheit.

I pounded the pavement dressed in my best clothes (jacket optional). To complement my dress was a smile, a positive attitude, the company standardized sales pitch, and perspiration evenly distributed in my shirt.

On my first day, my trainers from Boston took notice of my sales ability. I sold all my solar-powered radios and returned to the warehouse for more. I was wearing my best poker face when I tossed him the empty box while complaining that I was unable to handle this job. He was startled at first and then laughed and said, "You got the juice! Juice by you, good job. From the day I interviewed you, I could see the intensity in your eyes. You are definitely vice presidential material." What my trainer did not tell me is that from then on, I would be viewed as his rival.

Within days, I was not only training people but also setting the pace. In addition, I was called on to direct daily morning meetings and give pep talks to the army of salespeople getting ready to tackle the road. There were four other Bostonians working in Jamaica to open new merchandising locations. I had had a window into the American work ethic that I best summed up using the unofficial motto of the US postal service: "Neither snow nor rain nor heat nor gloom of night stays these couriers from the swift completion of their appointed rounds." The Jamaican worker in the US is usually among the most productive. However, while working in Jamaica, the ethic seems to suggest, "no problem, mon, don't worry, it will be done." If you should ask "when will it be done?" the answer is usually as soon as the rain stops or the sun cools. Working with the Americans in Jamaica was also enlightening.

The American leaders from Boston got involved and rolled up their sleeves and were relentless in maintaining standards. They often won the respect of the team and got a higher response from the staff because they led by example more than a typical Jamaican leader would. They were also inflexible, and it sometimes took repeated failures to convince them that adapting to a different culture was a requirement for success.

Few people noticed that these foreigners worked illegally in Jamaica. They worked very hard, often venturing on foot into areas of Kingston that locals who were not residents typically avoided. On one occasion, one of the trainers, Phil, was working in one of the most crime-ridden areas in downtown Kingston. A child faked an interest in one of his watches before running off with it. Instead of leaving it alone, Phil gave chase and cornered the kid in an alley where he retrieved his watch.

The residents were impressed and affectionately nicknamed him "White Knight." Soon, he made several friends, including local fishermen who invited him to go fishing with them, play dominoes, or attend local dances.

Phil and the others also opted to eat in the local shacks and other "holes in the wall" instead of fine dining restaurants. This was first done out of necessity, given the proximity of the office to nearby restaurants. However, such daily patronage helped to cement bonds in some of the most difficult neighborhoods, and soon they were protected when they visited any of these areas.

I had my share of experiences with the criminal class. I was alone selling solar radios in an area of Kingston that I considered virgin territory. It was not long after I had arrived that a young man took off with one of my radios. I refused to leave and was repeatedly advised against hanging around. I explained that I would have to pay out of pocket for the radio and could not afford to.

Soon, I was surrounded by a gang, who decided to explore what other merchandise I had. Shortly after, the person I considered the leader arrived. He was older than the others, better dressed, and wore a calm, self-assured demeanor. He was treated with reverence and was listened to when he spoke.

"Sir," I began as I addressed him directly. He listened to my short complaint then held up his hand and instructed the members of the gang not to touch my merchandise.

"You guys must learn who to steal from. This guy is a student trying to make a life." He insisted that whoever took my radio should bring it back. I interjected to describe the thief and the incident.

"You see what I mean? He knows who it is, knows the bicycle he rode, very soon we could have police turning over this place over a *radio*. Bring back his radio now!"

I was amazed at what happened next. Less than five minutes elapsed before the boy who stole the radio was escorted back with little effort. He walked humbly back like a dog with its tail between its legs. He handed me the radio, and I thanked him. I thanked "the don" and shook his hand and the hand of the thief. The gesture was aimed at assuring them that I was leaving with no malice, but I did not hesitate in exiting the area.

I scolded myself as I left and thanked God, since the outcome could have been different.

I did not know Kingston very well, but is was clear that this was one of the so-called garrison sections of Kingston. (Garrison constituencies were constituencies where elected representatives had over 100 percent political support. In return, they turned a blind eye to crime and drug trafficking.) In these lawless enclaves, the dons had more influence than the police.

I recalled another incident in which my merchandise was stolen in another area of Kingston. I found and pointed out the thief to the police. The police refused to arrest him, saying it was clear the guy was a "madman," and they did not want to be injured arresting a madman. As I compared the two incidents, I wondered, if I lived in an area that the dons controlled, would I be better off paying taxes to the dons? I was glad that I didn't have to answer that question.

Hooey was a comedic character among the Bostonian bunch. He was an Italian American who had a prison record and found it difficult to get a job. George, the owner, gave him a job, and they became friends. Hooey and the others spoke in hushed reverence about George. Many of us had not met George, but it was clear from the five Bostonians present that he had earned their respect.

Hooey was doing very well in Jamaica, but he had not mastered the people skills necessary to function in a business setting. He still believed in jailhouse discipline. During a morning meeting, Hooey threatened to beat someone who was not paying attention. That statement ended his management prospects when George heard about it.

Hooey told several horrific stories about his girlfriend whom he had left in Boston. According to Hooey, he was half asleep one night when he had a strange feeling of someone over him. He opened his eyes and immediately grabbed the raised hand of his girlfriend, which contained a knife. Weeks after he told the story, his girlfriend traveled from Boston to visit him. Everyone who had heard some versions of the story eyed them for potential drama, but luckily none was on display.

ii.

A few months after I joined the company, the owners of the company visited the office in Jamaica. I met George for the first time and immediately connected with him. His personal story appealed to me and was another highlight in the American dream.

George had grown up in Grenada and moved to the USA illegally. He worked in an auto shop, and soon he excelled to own the auto shop and even an auto dealership. Even though he was not Jewish, he became known as "the black Jew." After his first marriage failed, he married Robin, a Canadian, and together they diversified and built a merchandising company. They told this story several times to inspire new recruits.

George did not have a formal education, but he was charismatic, street smart, and read people very well. After their visit to Jamaica, four of us (pacesetters with visas) were invited to visit the home office in Boston. The four were Amoy, John, Judy, and I.

iii.

I was excited to be traveling again. When we arrived in Boston, George and his wife, Robin, put on the charm offensive, opting to pick us up using their convertible Mercedes Benz and Porsche. As we pulled into the driveway of their home, I wondered aloud why they had not used the minivan parked in the driveway since our luggage could barely fit in the two cars. Judy gave my arm a friendly squeeze, and I took that as a signal not to amplify or repeat the question.

***Lesson 15:* Sometimes, you have to first show style before others are able to see your substance.**

The house was a modest middle-class suburban home that was sparsely furnished, which was understandable since George and Robin spent more time traveling and in hotels than at home. They had organized several locations in the USA and were now looking for international opportunities. Behind their home was a deck and a swimming pool. George wasted no time insisting on removing the covers and then cleaning the pool, despite the temperature hovering in the sixties. Neither he, his wife, nor any of us coming from Jamaica were about to get into a pool at that temperature. It finally occurred to me that George was attempting to show what was possible if we worked hard. The objective was to sell the appearance of success to fire us up to work even harder.

My three colleagues from Jamaica were diverse. Amoy was a vivacious woman, and her dominant Asian characteristics did not hide her mixed racial heritage typical of Jamaicans. In fact, many view the Jamaica's motto "out of many, one people" as an explanation of Jamaica's mixed heritage. Judy was an elegant and poised lady. Her sweet smile encouraged several unintended purchases. John was an Englishman, and ex-military. He had followed his girlfriend, who worked for a large company, to Jamaica and was now seeking his footing. John was a natural leader who was not afraid to take charge. I watched him keenly and decided that he was someone to learn from.

All three had owned cars, and were at a distinct advantage selling in Jamaica. I had personal drive and youthful naïveté that saw boundless possibilities. That outlook on life made walls obstacle courses instead of limits.

George and Robin had gotten in early into a business that utilized the Amway model. If you did well, you could open new locations with people you trained. You would continue to get an override as you built the pyramid.

This model worked very well for those at the top who source cheap merchandise from China and Taiwan. They bought millions of units, then broke the bulk and dispersed it to several locations. In a few weeks, the sales staff would move the bulk, and it would be replaced with shipments of other items. This model utilized cheap production labor, with sometimes low-cost products of inferior quality, low storage costs, and near-zero marketing costs.

George and Robin had many weapons in their "charm arsenal." During the weekdays that we stayed with George, he took us to dinner. On the weekends, he and Robin fired up the barbecue in their backyard. We stayed home Sunday night and congregated on a pull-out bed in his basement to watch a movie. While the expensive cars did little to appeal to me, the experience of simply watching a movie did. I did not realize how much of a need to belong I had developed. I felt that I was becoming part of a family, and I made a conscious effort to remind myself that I should not get carried away. This was business.

When I returned to Jamaica, I was motivated. George watched us talk about our experiences and noticed that I was sold. I took my team on road trips, and our performance rivaled that of the home office. Soon afterward, John and I were promoted to assistant managers. I was on a natural high.

I realized that I was not secured. I needed my own office. I made overtures to locate an office in my school hometown in Mandeville. I found a real estate representative who found a warehouse and I put the agent in touch with the company's attorney. George loved the initiative, and very soon I was on my way to managing a location in Mandeville.

CHAPTER 13: MANDEVILLE

i.

My start as a manager was exhilarating. I had a well-trained sales team that accompanied me to Mandeville, and we promptly started additional recruiting. We took the territory by storm. The persistence and professionalism of the team were evident, as members of the staff repeatedly got job offers as they prospected in the field. Despite the fact that Mandeville had less than 20 percent of the population of Kingston, we generated more than half the revenue, and some weeks we topped the sales chart.

My old college was taking notice. I interviewed current and former students for jobs. When my college economics professor showed up for an interview, I was reminded of a warning a teacher had given me several years before. The warning came after I shoved someone I considered a brat. My teacher reprimanded me and told me that my behavior was surprising and "bully-like."

"Never take advantage of someone else because you can," she said. She continued with the moral suasion of "whatever you do to the least of these, you have done it to me (God)." I had heard this all before, but the next sentence stuck with me. "Life is funny," she said. "You might find yourself working for the same little guy you are now mistreating. Be careful."

Nah, I thought, that is never going to happen. It never happened that way, but it felt surreal to interview my professor. We had had a great relationship and I had a great deal of respect for him, and I had enjoyed his classes. However, I could not escape the irony of life of my professor seeking employment from me. Previously, I had interviewed and offered a job to a fellow past student who used my father's imprisonment to belittle me. Life is filled with twists and turns, I thought.

Business leaders also took notice and sent me invitations to join local business groups and to attend some functions. Women also took notice and so did my family. I smiled at how my level of attraction had changed, even though I wore the same clothes and maintained the same modest living.

I made grandiose long-term plans that would have seemed impossible only months earlier, but were now within grasp. Nothing, however, would prepare me for the lesson I needed to learn about success. Success is not all about climbing the ladder, but also the skill of staying on the ladder long enough to make a difference. While on the ladder of success, there are always people and other environmental forces trying to shake you off. However, sometimes, the greatest challenge to your success is you.

I love traveling and was pleased with the opportunity to attend a conference in Atlantic City. It was winter in the USA, and I made sure I packed a jacket that I had purchased in New York. Even though the conference was in Atlantic City, my itinerary had me going from Kingston to Boston, the home office.

From the plane I saw all the snow on the ground (my first experience with snow). When I landed, I realized that my jacket might not be adequate. I waited outside the airport for what seemed liked hours to be picked up. Occasionally, I ran back inside the airport to warm up and added a layer of garments from my suit bag. I had watched several movies and news reports of what it meant to be cold, but feeling was believing.

ii.

After a short meeting in the office, I set out with two of the salespeople and rode to Atlantic City. I sat in the back of the car. The left back window had trouble, and I had cold air hitting my face from Boston to Atlantic City. The driver and the passenger chatted for most of the way, ignoring my agony. At the end of the trip, my nose was clogged. I would not breathe unrestricted through my nose until I returned to Jamaica days later.

When I returned to Jamaica, my team and other Jamaicans were anxious to hear about the conference. In addition, they wanted to hear something of vital importance. Did I sign an ownership contract with George? I had not. No one in Jamaica had.

I was not an owner yet, and I had the loyalty of many Jamaicans, who were concerned. There was a possibility that I could contact the distributors directly and launch out on my own. I was a good saver and was building a small fortune.

Two issues developed that would change the dynamics of my relationship with my boss forever. First, my administrative assistant was invited to Kingston for training. I was not told directly about the invitation to go to Kingston. George told my assistant during one of his many conversations with her. I suspected that George used his personal charm with administrative assistants in a number of offices to keep tabs on what was going on.

However, when my assistant expressed reservations upon being asked to stay in George's apartment, I intervened and made alternative arrangements. Not only did she fear jeopardizing her relationship with her fiancée, but there were also rumors about George's advances.

The second issue was a car. I had still not gotten a car, and I know my office could do a better job with a car. A member of the Boston staff was now managing the Montego Bay office and had tried to have his car shipped from Boston to Jamaica. He was headed back to Boston and decided against clearing it from the wharf. I was offered the car if I paid to have it clear customs. I had no knowledge of what I was buying, and I made what would be a most costly error in judgment as I took the bait.

My boss was previously in the car business, and I trusted his judgment. Little did I know that my saving habit was a perceived threat. Since I was saving, it was feared that I could source merchandise directly without his involvement.

At the request of the company's (George's) lawyer, I provided the funds to clear the Chrysler Lazer and depleted my savings. Import duties also provided windfall for the Jamaican government. The duty was 100 percent of the car's last invoiced price. The sales invoice was four years old and no adjustment was made for depreciation. (Import duties have since changed.)

To add insult to injury, the car would not pass inspection with major work, and my savings was further depleted.

iii.

"Why are you going to the Dominican Republic?" some of my team members asked. "Do you really think that is a good idea? The big man (George) has not kept any of his word. Why do you think he will not give away your office when you are gone?"

"I will only be gone for two weeks," was my reply. "Besides, Daniela, who is visiting from Boston, will be in charge. She has no desire to stay here." I was right in my calculation that Daniela was bored in Mandeville. As a fast pace Bostonian of Italian decent, she had little interest in the town. I thought she had found some stability when she started dating Job, a friend from college who had set up a gym in the town.

In a week after my departure, the office was at its lowest production level, and staff were leaving because they didn't like her style. Daniela decided that she had had enough and packed up and left not only the office, but also her new boyfriend. This occurred while I was in the Dominican Republic, and despite my plea, George insisted that I stay there.

"You need to help get the office in the Dominican Republic up and running. I'll send somebody from Kingston to get your office up and running again," George said.

"My office?" I quibbled. Not only was I not getting any overrides as promised, but I was now also a sales staff member again in the Dominican Republic living off my daily sales proceeds.

Despite the fact that I didn't like the changes made to the original plan, I decided to give the Dominican Republic my best shot. Maybe I could take some time and learn Spanish. If I were successful at that, I would be at a tremendous advantage.

People in the Dominican Republic were similar to Jamaicans in their friendliness and love of music. The meringue dances seemed more coordinated than reggae and calypso with which I was accustomed. Any sound of meringue seemed like a summons to groove as people danced on buses, in the street, or wherever the music sounded.

My effort to learn Spanish was complicated by the desire of the locals to practice their English with me. However, they responded to my prepared sales pitch, and I was instantly among the top sales producers.

Church in Spanish was more problematic, but I followed the program contextually. My new friends summarized the sermon and I was offered a Spanish Bible. Church also reminded me of an unresolved issue that would continue to be a tug of war between faith and my choice of a profession. Other members of the office worked Saturday, and I took off most Saturdays.

After twelve weeks in the Dominican Republic, having had enough of George. I didn't like the idea of quitting, but there were no guarantees I'd get the ownership that I was promised. I traveled to Santiago to convince myself that I would stay to aid in the development of an office there, but I had lost the fire. I returned to Jamaica days later.

iv.

Within weeks of my return, I was working again. This time, I was supervising the business of one of the business leaders I had met earlier. For the next two years, I worked at a job that I knew had no future. My employers were nice people, but with that job, I would barely make ends meet.

As each day passed, my opportunities in Jamaica seemed smaller and smaller. After one had bitten into the fruit of what is possible, it is difficult to settle down into the mundane. Was it this feeling that triggered Big Mac's many moves? I wondered. I felt like I was suffocating. The world is a big place, and I loved Jamaica, but I couldn't be confined; I needed to be free. I had a visitor's visa to the US and could travel. However, I decided against traveling or overstaying since I did not want to live in the shadows illegally.

I considered graduate school in the USA. Many industries in Jamaica had graduates of US institutions who had gained international exposure. Since my funds were almost depleted, the question was, where would the funds come from to attend school? I had considered Andrews University, operated by my church, and also Howard University, after learning that a number of Jamaican leaders had studied at Howard.

The economic climate was not supporting my saving objectives, but it was providing me important lessons in finances, specifically with foreign exchange and devaluation. Each time I saved the equivalent of US $1,000, there would be a corresponding devaluation in the local currency. In two months, my $1,000 would be worth $750. I decided to hedge against that by opening up a foreign exchange account in Jamaica where my savings would be maintained in US dollars. Since many business people were also doing that, it created more demand for US dollars and fuelled greater devaluation.

I was paid in Jamaican dollars, and my pay would buy less and less. A spiraling effect was created as the government printed more money resulting in more Jamaican dollars chasing fewer and fewer good services. An economist was not needed to explain the inflationary result of such polices. The combined effects added more pressure on the Jamaican currency and fueled even sharper devaluation. I concluded that my destiny could not be left to the mercies of macroeconomic policies, and I had to chart my course once again.

From this analysis, I knew I would not be able to save my way to an education. Within weeks of acceptance into Howard University School of Business, I obtained a student visa and booked a flight to Washington, DC. I had no knowledge of how I would pay for school, but a step of faith was necessary.

CHAPTER 14: WASHINGTON, DC

i.

The flight to Washington DC did not endear the level of anticipation as my first flight to New York. The truth is I was scared. How would this chapter in my life end? How would I get through college when I couldn't even pay my first semester's tuition? Why had I chosen Howard University knowing how expensive it was likely to be? Where would I live? Why had I depleted my savings trying to buy a car I had not even seen—for cash? That money would have been good for more than a year of school. Why did I leave my office and go to the Dominican Republic?

Stop looking back, I admonished myself. It was not productive to second-guess decisions over which I no longer had control. "Sunk Cost" was the term my economic instructor, Archie, bellowed before introducing the concept. There was no turning back now. All my energies would be needed to move forward and survive. It was not going to be easy, but this was my life, and I would live it my way.

I exited the Dulles Airport and utilized the most cost-effective way to travel, by bus and the DC subway system. My destination was a DC student hostel that I had located in my hostel guide. Even with my mental preoccupations, I still noticed how much cleaner the DC subway system was compared to New York's.

Immediately after checking in, I made another futile effort to contact my aunt who lived nearby in Maryland. I did not expect her to support my college effort, but I thought it would be helpful to have someone in my corner. The next day, I went to register for college and could only afford a part-time schedule, which provided an immediate concern to my immigration status. I would also need a job to survive, also an immigration concern.

My instinct was to obtain a job on campus, consistent with the terms of my visa, but I was unsuccessful. The process, however, led me to find opportunities for jobs as a valet parking attendant to work different events throughout the city. I obtained a driver's license immediately and was pleasantly surprised with the speed of the process.

My next task was to find a place to live, which I found in a not-so-great part of town, and rented. I shared the house with four men who were not students. Two of them told me that they were president and vice president of a new company they had just formed. However, when I saw the amount of booze that they bought with their welfare checks, I felt compelled to change my living arrangement as quickly as I could. So I called the Landlord to explained. The conversation was not going well and I shifted gears.

"Sir, I cannot continue to live in this house."

"What do you mean? You signed a contract!"

"I am sorry, but I promise if you return my deposit and prorate my first month's rent, I will not call the rent board to render the house unsafe to live." He complied without protest.

I settled into another house inhabited by other students near the campus and was much more comfortable. Later, another roommate, Barry, and I would work out an arrangement with the owner to collect rent and help with the general upkeep of the house. Though the incentive was small, I felt justified cleaning up and organizing cleaning schedules with the other roomers.

Since I was attending school part-time, I decided I should focus on the CPA exam and obtain another job. I had studied accounting in Jamaica; however, the US tax laws were different and so were methods of preparation. The CPA exam (at that time) required candidates do all four parts in one sitting. If you failed three parts, you were not allowed to keep the part that you passed. It would take several sittings before I finally conquered all parts of that exam.

My second job was at a French bakery and deli in L'Enfant Plaza. Shops on the plaza provided coffee and lunch and other refreshments to a number of federal workers. It was there that I would become fairly familiar with the acronym SPAAF (Single Professional African American Female).

ii.

Like Northern Caribbean University (NCU) several years earlier, my first year at Howard University was interrupted by a major act of nature, a blizzard. Washington and the northeast were blanketed by more than three feet of snow. Many of the roads and the aboveground area of the subway system were impassable.

I loved the experience frolicking in the snow and felt protected walking the streets in my new Timberland boots. Andy, a colleague at the restaurant, had recommended them. Not only did my boots provide warmth, but I suspect I also became more hip and fashionable with the hip-hop culture that fancied these boots all seasons of the year. My hipness would not include the baggy pants falling off my butt. But as my boots survived the years, I was convinced they were a good purchase.

As I had done in Jamaica during natural disasters like Gilbert, I lent a hand wherever I could: helping people to push cars that were stuck in the snow; and clearing driveways and sidewalks for the elderly. A major paradigm shift was in store for me when I noticed that some people were unable to view the gesture as neighborly.

Oftentimes, as I approached people and offered my help, some halted their activities and were puzzled as they tried to figure out what I wanted or what my motives were. Some, after accepting my help, offered a couple of dollars, which I politely refused.

After I helped one guy to push the car that his girlfriend was driving, he avoided eye contact, didn't say a word, and jumped into the passenger side as they drove off. Another rolled down his window just in time to quickly apologize that he didn't have any change, and then rolled it up again. As I approached some drivers to offer help, the automatic locks clicked and some waved no thanks.

My annoyance was growing, and I soon caught myself passing by people who needed help. I felt guilty and chided myself for allowing people's attitudes to change my feelings and behavior. I finally concluded that they were entitled to refuse my help, but I should continue offering.

Cleaning up after a blizzard, Washington DC

After helping an elderly man clear the steps to his house, I asked why people always assumed that I wanted something or seemed to question my motives.

"Young man," he replied. "You have good intentions, but there are a lot of junkies around here. They break into people's cars and houses. You see all those broken parking meters," he continued, while pointing. "They remove the meters and steal the coins. They talk a good game and then try to guilt people into giving them things."

That insight gave me a new perspective. I smiled at the thought of me in my cheap winter gear being viewed as a junkie. Simultaneously, I realized that such a lifestyle resulted from people who felt broken and defeated. With no support in the city, that could become my fate. My resolve was now stronger than ever. I had come too far; failure was not an option.

The snow was fun when it was fluffy and soft. It not only blanketed the city, but it also covered the garbage that littered the streets. For a time, it looked clean everywhere. After days of melting and refreezing, what remained was solid, treacherous ice. The novelty of my snow experience and the fun from frolicking was gone. A number of events were cancelled, which affected my parking jobs. While I didn't spend much time at home, I understood the catch phrase "cabin fever."

My valet parking experience turned out to be interesting. I went to several events and met several members of Congress and the media personnel as they attended events all over Washington, DC. "Look, I think that is Senator Dole, and Senator Graham," fellow valets would say to each other. Or, "Reverend Jackson, it is great to meet you." "Do you know that this is John McLaughlin's house?" "I can't believe Cokie Roberts only tipped a dollar."

Before long, I realized that addressing these personalities by name encouraged generous tips. Sometimes, the clients of these events would pay by credit card and added extra for the hardworking valets. Unfortunately, like trickle-down economics, these tips rarely trickled down to the valets for whom they were intended.

"Congressman, it is a pleasure to meet you," I would say. Some politicians lingered an extra minute to create small talk and to joke and cultivate the image of a congenial people's representative. Others would be so preoccupied with their thoughts that it would not have mattered if the sidewalk or pavement returned their keys.

The highlight of my parking experience came when I met General Colin Powell. I had read his book. One valet got the door for his lovely wife, and I got his door.

"General Powell, I was expecting a Volvo," I joked. He paused long enough to discern the source of my accent and then laughed. In his memoir, he had talked about how he loved fixing his old Volvo. I surmised that since his book had done well, he now sported a nice car. After the event, I promptly retrieved his car. I didn't have to go very far since I had reserved the best spot for him. He had come out ahead of his wife to make sure she didn't wait in the cold.

As I accepted his generous tip and bade them goodnight, I couldn't help thinking what many Americans were thinking. This man could have been, or may become, the President of the United States of America.

Capitol Hill Church, with Friend Brian, Washington DC

iii.

"Enjoy our new soup in a bread bowl," I said to members of the crowd of mostly government workers as they gathered for lunch at the Au Bon Pain restaurant at L'Enfant Plaza. I was working the cash register that day and engaged patrons as they lined up for coffee, sandwiches, and soups. "It is environmentally friendly," I continued. The crowd laughed, and before long, the other cashiers, with the support of management, were using some of the phrases I had coined. Among those laughing was an attorney I had met a few days before. She had lingered at the cash register long enough for me to ask her name and for us to talk briefly. She wore a sweet smile and a calm, unassuming demeanor.

"You are enjoying your job, aren't you?" she asked.

"Well, I try to give every task my best shot," was my reply.

"Where in Jamaica are you from?" she continued.

"That obvious, huh?" I said, smiling.

"Well, I am from Jamaica, too," she said, laughing. "Or better yet, my dad is from Jamaica. I come here two or three times a week for lunch or coffee. I'll see you soon."

"What's your name?" I asked. I wanted to continue the conversation, but the line was growing.

"Althea," came the reply. "See you tomorrow."

Several weeks would pass before I finally asked Althea out. She wanted to play tennis. I didn't play, but I told her I wanted to learn. Since tennis partners were difficult to come by, she figured I could at least get the ball over the net to give her some exercise. She was wrong. Though she was never critical, it was obvious that our session frustrated her, and she never played with me again. I was disappointed, and my pride sufficiently bruised to encourage me to learn the game.

One morning after my tennis experience, things were not going well at the restaurant. The employee who came in earlier had noticed that the coffee grinder was not working. I suggested to my manager another method to grind the coffee using another machine. It was a much slower process and would not produce the quantity we needed. After half an hour, he abandoned the idea. That turned out to be a decision he would regret.

The store opened, and federal workers started filing in. People were not as chirpy or responsive to chirpiness. I overheard the conversations they were having among themselves and finally made a connection to what I had seen on the news. Speaker Newt Gingrich and President Bill Clinton were at an impasse with the national budget. Speaker Gingrich and the Republican Congress wanted to cut Medicare and Medicaid spending to balance the budget and refused to raise the national debt ceiling. President Clinton, while supporting a balanced budget amendment, did not agree with those cuts. The continuing resolution was nearing expiration, and if a budget deal was not reached, the US federal government would shut down. Naturally, the employees were concerned about their jobs and were in no mood for small talk.

Soon, the manager made an announcement. "The coffee grinder is broken, and we will not be able to provide coffee this morning."

"This is fucking amazing," one man said as he walked out with the empty cup he carried with him from his office.

"You have got to be kidding me," said another.

"Did you hear, they are out of coffee? And . . . "

"Out of coffee, how is that possible?" The smiles that I saw daily in the faces of these people were now replaced with glares and expression of disdain. This was going to be a difficult day.

An older lady who had not heard the earlier discussion walked up to the counter and was apparently pleased with her luck to be able to walk up to the register. (At that time of the day, the line would stretch nearly to the door.) She lifted her cup to place her regular order. I tried to preempt her and broke the news, but she apparently thought I was joking. She looked at me and realized I wasn't moving. With sorrow in my voice, I repeated my earlier statement.

"We are out of coffee because the . . . "

In anger, she shook her cup, and screamed. "This is a coffee shop, how can you run out of coffee, what the . . . " Her voice faded as she stormed out.

The symbolism of the situation would cause me to pay attention to the national deficits and debt from that point. I made three observations. (1) Americans are addicted to coffee; (2) Americans are addicted to debt; and (3) policy discussions are not only academic exercises, they affect real people.

iv.

Discussions about sports are used to break the ice at work, school, and church just about everywhere. Unfortunately, I found myself at a distinct disadvantage, because even though I was a sports fan in Jamaica, my events of interest were not popular here. In Jamaica, the major sporting events were cricket, soccer, and track and field. I never followed America's most popular sports—basketball, football, and baseball—while I lived in Jamaica. I remembered my insensitivity to a request to watch the Super Bowl via satellite at a friend's house from one on my boarders at Belair in Mandeville. I now had an interest in learning about the game, but with school and two jobs, it would be difficult. Trying to watch TV to learn the sports was frustrating.

"Tell me," I said to a roommate, Barry. "How can a game like basketball that lasts for an hour translate into three to four hours of television viewing? That is absurd," I complained.

"Well, wait until you see Super Bowl, man. Many of the viewers watch specifically for the advertisements. In baseball, the broadcaster stops the live game to advertise."

"And the fans in the stands don't complain?" I asked.

"No, it is accepted. You don't have advertising during soccer and cricket?"

"Yes, in soccer, the real football, for only ten minutes at halftime, and the game typically lasts for ninety minutes if there is no overtime. But those ten minutes are a natural break."

"You mean like when you break for tea? How long is cricket anyway?" he said sarcastically.

"Some games last a day, and some last for up to five days," I said reflectively.

"Five days, really? And you are complaining about four hours?"

"But, dude, that is the game, not the advertisements. The game is the bulk of the time."

V.

Althea invited me to attend Thanksgiving dinner at her parents' house. It would be my first Thanksgiving celebration, and I was excited at the prospect of some Jamaican cuisines. It became apparent to me that Althea was feeling the pressure from family members to find a mate. She had been through a divorce, years earlier, and was obviously cautious about another relationship. In addition, she was slightly older, and it's quite obvious to me that I had not yet attained her refined taste. After dinner, she sat beside me on the couch in her parents' basement, and I put my arms around her. My heart warmed, and I closed my eyes to savor the moment and fought back my analytical tendency and critical thinking.

As the moments slipped by, so did my resolve to avoid critical thinking. Despite her very kind and thoughtful overtures, I started to ask myself the same questions. Was I here to keep her parents and siblings off her back? Could I really survive in a relationship where I was not economically dominant?

All my life I had cultivated the belief that women wore the invisible label "Fragile, Handle with Care, Do Not Drop." Would my chivalry be considered sexist? I had always viewed myself as a non-traditionalist who worked with my partner in defining our own roles. However, when faced with a real situation, not an academic discussion, would I be truly comfortable? Would my current situation sabotage the possibility of a relationship? Gosh, why I am overanalyzing this? I thought. Maybe the sorrel had too much rum and . . . My thought process was interrupted when a player shattered the backboard of the basketball rim and galvanized everyone's attention to the television set.

After dinner, Althea drove me back to the subway station where she had picked me up earlier.

"I enjoyed my time this evening," I said, trying to keep a conversation going.

"I am glad you did," came the reply.

"And I am also thankful for your parents' house."

"Why is that?" she inquired.

"Well, if it was not for your parents' house, I may not have had an opportunity to put my arms around you." Althea smiled as the car came to a halt. I thanked her again and leaned over to hug her good night. She simultaneously leaned forward in anticipation of being kissed, and my shoulder slammed into her chin. Feeling like a complete dork, I apologized, completed the awkward hug, and opened the car door.

"Shit!" I bellowed as I walked in the direction of the train. "What the hell is the matter with me?"

Althea was off the next day, and I called her to find out if she was up for a movie. She was. I told her I was working most of that weekend, and she accommodated my schedule. We talked about her work briefly before she reminded me how happy she was to be off. The subject of how I could work two jobs plus attend graduate school came up. I decided that this was as good a time as any to tell her my situation.

I expected some pull back or a gentle let down and was surprised that she was instead inspired by my story. She talked about her father and his evolution. When the conversation shifted the politics, she was not surprised by my views. Most people from the island are very conservative when they arrive, she declared. "I'll give you a few years, and like my father, your politics will change."

"Really?" I said. "Why?"

"You'll see," she responded confidently. "By the way, Joseph, you might want to consider having me pick up the tab if we go out. I am sure if you were working and dating someone in school, you wouldn't have a problem paying for her, would you?"

"Of course not! However, I don't want you to think that I explained my current situation as an invitation for you to pick up the tab. You really don't have to do that. We can consider inexpensive places for fun."

"I am not talking about the Hilton or the Ritz. But if I can afford some of the finer things, why should we deprive ourselves until you can?"

"Well, what you are saying makes perfect sense. But having you pick up the check is not the same thing since . . ."

"Why isn't it, because you are the man?"

"No, because I am the one inviting you out."

"I don't see the difference. If you had lived here longer, you would not have second thoughts about it. Like I said, the longer you are here, your views, like your politics, will change. Anyway, I'll have to go, my brother is calling. We can meet in front of the theater at Union Station."

vi.

I always knew I had an ego, but I was sure I did not have an ego problem. However, as someone who had worked for almost everything since I was eleven years old, it was evident that I had some learning and pride swallowing to do. Some of the independent streak would have to go for me to form a viable partnership with an intelligent, successful, and attractive woman. I was willing to learn, but would she be patient? Why should she? The tennis experience already provided some indication to that question.

I continued a mental conversation in her absence. I don't think she really understood the distinction I was making. How ridiculous it would be for me to call her up and invite her to a great restaurant and then expect her to pick up the tab. That is something a child would do. I did not refuse an invitation from her. She invited me to her parents' house, and I went. If I were invited to a restaurant, I would go, as long as I was not working that night.

I continued my mental dialogue and then paused to acknowledge a parallelism I was sensing with Christopher Columbus. Columbus claimed to have discovered the New World. Though new to him, the "new world" was already inhabited. My discovery was the high correlation between economics and relationships, a concept that was already well known to many. Another discovery was that dating in America could be a very confusing proposition for a man.

I was on time for the movie, and she was already waiting along with two tickets. "You got us tickets?" I asked as I hugged her.

"Not really, there was a guy in line, and I suspect that his date didn't show, and he walked up to me and offered them to me. We can watch something else if you prefer."

"No, that's fine, we don't have to."

"Really, if you want, we can watch something else."

By now, I was in a lose-lose situation. She seemed already convinced that I didn't believe her story. If we watched the movie for which we had the ticket, I might inadvertently confirm that suspicion. If we chose another, she might try to get something that she didn't care for, but thought I might like.

"What other movies would you be interested in if we didn't watch this one?" I asked.

"I don't have a preference. I would be fine with whichever one you choose."

"I think we were lucky to get free tickets," I said. "I will get drinks and popcorn."

That night, when our date ended, the only positive spin I could come up with is that my conflict and conviction for my church's teaching for abstinence from premarital sex would not be tested. I was now learning baseball and had an analogy. If I couldn't make it off first base, how could I even plan for third base? If I didn't strike out, maybe I would be walked.

vii.

It was Friday night and I was on campus with a group of similar-minded Christians who met for vespers. We testified and shared our experiences and prayed together. I shared an experience I had at work.

I had gone to work at the restaurant that morning and noticed that Roy, one of the employees who came in at 4:00 a.m. each day to prepare before the restaurant opened, was not there. I inquired as to his whereabouts, but was not prepared for the answer.

"He was shot in Anacostia last night," Monica had told me.

"What do you mean . . . ah, ah?" I responded in disbelief.

"Like shot, shot in front of his crib."

"Is he in the hospital?" I said, trying to process what I was hearing.

"NOOOO, idiot, he is dead," Monica said, projecting a strong exterior, but visibly hurt; she lived in the same area of the city.

After I related the story, others spoke. Violent crimes were regular occurrences in the city. Some were saddened at the observation that the only time outrage was voiced by civil leaders or reported by the media was when the police were involved in the shootings or the crime had racial overtones.

I continued my dive into the culture wherever I went. After morning Sabbath service, I accepted an invitation for lunch at the church. The congregation was a mix of professionals, blue-collar workers, welfare recipients, ex-junkies, ex-convicts, and students from Howard and other universities in DC. The experience provided a colorful look into American life, especially from the African American perspective.

I had enjoyed the sermon. "Church," the pastor had said, "is like a hospital. It is an institution for the broken and spiritually sick. If you are not spiritually sick, you are in the wrong place. Let me correct that! If you feel self-righteous and look down with contempt at others who are here, then you are in fact in the right place. Because pompousness and self-righteousness are symptoms of spiritual sickness and are indications that you also need healing."

During the potluck, several topics were covered. It was jaw-dropping for me as some very articulate participants talked about different issues. A major topic of discussion from Cynthia and other law students was the lack of viable African American men for husbands for single professional women. The reasons put forward related to other social issues.

There was a growing prison industry in the US with nearly two million incarcerated. More black men were in jails than colleges. Society's move to privatized prisons was viewed suspiciously, and black men were viewed as the grease to keep this industry going. Despite affirmative action, studies showed some black men, without prison records, did not find it any easier to obtain jobs than whites with criminal backgrounds. After hearing these numbers, one student lamented that it was no wonder a number of young black boys felt the incredible pressure and decided to give up before they even started. Of course, giving up perpetuated the problem and became a self-fulfilling prophecy.

The discussion continued highlighting the percentage of African American males who were gay and those who were broke and dating and marrying white women. If black men shaped up, life would be great, the women theorized. After all, one student concluded, black women had the same economic and social conditions, so why all the excuses?

It was at one of these potlucks that I sought to understand why African Americans voted so overwhelmingly for the Democratic Party despite the fact that it was Lincoln, a Republican, who signed the Emancipation Proclamation. Wasn't it better to leverage votes, rather than have one party totally ignore you and the other take you for granted? We discussed the civil rights movement and how that had transformed American politics and changed the allegiances to the parties. The Republican Party had started to appeal to whites who were upset with the civil rights movement.

Since I had met General Colin Powell, I mentioned his name to a middle-aged lady at the potluck as a possible candidate for president. Her eyes lit up.

"Yes, I heard a little about him. He seems like a respectable man."

"So, would you vote for him if he ran as a Republican?"

"He is a Republican?" she said, shocked, surprised, and dismayed. "Well then, he ain't going nowhere.

Besides, that party would never nominate him. They would kill him first."

viii.

Althea and I would remain friends, but our relationship never moved an inch. We talked to each other on the phone and my heart rate would speed up whenever she entered the restaurant. She made several trips to Chicago, and she later told me of her longtime interest in someone there. Unfortunately, their goals were not congruent. She wanted children, and he did not, at least not with her. Her desire for children had led her to consider insemination and other methods of fertilization.

"Hypothetically," she had said to me. "If a tall graduate student wanted to focus exclusively on college and wanted his bills paid, do you think he would consider fathering a child?"

"Well, a graduate student might not want to have a child of his that he cannot support," I said as I tried to grasp the gravity of what we were discussing.

"Well, as an attorney, a contract could be extracted to protect that student from any future responsibilities for the child."

"Well, that student may not feel comfortable that he had brought a child into this world and didn't share in the parenting responsibilities." We talked politely for a few minutes before she opted to take a call from her sister. As I hung up the phone, I marveled at what I had just heard. I was not offended by the questions, and in fact, I felt closer to her that she felt open to discuss her innermost needs with me.

ix.

"U Street-Cardozo Station, this is the end of the green line. Thank you for riding metro." I had gotten off at this station on my way from work and had heard the announcement numerous times before. Tonight was no different. It was after midnight, and the next bus wouldn't come for at least half an hour. I decided to walk the two miles home as I had done many times before. As I headed onto Eleventh Street, I saw the sight now familiar: junkies buying drugs or offering sex to earn money to buy drugs. I was dressed in my valet parking uniform and crossed to the other side to avoid the small gathering on the sidewalk.

"Hello!" a voice from behind called out. I looked back and saw someone that I had seen on the train earlier. I didn't know him, but had seen him and said hello several times before. I knew he lived in the same area since he had gotten off at the same stop. I surmised that he was coming from work also and wanted to avoid the gathering on the street. So, I slowed for him to catch up. We chatted politely and walked briskly.

"Are you coming from work?" he asked.

"Yes!" I responded. "You?"

"Yes. Anyway, man, I am charged up, and my house is right over there." He was pointing a block away. "I want some tonight." I laughed, and as we passed the group of prostitutes and addicts, I thought that shouldn't be difficult.

"I will make it worth your while if you stop by my house," he continued.

"What!?" I said, making sure I had heard him right.

"Yeah, I'll pay you—twenty dollars?"

"You were kidding me, right?" I said, hoping for a punch line.

"How about forty? You will be happy!"

"Hold on!" I said as I halted my steps. "What the hell made you think that you can walk up to me and proposition me like that? Here is the deal, the next time you see me on the train, don't say hello and don't talk to me. If I am on one side of the street, cross to the other. If you bring that conversation to me, I will knock your fucking teeth out!" With that I crossed the street and was still fuming when I got home. I was also upset with myself for losing my cool and for using the word *knock*. This word was frequently used by my father, and the thought of me becoming him scared me. I had vowed to avoid acting on impulse as my father did many times, resulting in violence. I knew Big Mac would have knocked him cold. I had felt little fear and had wanted to knock his teeth out.

Though I was comfortable in my sexuality, I questioned once again, was I homophobic? I attended a college where several students were openly gay, and I felt no hostility toward them. Was this how women felt when unwanted advances were made? Wrong timing and bad example, I thought. This was not the time to get in touch with my feminine side.

In an effort to distract myself, I turned on the TV in my room. The television provided some comedic relief as I scanned through the channels. I stopped on the movie *Indecent Proposal*. I had seen the movie before and laughed at the irony. This guy gets offered a million dollars for one night with his wife. I get propositioned for $20.

My thinking continued as I showered. Maybe I was too nice and behaving like I was still in my little district in Jamaica. I might have been sending the wrong signal. I was in a new city, and I was lonely. I thought about Althea, and how much I needed her. Maybe I should call her and let her know how I feel about her, I said to myself. I can't do it now; it is now after midnight. Oh hell. If I don't do it now, I will talk myself out of it.

I picked up the phone and raced to call her before my logical side caught up with me.

"Mmm . . . Hello . . . Joseph?"

"I am sorry to wake you."

"What happened?"

"I just wanted to hear your voice . . . ah, I think I am in love with you."

"What, what time is it?" she said, yawning.

"Oh, I am sorry. I should not have called you."

"Are you alright?"

"Yes, I didn't realize how late it was. I'll talk with you another time. Goodnight!"

"Okay!"

The next day, I was working the cash register in the restaurant when Althea walked in. She joined my line. My heart was racing. Monica's register became open. She said to Althea, "Ma'am, I can take you over here."

Althea walked toward Monica's register, and I was relieved. I knew I had acted out of impulse last night. My timing had been bad, and I knew I had set back the possibility of a relationship. I sought justification that it was probably for the better. I recalled a discussion we had had about her previous marriage. "Been there, done that," she had said. "I don't want to do that again."

Maybe my sperm was all she really wanted. I smiled at a new American statement I had heard: "You are not in Kansas anymore." Joseph, you are not in Jamaica anymore, I thought to myself.

A few weeks later, I attended a potluck with some of my friends at college who shared the same faith. During lunch, one of the female students went outside to her car. Moments later, she returned along with one of the guys loitering outside the apartment complex. He sat in the chair next to me and joined in the conversations. He related his experience that had landed him in jail. When the conversation shifted to the church's teaching on gays, he offered his own experience. While in prison, he had been raped repeatedly. Now he was gay by choice and sometimes sold his body.

I was moved by his story, but after he spoke, my first thought considered the probability of him walking into the room and finding a seat next to me. I was angered by my earlier proposition and didn't like to be reminded. It became clear to me that my self-righteous attitude was not reflecting the philosophy of Jesus Christ. I felt ashamed. When it was time to pray, we formed a circle and held hands. As I held his hand, I realized that somehow he was there to teach me the meaning of acceptance. I didn't have to embrace his lifestyle, but I had to show love. After all, that is what my religion taught. Isn't that what Jesus would do?

X.

Andy, my colleague at the restaurant, walked over to me from his register and whispered, "These ladies seem to like you, don't they?"

"What are you talking about?"

"Well, that lady was asking about you? I think she is a contract lawyer at the post office."

I smiled and walked away toward the sandwich bar where Daryl worked. I gave him instructions for an order, and he pretended (as he had done several times before) that he couldn't understand what I was saying.

"What?" he said, leaning in my direction, and asking me to repeat myself. I knew I had an accent, so I spoke more slowly. But his emphasis convinced me that he was making a point.

"Daryl, you really don't understand me?" I asked.

"Joe, if you have a problem with me, we can take it outside."

"Are you kidding me?"

"No, I'm serious," he said. "You think you are all that."

"You seem to have a problem with me," I said. "Since you always pretend that you don't understand my accent."

"Yeah, so let's take it outside."

"You can't be serious," I said. I suspected this was one of those alpha male fights for territory. I have to get out of here, I thought to myself. I need to find another job. There is just no way I am going to get in a fight with some guy for a reason that I can't really understand and he can't explain.

I suspect Andy had carried the joke about women constantly asking about me too far. If that was Daryl's problem, I was prepared to cede territory. If he attacked me, I'd kick his ass, but volunteering to go outside and fight was another matter.

A few weeks later, I was on the register when I heard screaming in the back. The manager had just fired a member of the staff, and she had attacked him. She followed him to the front and tossed coffee, coffee pot, and everything she could at him.

"You think this is funny," she said. "This is my life." The manager ran past me, and the coffee grinder handle that followed him caught me in the back. The manger suffered cuts and bruises, which were more visible on his white skin. As I felt the bruise in my back, a security guard from the mall came and asked me if I needed an ambulance, and I said no. A colleague pulled me aside and lectured me.

"Are you crazy? You could get at least four thousand dollars of workers' compensation. You want money to attend college, and you are passing up this opportunity? Man, you are not in Jamaica anymore!" Not only was I not in Jamaica anymore, but this would be the start of my learning about the workers' compensation, health care, and tort systems of America.

xi.

The familiar announcement came with the blinking lights as the train pulled into the final station at U Street-Cardozo. I had done a fair amount of running while parking cars at the Cochran Gallery and wasn't looking forward to walking an additional two miles home. I walked to the bus stop and was disappointed that there was no bus present or in the distance. I turned around to continue my walk when a car honked to gain my attention. It was a taxicab.

"Would you like a ride?" the driver asked.

"Well, I cannot afford a cab."

"That is fine," he said. "Hop in." I did not know the driver, but I got in.

"That is interesting," I said, laughing.

"What is?"

"Well, I was in Adams Morgan a week ago and tried to get a cab home. None of the drivers would stop for me. The funny thing is the majority were black drivers and drivers from other countries."

"And here you are tonight, being invited into a cab by the driver who is not charging you," he said, laughing. "Life is funny indeed! I saw you glance at the bus schedule and started walking. Since you were headed in the direction I am going, I thought I would offer you a ride."

"Thanks for the ride, man," I said as I got out of the car two miles later. "I had offered him the equivalent of my bus fare, but he refused. "All the best to you, man."

The gesture was a good lesson. In Adams Morgan, the week before, I had walked in and out of bars and clubs trying to mask my loneliness. I didn't like clubs or bars, not only because I didn't drink and I hated the cigarette smoke, but also because my church advised against these venues. At one of the bars, a lady offered me a drink. I was not familiar with the pickup line and politely refused.

"I am sorry," I had said. "I don't drink."

"Why are you in a bar then?" came her curious question.

"I just want to listen to some music and meet people." We chatted for a few minutes, and then she moved on. Talking with me would not satisfy her needs.

It was 2:00 a.m., and as I got out of the club, I decided against walking the five miles home. Several patrons were also trying to get home. What I saw infuriated me. The cab drivers were passing all the black passengers in favor of the white ones. Some whites hailed cabs and offered them to blacks having difficulty obtaining cabs. On several occasions, as the black passengers got into the cabs, the driver pulled away sometimes with the door still open. I was in disbelief.

My shock propelled my next action. I stepped into the street and blocked the next cab and got in. I sat down, and the accented driver asked where I was going. After I told him, he requested the fare up front.

"You want my fare before I get to my destination?"

"Yes," was his calm reply. I complied, and he drove in the direction of my address.

"Sir," I said. "Can you tell me how you can justify passing a black passenger in favor of whites, or requesting my fare up front and not to others?"

"Well, my friend, I don't like the practice. But I have four kids and a wife to support. Like you, I am from a foreign country, and I have to work hard to feed my family. I was robbed twice in four months. My friend who also drives a cab was shot. You cannot believe the number of black youths who ride our cabs and just run off without paying."

"Well, I think requesting fares up front might be a better solution rather than just passing people on the street," I said. I was sympathetic to his situation, but I didn't like being responsible for all black males who had cheated cab drivers out of their fares. At the same time, I had a sinking feeling that contemporary civil rights leaders may be missing an opportunity to emphasize personal responsibility and parental guidance.

Many of these drivers did not grow up in America. Behaviors such as this were formed out of their experiences and the will to survive. Legislations, however well intended, would not alter behaviors when the root cause was not addressed. The behavior would change when the percentage of black youths who ran off with the fares was not larger than that of the general population. The irony was that black youths who just wanted to go about their daily lives and do the right thing resented being treated differently based on the behaviors of others. Sometimes, they lashed out, which fueled even more suspicions of black youths.

From my vantage point, it was evident that the issue of race permeated almost every part of the fabric of American life. I considered myself privileged to have had the benefit of an outside perspective. The perspective allowed me not to see race as the first issue in everything. I saw police brutality in Jamaica and recognized that it was directed at the poorer and uneducated class. In America, when it was directed at blacks, it was almost always considered racist. I recalled my own experience working parking cars at a house in Georgetown. A cop pulled up and asked what I was doing there and then turned his floodlight in my face.

<u>Lesson 16:</u> The choice is not always black or white.

"Sir, will you please get that light out of my face," I demanded. When he complied, I walked up to the car and explained my purpose. I told him that while I understand the difficulty of his job, it was inappropriate to assume that a young black male in a predominantly white area had to be up to no good. "Maybe he is just working for a living," I continued. The black officer apologized and left. After that incident, I decided that there was a great fear of the young black male in America. As unfair as it was, I had to assume the responsibility to put police and people at ease to ensure my own survival. If earlier leaders were placed in jail for my freedom, then despite the obvious humiliation, maybe I could show the police some courtesy that would reduce the likelihood of incidents. It was unfair, but that would be the price I would pay, so the next generation wouldn't have to.

I did not have to fight Daryl, and I gladly ceded territory. I took a new job with a temporary staffing agency. This agency placed me on temporary assignment with numerous businesses in DC and the surrounding areas. I performed accounting, clerical, and other office duties as required. Before long, I realized that I would be unable to perform my parking job, and so I gave it up.

At my new job in Rockville, I went out to lunch with a white colleague and did not anticipate another racially humiliating experience. He was driving his Explorer, and while we were at a stoplight, he asked me if I could ask the lady driver in the car next to me for directions. The lady sat motionless, looking ahead, and did not roll her window down. Despite my formal attire, she would not respond. My white colleague leaned over, and she immediately complied and gave him directions. I was taken aback by the behavior and fought hard to remain calm despite my boiling anger.

That night, I prayed for the strength to remain in control and not allow people to push my buttons. I didn't have to like what they did, but I resolved to remain in control of my behavior. That incident, I thought, gave me a peek into the psyche of the early civil rights leaders. Self-control in the face of disrespect and injustice required inner strength, perseverance, and diplomacy. Being an angry black man was easier, and when you had legitimate grievances, it felt justified to lash out.

xii.

The new job was a better-paying job, and I sought to obtain a car to be able to travel to different work sites. I went car shopping with two requirements for the car that I wanted. It should be reliable, and it should be inexpensive. I settled on a 1996 Geo Metro with thirty-three thousand miles, and my exploration of America continued.

My car was not only efficient on gas, but it also provided comedic relief for many. I would be asked questions like "how tall are you?" My answer of "six–foot-two" was followed by "do you really fit in that car?"

The car brought many changes. It gave me a new perspective of Washington, DC, a perspective lost to a regular rider of the subway system. I gained friends who sought me out for rides to church and other activities. I visited other churches and met other singles. In addition, I realized the difficulty of finding parking in a city, as my number of parking tickets increased. The speed limits, I would later realize, were not just guidance.

I was on I 495 on my way home after spending the evening with a new friend, Marcia. We had talked for hours. We laughed about an experience the prior week. After church, I got into her car and rode with her to a local park. We had lunch and then walked around for a few minutes. It was getting cold, and I offered her my jacket as we went back to the car.

We sat in the backseat and pushed the front seats forward for more room. I had my feet on the back of the front seat. Marcia was still wearing my jacket pulled tightly around her petite body. Her legs were comfortably crossed and rested on my knees. As I adjusted my position, I noticed a police car parked behind us. We were in a highly visible area, so I expected that he would move on.

When he didn't, I wondered out aloud why a police car was parked behind us. Marcia sat up and peered through the back glass. Instantly, the police car door opened, and a cop walked to my side of the car. I wound the window down and addressed him.

"Officer?"

"Are you all alright, ma'am?" he asked Marcia.

"Of course!" she said.

"Sir, may I see an identification?"

"Why?" I protested.

"An identification, please, sir!"

I was not in the mood to cooperate, so I handed him my school ID.

He smiled and then asked, "What's is this?"

"An identification," I responded with a sarcastic grin.

"Your driver's license, sir."

"I am not even in the driver's seat," I said as I produced my driver's license. I did not want to tell him this was not my car for fear that he would start interrogating Marcia.

"What's the reason for your questions?" I demanded.

"Well," he said. "I saw your heads pop up looking back at me, and I just wanted to check on safety."

"You find it unusual for someone to look back at a police car parked behind them?" I asked in disbelief. "And given your concern for our safety, how come you did not ask me if I was okay?"

He explained that we were not in a regular parking spot, and that had sparked his curiosity. I thanked him for his concern and assured him that we were fine as he left. I generally appreciated the difficulty of the police job. However, after feeling that I was constantly suspected for doing something wrong, I was losing patience.

xiii.

I was still on the beltway when the flashing light in the rearview mirror interrupted my reminiscing.

"Gosh! Each time I see Marcia, I get a visit from the police." I looked at my odometer, and to my horror, I was well over the 55 mph beltway speed limit. There was no doubt this time.

Previous encounters with the police were not as clear-cut. In one case, I was accused of running a red light—an accusation that was dropped when I explained to the police the impossibility of that accusation since I had not come from that direction. The irony was not lost on me that I had earlier debated students who complained about racial profiling. "You can't be breaking the law and then complain when you are caught," I had said.

Now I was becoming a lot more sympathetic to their concerns. I now fully understood that if you scrutinize a segment of the population at a higher level than the general population, then it is likely that you'll find a higher percentage of lawbreakers in that segment.

xiv.

It was Saturday afternoon, and I had just finished church. I told my friends that I was on my way to the Washington Mall to help a church group pack some supplies to send to Haiti.

I had seen how the church responded with the relief efforts after Hurricane Gilbert (when I was in Jamaica) through its relief agency, ADRA. I was eager to be on the helping side. "Would you like to come along?" I had asked.

"Which church is organizing that, a church in the white conference?" came my friend's rhetorical question.

The question startled me. I snapped! "I don't think the people in Haiti care whether the white or black conference sent them help." The response did not win me support and I attended alone. However, the incident prompted me to examine the organizational structure of my church. Several years ago, I had looked it up in the encyclopedia, and had found it less than flattering when the church was described as a cult.

The Seventh Day Adventist church is an evangelical movement that was formed in 1863. Current membership is over seventeen million in over two hundred countries. One of the church's most famous members is neurosurgeon Ben Carson. The church has fundamental doctrinal beliefs, but distinguishes itself from other protestant Christians by emphasizing the Judeo-Christian Seventh Day Sabbath—the day of rest. Worldwide, the church operates a number of colleges and hospitals.

I found it amazing that despite the church's global appeal, it had not settled its racial structure in America, the country of its origin. It was not that blacks and whites were hostile to each other. In fact, they worked closely together and were respectful and helpful. When I visited predominantly white churches, it was not unusual for people, trying to be helpful, to suggest other churches in the area—I suspected to make me feel more comfortable. I often joked with friends that I would wave from the black side of heaven.

I understood that styles of worship were different. I recall measuring the time it took to get through the program at black churches as compared to whites. As my process-improvement knowledge developed at college, I found myself constantly mentally re-engineering the worship process as the prayers and sermons dragged on and on and on.

At 2:31 p.m. on Sabbath, I walked out of church, as a pastor had had the audacity to announce that today was the Sabbath, and we had nothing better to do than to be in church. Normal worship, according to the conference guide, ended at noon. In many black churches, the accepted norm was 1:00 to 1:30 p.m. The preacher had related his experience in Vietnam and how he had done all the drugs to numb himself during his tour. Jacqueline, a fellow student, had whispered that he must have been having a relapse today.

As I left and complained about the intemperance of dragging out the service, a fellow student and social worker, Andrew, explained that he had been "touched" by the sermon as he felt that it had been tailored to him. From then on, I realized that hearts are spoken to in different ways. While I was bored, someone was being reached.

My evaluation of my church structure continued. I was not surprised or concerned to see predominantly white or black churches in different areas, since churches reflect communities. What surprised me was that the central governing body of the church, the conferences, were organized to accept segregation.

The system was initially formed out of a genuine desire to make sure black pastors could serve black population during segregation. As the system became more entrenched, black leaders refused to relinquish the power and prestige of the dual system. I would later be told by a white pastor that black pastors could choose from two different pension systems while they had one option.

King Solomon was right. In Ecclesiastes 1:18, he wrote that for in much wisdom is much grief, and he that increaseth knowledge increaseth sorrow. The more I learned about my church, the more disillusioned I became. Like my father before me, the church was now revealed as an imperfect body. I had seen the good works, and now I was seeing the less flattering structure. Government had led the response to civil rights demands forty years earlier. Members of churches across America continued in an accepted segregated pattern.

I was also to discover that the most intolerant views on race were from a region of the country that considered itself the Bible belt. In the past, some well-intended Christians in these states worked with their local governments to continue their "God-given" rights of segregation.

My visits to a church in Alexandria, Virginia, became more frequent. Pastor Wright's church was predominantly black, but he was organized in the white conference. His church boasted people from many different countries. I recall my surprise when a member of the church expressed his concern for his family during the genocide in Rwanda. Up to that point, I considered myself pretty knowledgeable of current affairs and was surprised that it was not a major story in the US media. With Ken Starr and Monica Lewinski, nothing else seemed to matter to the myopic media outlets.

Pastor Wright was prepared for his sermons, and he focused on process and respected time. His sermons were easy to follow and were not never-ending ramblings or attempts to entertain. Each sermon presented an opportunity to learn. His focus was holistic teachings: health (physical and emotional), spiritual, financial, and social. He recruited experts in health, finance, legal, and other fields to help his congregation make better choices. This was different from the focuses of other churches, which I had evaluated for process improvement, and I loved the format. There was also another pull: June.

XV.

June was a confident, attractive, and single African American lady. She was poised, articulate, and friendly.

She was a go-getter, and her attitude reminded me of my eldest sister, Jenny. The church was planning a singles hiking trip on the Shenandoah Mountain, and I was not going to miss it, especially after learning that June would be in attendance.

Sam, Andrew, Shannon, Brian, and I had developed a bond. We were all students at Howard and shared the same faith. We all agreed to attend the hiking trip. The group met in a parking lot and decided to carpool. We stood in a circle, prayed, and then introduced ourselves. The introduction taught me a powerful lesson in humility. All the current students proudly articulated their areas of study in our introduction: Brian, final-year law student. Andrew, Masters in social work. Sam, law student. Joseph, MBA student. Then, I noticed a change in the way the non-students introduced themselves.

"My name is Dale, and I hope to have a great time today." I was deeply surprised at Dale's humility because I had learned earlier that he was a physician working in a DC hospital. That set off an interest for me to find out about all the people who had just given their first names. As it turned out, all the humble folks did not have to flaunt it because they had it. They were highly accomplished professionals and entrepreneurs who did not want to scare off prospects by highlighting their accomplishments. One such person was Karen.

"Joseph, would you or anyone else like to ride with me?" Karen asked. Two of the other guys had ridden in my Geo to the meet-up site.

"Thanks, Karen, but we are all sorted out," I told her. We packed ourselves into four cars and were ready.

"Do you know who that was?" Andrew asked me.

"Yes," I said. "That is one of the sweetest ladies you will ever find. Her name is Karen."

Andrew was not done. "Do you know that she is a doctor?" He paused for effect. Then, he continued. "Do you know she is June's cousin, and my guess is that she likes you?"

Andrew suddenly had my attention. I would not be surprised if he was right. Life always threw a curve ball. My eyes were on June, while, if Andrew was right, her cousin had her eyes on me. Little did I know that since I had met June, my decision-making abilities were impaired. It is only in retrospect that I can fully appreciate how much of my decisions were influenced by my desire to be near her.

June was one of the drivers, and everything she did intrigued me, least of them the way she donned her cap front to back. She wore short blue jeans revealing long, smooth, unblemished legs. Her buttoned-up blouse was tied at the bottom. It occurred to me that it was the first time I had seen her in casual wear and concluded that her clothes did not enhance or detract from her natural grace and elegance.

We got to our destination, got on the trail, and walked for over an hour. June led most of the time, and I immediately realized that she had a competitive streak. After lunch, the girls lingered behind, talking, while the guys went ahead on the path. I found myself alone and at equidistance between the two groups of hikers. My position reflected my internal conflict. Before me were the men, and I fully appreciated the need for male bonding. Behind me were the women, including a woman in whose presence I reveled in great anticipation.

My internal turmoil manifested itself into a boyish prank. I weighed the decision briefly and thought I'd risk the women hating me. However, my boyish desires were stronger than logic, and I set the plan in motion. I hid behind a rock near the path and picked up a rotten tree trunk. As the women approached, I rolled the trunk into the path followed my low moaning bear sounds. The rotten trunk crumbled into little pieces and created the desired effect. Some of the women screamed and others bolted. I quickly revealed myself to stop the panic. I was greeted with expression of "Oh, Joooseph! Gosh!" plus other words not typical of a Christian's vocabulary. I resisted the urge to laugh as some of the men hurried back to investigate the reason for the screaming.

Weeks would pass before I summoned the courage to invite June out on a date. I promised myself that I would not sabotage it the way I had previously done with Althea. I had a tendency to hide my nervousness by becoming aloof and cerebral when in the presence of an attractive woman.

Our first date was uneventful. It was a typical dinner and a movie. I picked her up in my Geo and followed her direction to an Olive Garden restaurant. After dinner, she made no fuss about my picking up the tab, but I felt her scrutiny during dinner, observing if I ate first, or if I was expecting her to dish out my salad when I offered her the bowl first. Initially, it felt like a dinner interview where a prospective boss watched your every move to find a reason not to hire you. The irony was that she was a recruiter for her company, and it was evident she was using some of the same techniques to determine my eligibility. I smiled to myself and thought, this is too mental. We both relaxed when I started deliberately exaggerating and sabotaging the process by doing things that would be considered unacceptable in any interview context.

As we talked, her tough, confident exterior peeled away, and a more vulnerable woman with ordinary needs emerged. We left the restaurant and walked to the movie theater to see *Good Will Hunting*. I felt a great sense of pride to have her by my side.

xvi.

Life was good even before my date with June. I had reconnected with my aunt Eunice, who lived in Maryland, and she invited me to stay at her house. Eunice worked almost twenty-four hours taking care of an old lady in DC. She seemed eager to help and gladly cosigned a loan, and I was able to resume school full time. It was not a student loan, which meant I would commence repayment immediately. She bought me a computer, and I was on my way.

Eunice made it home once weekly and thought it was a good idea to have someone at her house. I thanked her and insisted that I continue to make rent payments. I also suggested that I pay an additional allowance for the groceries I used from the stock of groceries she had amassed. She spent a lot of her free time shopping and amassed a number of things to mask her loneliness. Retail therapy, it was called.

Eunice was divorced. Two of her three children lived in DC and the other in New Jersey. Her two sons who lived in DC were older than me. but I had played with them, as we visited each other during the summers while we were in Jamaica. Eunice had worked as an au pair for several years before she eventually moved her family to the USA. I was baffled when none of her children, especially the boys, reached out to me despite my efforts to contact them. I wondered if America could have changed people to that extent. It surprised me when I learned that she had not spoken to one of them in three years, considering that he lived less than twenty miles from her. As I packed my things to move, a fellow student suggested that my move was more for her than for me. “I don’t really care,” was my reply. “She is family.”

My first attempt to move came Saturday night after church. I arrived at her townhouse later than I expected. My books and belongings had taken longer to fit in my Geo than I expected. It was near midnight when I rang the doorbell, and Auntie didn’t respond. I knocked then rang and still no answer. Eventually, I returned to DC and called her the next morning. She was in the house at the time I had rang, but was upset that I had arrived later than I was expected. I apologized and resumed my forty minutes’ journey to Upper Marlboro. On my way, I had a strange feeling that I was making a big mistake. Could I live with someone who was not prepared to make any allowance for deviation? Don’t worry, I concluded, she is family.

My aunt started coming home more frequently now that she had company at home. We would talk late into the night, and I would cringe to myself since I had assignments to prepare for school. She told me stories about how she had made it in the US, and I was impressed with her effort. She told me that she was disappointed with her children who had come to this country and had not yet all made successes of their lives. Her daughter thought freedom in America meant that she could just purchase anything she wanted with her new approved Visa card. Soon after her daughter was married, she and her husband lost their home and filed for bankruptcy. One of her sons (without her knowledge) dropped out of the navy. Her other son held a steady job. However, Auntie did not like the woman he had married and made it known each time they met. The result was that he had stopped talking with her, and Auntie couldn't understand why.

Auntie also couldn't understand how her sister's son (me) had come to America to college, while her own children didn't grab the opportunity. I tried to avoid such discussions and assured her that we were family, and that my success was her success, and that I appreciated how she was helping me.

However, as the story repeated itself, so did Auntie's annoyance with me. Her annoyance with me grew over routine issues, such as when the bank forced her to take a fingerprint when she attempted to cash a check I had written to her from the new consultancy practice that I had formed. I had started to contract my services directly to companies rather than go through an agency.

Then, Congress and the Clinton administration decided to overhaul the immigration laws. Students who had come to the US and were not in school full time were now out of status. The law applied retroactively. I was now full time in school, but I had been out of status previously, and the new law affected me. Also, only work on campus was tolerated for anyone on a student visa.

I immediately told my aunt of my predicament and the fact that I had to apply to Immigration to get back in status. If my application with Immigration were successful, I would have to apply to get a job on campus. In the meantime, I could not work. I had less than a year to go, and I believed my GPA would make me eligible for a scholarship the next year.

When I stopped working, I was unable to pay my rent, but I continued to focus on school. Immigration also wanted me to find a US sponsor who would agree to step in if I fell on difficult times, so that I would not become a burden to the state. Auntie refused to sign, but fortunately, Basil, a friend I had met at work, did so gladly. "I'll marry you if you want, Joseph," some female friends had joked as I searched for a US sponsor.

Auntie was not thrilled when she learned that I had obtained the required sponsorship. Since I could not work, my rent was late again. One night after Christmas when I came to her house, she asked me to leave.

"Are you serious, Auntie?" I had asked in disbelief.

"Of course, I am serious!"

"Why?"

She did not have to give me an explanation. It was her house. Auntie is a generous woman, and the action took me by surprise. However, I realized that she was very controlling and vindictive. Her children stayed away for that reason. I suspected that she thought if she increased the pressure on me, I would have to beg for help. Her gifts were the price she was willing to pay for undying loyalty and affection. But with me, she had miscalculated.

I reached out to my old roommate, Barry, who had moved with another roommate, Ernie, to Maryland. Barry had just joined the army and told me his room would be empty, and that I could have it and pay when I could. I got on my knees and thanked God. Other students also reached out and offered to share their rooms.

When I got back to the house, Auntie had taken my computer with everything on my hard drive. She had never used a computer in her life, but had now taken the one she had purchased for me. I picked up all I had and moved to Barry's room in Oxon Hill. The next day, I returned to collect my mail and to return my keys. I thanked Auntie for her help cosigning the loan to get me back in school. I told her that less than $700 was now outstanding, but I would continue to make payments as best as I could.

"Would you like some soup?"

I thought, you have got to be kidding me. But instead, I replied, "No, thanks, Auntie, I must go." I didn't totally understand what had happened, but I thought loneliness and jealousy of her sister's son might have provided some explanation.

In America, loneliness seemed more of a problem than in Jamaica. In Jamaica, you hoped that your neighbors and relatives stayed away. In America, you moved to the suburbs to avoid people, and then talked their ears off when you met them or talked on the phone. Auntie made several trips to the doctor, who eventually told her that she was fine, and that all she needed was companionship. She was a strong woman, but she had succeeded in pushing away her husband and her children and now me. I knew deep down she was hurting, but I was now concerned about my status in the US, and I had to save myself.

When I moved to Barry's apartment, I again met Ernie. Ernie was an engineer who appeared to be in a state of depression. He had lost his business and owed the IRS and other creditors. For two years, he spent time driving his car and delivering packages as a courier until his car died. I saw his talents and was amazed at how he had been beaten up.

I referred him to one of the staffing agencies with which I had worked and gave him my car to find a job. Before long, he was working again, and his confidence improved. He turned out to be glad that his car had died. For two years, he had been on a treadmill delivering packages and getting parking tickets as he tried to survive, and had been slowly forgetting his true worth.

I continued to see June at church, but with all that was going on, I never went out with her again. We talked occasionally on the phone, and I told her about my immigration problem. Shortly after, June told me she was moving to Georgia. My response was a lame effort at humor. Even though June typically had a good sense of humor, she did not think it was funny when I inquired if she was leaving on the midnight train. (I was referencing Gladys Knight and the Pips—"Midnight Train To Georgia.") Despite my attempt at humor, I was devastated, but found some comfort in her invitation to attend her going-away party.

xvii.

My friend Brian had graduated from law school and was working with the federal government. He helped me prepare my affidavit for Immigration. Despite our effort, Immigration rejected my application to work under a hardship provision. My only recourse was to return to Jamaica and renew my status. I alerted my professor that there was a possibility that I might not return in time to complete the semester. I handed my car key to my roommate as he dropped me at the airport. If I were not able to make it back, he would have a free car. As I walked into the airport, I reminded myself that I was very close to the completion of an MBA degree and that I wanted to see June again. I had to succeed.

At the airport, I went into the restroom and changed into more tropical clothes. I would not need the heavy sweater in Jamaica. I had a strange feeling that I was being watched when I noticed a guy at the urinal taking a longer-than-normal time. I left the restroom and proceeded to the gate. Boarding had already commenced. My suspicion about being watched was confirmed when three FBI agents charged and surrounded me, shouting "FBI, FBI." I was startled, but calm.

"How may I help you?" I asked.

"Identification please!" I complied and answered all their questions, and they retuned my document shortly and told me to enjoy my trip. What was that all about? I wondered as I boarded the plane. I did not know the answer, but concluded that maybe they were trying to catch someone trying to slip out of the country. Whatever it was, my focus was on my own problem.

A week later, I returned to the US. My new student visa was issued to give me just enough time to complete my degree. There was no margin for error. Usually there was an additional two years allotted to allow for work and training after school. That was now gone.

When I returned to Howard, I fought to get my bills paid. I obtained a job on campus working in the financial aid office. I was also now made aware of student loans that I could apply for as an international student. All that was needed was the signature of a US resident.

I turned to Dale, whom I had met earlier at church and on my visit to Shenandoah Mountain with the singles group. Before then, Dale did not know me beyond the casual hello. As a physician, he worked long hours. However, he was also from Jamaica and knew the president of the college I had attended. He explained his inability to cosign a loan. Instead, he wrote a check for the amount of my tuition with the condition that I would pay him back when I secured the funds from the student loan office.

Brian also provided a loan to finance my living. Sophia, a friend I met at church, finally cosigned. A third of the loan was not paid back during the three-week timeframe I had promised. In fact, it was after graduation and after the start of a new job before I was able to repay. Without being asked, I produced a 10 percent interest as a token of my appreciation for their generosity and patience. I will forever be grateful to these folks. Without their help, my college dream might have ended in failure.

xviii.

June returned to Washington, DC to visit a few weeks after she left. She came directly to the church with her luggage. After the evening program, I escorted her to her hotel. We had agreed to meet after church. She was in a foul mood. She didn't like the hotel room and sought to have it changed.

I followed her to her room, walking behind her with her luggage on the cart. She entered the room and then slammed the door shut, leaving me outside. I wasn't sure what to do. Should I leave? Moments later, she opened the door and apologized and invited us in, her bags and I. The hotel was her employer, and she was in management. I suspected she was straightening someone out. She didn't provide me an explanation, and I didn't ask.

I entered the suite and sat down in the living area. She complained that she was exhausted, and I volunteered to leave, so she could rest.

"No, I don't want you to leave, but I don't feel like going out. Do you mind if we stay in?"

I didn't. She ordered room service and prepared to take a shower. I picked up the remote and tried to turn on the TV. The remote didn't work, so I got up and turned the TV on manually. She emerged from her room in an oversized T-shirt and shorts accompanied by a delicious scent. She inquired about what I was watching.

"Nothing," was my reply.

"Let's order a movie," she said as she grabbed the remote, only to discover that it didn't work. She left to her room again, and I could hear her on the phone. Moments later, dinner came, along with batteries for the remote. I picked up the batteries and the remote, and she yanked them from my hands and installed them. We ate and chatted, and she relaxed.

"Joseph," she said, "I really appreciate your flexibility tonight in letting me stay in. I was so exhausted."

I nodded and assured her that I really felt privileged to be in her company. That was the truth, despite the fact that her actions left me unsure of myself.

She poked me playfully with her fingers and I took her arm and pulled her closer, and we flipped through the channels for something to watch. We stopped on the late news, but my imagination was already making our own movie, starring Joseph and June.

In my mind's eye, I lifted her feet off the ground and into my lap, and rubbed them. I surveyed the contours of her legs all the way to the cleavage of her bosom. I was undressing her when her yawn brought me back to reality.

"I should go," I said.

"I am sorry," she said. "I am tired." I stood up, thanked her for allowing me to share her evening, pulled her into a warm embrace, kissed her forehead, and started to leave. I walked to the door and we hugged again, longer, and I felt her comforting bosom cushioning my chest. I didn't want to leave, and all my senses were on high alert. I walked to my car reluctantly and was destined to play that night over and over again in my head, hoping for a different ending.

June retuned to Atlanta and was traveling a lot for her new job. We rarely spoke. One evening, she retuned my call from a hotel. With the number, I located the address of the hotel and sent her flowers. When she returned the next day, she was first suspicious and then surprised. "How did you know where I was?" she demanded angrily. Moments later, she calmed down and thanked me.

A few weeks later, I sent her a birthday wish. "How did you know it was my birthday? Are you using some illegal database to track me?" she wrote in her e-mail. I reassured her that we had talked about this before, and I had asked Karen to confirm it. Why was she so paranoid?

Months passed, and I had not heard from her. She stopped returning my calls. I told her I had not been to Atlanta and would love to visit. She lived in a two-bedroom apartment and suggested that I stay at a hotel nearby where she lived. She made the arrangements, and I couldn't be sure if she really wanted to see me. Was she seeing someone else? Of course! I thought. Why wouldn't she? She was a beautiful woman. I postponed my planned visit, and she was furious. "Joseph, my suggestion for a hotel had nothing to do with me not wanting to see you. It is just the principle of me having a man overnight with me at my house."

These damn principles, I thought to myself. They are the same ones that prevented me from spending the night with you at the hotel that night. I know we both wanted each other but dialed it back. While we were not physical, nothing prevented me from sinning several times over and over again in my mind. My only disappointment was that it wasn't real.

We had written to each other several times. I finally acknowledged that the hotel was not the issue, but my own insecurities. I felt that I was imposing. As a broke student, I didn't feel as confident receiving favors from persons in whom I had an interest. Invading your space in your apartment was less objectionable to me than invading your pocket (she accommodating me in a hotel). She thanked me for being honest, but as our e-mail dialogue continued, I got too honest and less diplomatic.

Time was not indefinite, and after all, I had a longer horizon (referencing the fact that she was older than I was). When several weeks passed and she did not respond or return my calls, I knew it was a dumb thing to write. Am I becoming like my aunt who was sure that she was telling the truth while she drove love away? I wondered. Why hasn't she called? At church, I asked some of her friends how June was doing, and they all said she was doing fine. Maybe she had moved on, and I should have, too. But I couldn't. My heart was in Atlanta. I would go there. I had to see her, and I knew my Geo was up to it.

During the trip, I had a lot of time to think. I was grateful that graduation was now on the horizon. I had gotten a scholarship, and I would leave college with less than $12,000 in outstanding loans. Not bad, when a friend from dental school told me he was $88,000 in debt. I was also now working for the World Bank on a short-term assignment. My car note would be paid off soon. I had flown to the corporate office for two insurance companies and had received one offer. I was not thrilled about the job, but they had also agreed to sponsor me for a work permit.

I still had a desire to return to Jamaica, and I wondered if I were ever successful with June, would she even consider living there? Althea's predictions flashed into memory. She turned out to be right about so many things. She confidently predicted that my desire to return to Jamaica would wane just like that of her father.

The Geo was making progress and my mind was racing as I pulled into a gas station in Roanoke, Virginia. What was it about this city that I should know? I wondered. Oh, Nadine, whom I had met on my initial trip to New York, was from Roanoke. I wondered how she was doing. My thoughts were all over the place, and I realized that I had not given much thought to how I would get June to see me.

I couldn't just show up on her doorstep. She was already paranoid when I sent her flowers and birthday wishes. I was not sure if I wanted to give her that surprise. What if I showed up, and she had company? Was I prepared for that possibility? I decided to check into a hotel and call her from there. I would leave a message that I was in the area and would like to see her.

It was after midnight when I crossed into the Carolinas. Occasionally, I pushed my head through the widow to help me stay awake. Trucks would whisk by, altering the wind attack and causing the car to shake. I persevered until I pulled into a Red Roof Inn in Marietta and checked in. A couple hours later, I awoke to the morning sun and placed a call.

The phone rang once, twice, up to ten times before her voicemail came on. I left a message. Maybe she already left for church, I speculated. Maybe she's out of town. There were several churches in Atlanta, so it would be a gamble to find which one she attended. I fell asleep and woke up in another two hours and then called again and got no answer. I got dressed, ate, and started church hopping. I probably could just drive to her apartment. After all, I have her address.

The longer I waited, the more likely it was that I would talk myself out of it. Why should I make all this effort to see her? I am going to take a job from a company in Rhode Island, and then I am not sure where they'll send me. I should not selfishly awake a possibility with her only to leave again. My logical or rationalizing side was winning.

I consoled myself that since I enjoyed traveling, I had not wasted time in coming to Atlanta. This had also been my longest trip on the American interstate. In the end, I would create an anticlimax. I would not drive up to June's apartment. I instead would return to DC, excited about my trip to Atlanta, but would not disclose to anyone my main objective and the fact that it was not met.

I tried to forget June by actively dating. I dated women outside the church where I could avoid addressing my internal conflict with the abstinence question. I realized the pain I was causing after one weekend trip to Pennsylvania resulted in late calls asking what my intentions were. "You can't imagine the loneliness I felt after you come here to spend the night or the weekend and then you leave or talk to me until you want to visit again."

Up to that point, I did not see myself as the guy who took women's feeling for granted, and I certainly didn't want to become that guy. I knew, however, that my unresolved feelings for one woman were causing another's pain.

In the church bulletin, I read an invitation for singles to visit the home of the Browns (a young couple) and watch the "Songs of Solomon" DVD Series by Tommy Nelson—a study of Love, Sex, Marriage, and Romance. I signed up with little expectation. I did not have a steady girlfriend, but I knew I had the desire to start a family.

The Browns would facilitate a discussion after each lesson was presented on the DVDs. After the first session, I was intrigued and looked forward to the following week. I was learning to be verbally intimate. In addition, I was gaining perspective that I hoped would help me succeed in a relationship.

The Browns were very honest and forthright about their own personal lives. One of my most teachable moments occurred after the very articulate wife left the living room briefly to respond to a phone call. Her husband related an experience in the first month of marriage. "During the first month we were married, my wife told me that she didn't really love me and that she just wanted to be married."

This was a shocker to us, who saw a loving couple. Obviously, they had worked through it, since this was now three years later. We were anxious to learn how. When the wife returned and was cued in on the discussion, she expressed disappointment that her husband had shared that part of their lives. Then, she relaxed and talked about it. Little did I know how much I would benefit from their openness.

Happy Hour with Howard University Classmates

xix.

Despite the numerous challenges I encountered to graduate, my graduation passed without much fanfare. I invited Dale, Sophia, Brian, and my aunt. All except my aunt attended. I didn't expect any relatives to travel from Jamaica. Not only would the cost be prohibitive, but so also would the process to obtain a visa for those who didn't already have one.

I started a new job in insurance operations. My trainers were brilliant and made the information about Auto Homeowners and other personal lines products as interesting as possible. However, learning about insurance was like watching paint dry. But the paint did dry, and I stuck with it.

After the training was completed, the five surviving trainees expressed among themselves their desired preferences for assignment locations. The choices were Southern California; Phoenix; Arizona; Rhode Island; Connecticut; and Atlanta, Georgia. I toyed with the idea of California, but I knew I was not being true to myself when the time came to write down my preference. Atlanta, Georgia emerged as my first choice.

CHAPTER 15: **ATLANTA**

i.

Relocation to Atlanta was easy because I didn't have much to move. I packed my Geo and opted to ship my books and desk and save my new company the relocation expense. Hours later, I arrived in Duluth, Georgia, and took up temporary residence in a fully furnished one-bedroom apartment provided by my company.

After weeks at my new job, I felt underutilized. My training was focused on "how to" and very little "why." In addition, a lot of processes were in place to deliberately retard learning and prevent employees from gaining a macro view of the process. Because I was a macro learner, I found the training frustrating. I understood the reason for the separation of duties. It was designed to reduce the possibility of fraud and employee collusion to undermine the process. However, I still resented being told "this is how we have done things for years."

This resentment showed up in my job performance, and my supervisor wondered if I was up for the job. Some initially concluded not that I was underutilized, or that I needed to understand the "whys" of the job, but rather that I was another incompetent, affirmative action candidate who did not deserve the job. Since I was the only employee with a graduate degree at that level of the company, I wondered how I ended up in a job that did not require graduate skills. I was also below the median salary that graduates from my class were making.

My perspective changed when I started reminding myself how much I had to be thankful for. I had a job and was with a company that was willing to work with me through the immigration process. I decided it was time to look forward and give the job my best shot.

In addition to my job, I took on some higher-level learning courses. My success quickly dispelled any notion of incompetence. The regional manager responded with extra projects and support. He confessed that I was light-years ahead of where he was when he started, and that he had not mastered some of the certification ground that I had already started to cover. He promised he would work with me to keep me challenged and be as supportive as he could.

On Saturdays, I continued my search for a church home and visited a number of churches, hoping to run into June. Weeks passed. I saw several of June's look-alikes, but no June. Each time I called her number, I got her voicemail. Twice I left her messages that I had moved to the area. I didn't visit, because from all indication, she did not like surprises, and I did not want to be accused of stalking.

In one of my classes to obtain insurance licenses, I met Hallbrooke. He was a friendly guy who sought certification to become a financial advisor and was gaining his life insurance credentials. He was always seeking people out to make sure they were comfortable, and was good at making and maintaining friendships. We went to lunch and discovered that we were of the same faith. He then invited me to visit his church. Hallbrooke attended the Berean SDA church in southwest Atlanta. The church had a large membership. Over a thousand people were in attendance.

It was not my first time visiting. My last visit had resulted in my writing a letter to the pastor about overzealous ushers who blocked the exit for more than twenty minutes while the pastors conducted a long appeal. "Whose idea was it to put people under church arrest while making an appeal to come to Christ freely?" I had written. "How ironic that I was prevented from leaving the church on the day that was designated Church Liberty's Day."

I did not see Hallbrooke until after the service, but as I sat down, I noticed a familiar outline two rows ahead. My heart's palpitation confirmed that the stimuli from my sight were not an illusion; I was indeed looking at June. Our eyes met when she looked back. I waved, and she acknowledged me with an unenthusiastic bow. Karen was seated next to her, and after the service, I went over and greeted them. Karen responded with a warm hug, but June's demeanor was formal, as if we were meeting for the first time. We chatted briefly before I left to the sound of Hallbrooke's voice.

Hallbrooke introduced me to a number of his friends, including Meredeth, who had moved to Atlanta only two weeks prior. The Sermon on the Mount, which I had just heard, didn't deter my eyes from surveying Meredeth's brown eyes, her warm and flirtatious smile, and the cleavage she sported nestled between the gentle slopes of the dual mountains of her breasts. This survey happened in a split second while my hand extended simultaneously with the trite expression, "nice to meet you."

Shortly afterward, June came by and chatted briefly with others in Hallbrooke's circle of friends. She had regained her traditional congenial and enthusiastic self, which she had lost when she greeted me. I continued my conversation with Meredeth, and in my peripheral vision, I saw June leave. Soon after, Hallbrooke invited a number of us to lunch to be held at the home of a member, Terry

After lunch, the group chatted and then returned to church for an afternoon program. Then, it was dinnertime, and Hallbrooke's wife, Linda, suggested Harmony, a popular Chinese vegetarian restaurant located on the outskirts of Atlanta. A group totaling eight of us decided to go.

The meal at Harmony was great. It fooled the tastes of regular and past carnivores with dishes such as vegetarian steak and shrimp and other delights. Before we left the restaurant, Hallbrooke suggested that we all exchange numbers. This was a good suggestion since at least three of us at the table were new to the city. As I proceeded to my car, I saw Meredeth looking back at me, and as she drove away, she waved again. I think I'll give her a call, I decided as I waved back.

Two days later, I called Meredeth and secured a date for a movie on my side of town. We had agreed to meet at my apartment before going to the movie theater. I was a little apprehensive about meeting at my place since I had exhausted my temporary housing and struggled to furnish my new place. As Meredeth drove up in her luxury Acura Legend, I wondered about the impression that I was creating in my sparsely furnished apartment and my bright green Geo Metro car.

I tried to dispel the thought and comforted myself with the notion that I did not want any woman who could not see beyond the immediate accoutrements. Oh, how times have changed, I thought. History provided many examples of men who were spurred to greatness motivated by the desire to get or impress the girl. Now, as more and more women gained economic clout and traditional gender roles were abandoned, so were the hopes of many dreams of relationships, lost in the fog of uncertainty, misunderstandings, mistrust, and selfishness.

The sparsely furnished one-bedroom apartment did not seem to concern Meredeth. After the short tour ended, we left in her car for the movie theater. Watching a movie on a first date does not provide opportunities for talking, and Meredeth and I both recognized that as she made the short drive back to my apartment.

"May I use your restroom?" she asked as she maneuvered the Legend into the available parking space beside my Geo.

"Of course," I responded with little insight that our lives were about to change.

As I got dressed for work the next morning, Meredeth was still sleeping with a calm, ecstatic look on her face. I walked quietly back into the bedroom to collect my tie, and she moaned. I stooped down and kissed her exposed forehead protruding from beneath the blanket. A section of her hair hung over the edge of the exposed mattress and box spring.

"What time is it?" she asked.

"It is seven-forty, but you don't have to get up. I'll leave a key on the table. You can let yourself out."

I made my short drive to work while I recalled what had happened the previous night. We had talked late into the night. She was highly opinionated and assertive, which compensated for any shyness I had. Hormones raged, and we explored each other's bodies. Sexual repression and spiritual constraints resulted in sexual tension and frustration. My calm yet firm observation that she was using her body as a weapon did little to calm the situation. We had torn at the scab of wounded hearts and vulnerabilities. She had gotten up and walked toward the door. I did not try to stop her. We both knew that once the door opened and closed, so would our chances for resolution and the possibility of true intimacy. Intimacy beyond the physical. "Nakedness" was how Pastor Wright described it. Exposing your soul and revealing the ugliness of one's motivation.

Her advance to the door stopped, and she took a seat on the futon. Two hours later, we were still talking with less tension. She remarked on my ability to remain calm in a tense situation. She volunteered information of abuses from her past not known to her siblings or her mother. I talked about my childhood. From then onward, we were emotionally naked, and sharing our lives and bodies was natural.

At eleven o'clock that morning, I received a call from Meredeth. She had just left my apartment and was headed home. As an IT consultant, she traveled often, but was working from home that week. She would be working late that evening, but was available for dinner. We met for dinner every night for the remainder of the week. On Friday, when I got home, she was already in the apartment with dinner she had picked up from a nearby restaurant. When I went to hang up my clothes, the closet was organized with new hangers and other organizers for my ties and socks. I didn't figure her for the domestic type, nor was she, but I appreciated the gesture. Since we had talked for several hours, I dismissed the idea that we were moving too fast.

On Saturday after we met at church, she had invited a number of people to her apartment for potluck lunch. She hurried to her car with a sheepish look on her face.

"Is something wrong?" I asked.

"No! I went hiking with someone last Sunday, and he left a voicemail to meet for lunch after church."

"Well," I said. "Call him and tell him your plans have changed. If I were in his shoes, that is what I would want you to do. We are all adults here, so be forthright." Meredeth smiled and returned the call. She appeared relieved when she got his voicemail. Before we met, I had decided that I would not be an actor or facilitator in any games. Too many guys facilitated deception without realizing that they, too, could one day be played.

For the next three weeks, Meredeth and I saw each other every day. On weekends, we took long drives to visit her family in Miami, Orlando, and Thomasville, Georgia. Three months later, we agreed (formally) to date exclusively. I'd already adopted that conclusion months earlier.

Thanksgiving that year, I joined Meredeth in Minnesota where I met some of her friends. It was a great group, and I felt comfortable with them from the start. We talked about the Bush versus Gore election and how Florida's election was an embarrassment to the United State electoral process. I knew I was in trouble when I let it slip that Meredeth was registered in Florida (where she owned a house where her sister now lived) and had not voted.

While in Minnesota, I attended church and was in for a bit of tropical humor when the pastor thanked God for the heat wave they were having. People wore their jackets open, enjoying the nice weather of thirty-four degrees Fahrenheit—slightly above freezing.

I did not realize how limited my knowledge was about the nuances of the abortion debate until Meredeth and I had a discussion on the subject on our way back from Minnesota. I avoided political labels such as "pro-life" or "pro-choice." These labels seemed to miss the complexities of issues. At the same time, I revealed my own inconsistency by reasoning that it was simply incongruent to be Christian, following biblical teachings, and be anything but pro-life.

After Meredeth and I talked about this issue, I concluded that pro-life and pro-choice were not mutually exclusive. A woman can be pro-choice and not be pro-abortion because she believes that she is the best government for her body, not politicians. She is answerable to her conscience and her God about decisions she makes about what is inside her body. Her decision might be selfish and detrimental to the embryo, but the fact remains that her body is her body. Each individual is the government of his or her body.

The difficulty of this subject was amplified when I talked to Chinese relatives and eventually visited China and learned some of that country's history. There was a great famine in China that economists estimated was responsible for nearly thirty million early deaths from 1958-1961. Twenty years after the famine, the government instituted a policy known as the "one child policy," described as China's first step toward modernization. That policy, however, was responsible for preventing four hundred million births since its inception, and encouraged infanticides and abortions.

If China had not instituted that policy, millions could have died naturally from starvation and the country would not have experienced the growth it now enjoys. It begs the question, does humankind/government have the right to play God and control the environment, or should nature be allowed to take its course?

The conclusion to the discussion was that if one believes that God created humanity, then one might accept that God created human with the power of choice, including the choice not to believe in God or the creation story. Ironically, in the creation story, God created Adam and Eve with the power of choice. Their choice, as the story goes, resulted in the "fall" of man from the status of perfection, resulting in the death and destruction of millions.

It then begs the question that if an omniscient God, cognizant of the poor choices that humans would make, allowed those choices anyway, why should a freedom-loving country want to remove a woman's choice over her body? Certainly, individuals, families, and leaders (religious and otherwise) can and should exercise their freedom of speech and power of persuasion to appeal to conscience in encouraging women to make a non-abortion choice. However, that choice remains a woman's. Limited government does not mean one small enough to climb into a woman's womb to investigate her procreation choices.

Nine months had passed, and Meredeth and I had not aborted our relationship. The relationship was ripe for a new phase, and I proposed. I considered myself a romantic. However, the decision to ask her to be my wife was not. In fact, I used the decision analysis techniques that I had learned in graduate school to help decide if Meredeth would be a good life partner for me. In addition, I recalled a suggestion from Sam, a friend and law student who shared some advice from his father: "When contemplating marriage," he said, "you should think with your head and not your heart." As a romantic and an idealist, I was not initially warm to the idea. However, I had come to see some validity in that reasoning.

First, on the plus side, I reasoned that Meredeth and I were friends, and we could talk about anything. In fact, she taught me how to be friendlier and how to take steps to maintain and enhance friendships. She was very good at calling her friends and patient with friends I perceived as too needy.

We were of the same faith, of different cultures, but the same color. This was a country that emphasized race in everything, and if life could be less complicated for families and children of the same race. Oh, but on the con side, Meredeth did not want children. But I did not believe that she was definitive on that subject. I was convinced that she could be persuaded. After all, I looked forward to becoming a dad.

Meredeth seemed to understand partnership and was not concerned with keeping scores. She was outspoken and compensated for my mild manner. Because she was a US citizen, I would not need to continue to rely on my company to work through my immigration status. I was very careful about this issue for a number of reasons, which we discussed openly. One such issue was my belief in the institution of marriage. I had developed my own mission statement for family life, and I was not looking to use a long-term solution (marriage) to solve a short-term issue (immigration). On the con side, Meredeth was already a divorcée. Her earlier marriage had lasted for less than a month, and I wondered about her tenacity to fight to preserve her union and her penchant for fidelity.

The fact that Meredeth was born in the US and I in Jamaica was the only similarity needed for friends to quip that our relationship was an adaptation of *How Stella Got Her Groove Back* (a movie based on a book about a successful career woman from California who went to Jamaica on a last-minute getaway and met a Jamaican guy—twenty years younger—and later married him). In our case, I was already living and working in the US and was one month younger than Meredeth.

Meredeth loved to travel. She was a road warrior for her company. Although she complained, I always knew that she loved it. I loved to travel also, and I traveled for pleasure. On a given weekend, we were not always sure where we would end up.

In re-evaluating the con side of the analysis, I was convinced I had found someone whom I could spend the rest of my life with. I had some concerns, but I then concluded that a woman over thirty had better know what she wanted. Another of my concerns was whether I had resolved my feelings for June. I know that it was unlikely that a relationship would blossom between us, but it would be nice if we at least talked.

Meredeth was happy for the proposal, but decided she needed time to think. I was surprised. However, since we were considering a lifetime together, I thought it was only reasonable to give her time. Days turned into weeks, and I decided not to pressure her. When weeks became a month, I concluded that it was time to withdraw my proposal and free up us both to date others. In addition, my company had just suggested that I move to New Jersey, and I concluded that it was time to establish my loyalty with the company and jump at the request.

Within minutes of conveying my intention, Meredeth accepted my proposal and commenced planning for a wedding. In addition, she told me that she had no desire to move back to the northeast—definitely not to New

Jersey. I gave up the New Jersey option and reassured her that I wanted to spend the rest of my life with her. However, I was still curious about why she had waited so long to respond.

We announced our decision to our new church family located in Buckhead. The church was the brainchild of Brenda (a television anchor in the area) and her husband, Keith (a psychiatrist). Brenda and Keith encouraged community service rather than denominational differences and religious dogmas. They emphasized time management and encouraged diversity.

Despite the small gathering, we got involved in community activities, served in soup kitchens, visited prisons, and volunteered in hospitals. We played together and attended several fun events and retreats. I was impressed with the humility of members of the congregation, who were very accomplished, but did not seek the church for personal glory. These were some of the attractions that drew us to this church, and I suspect that the same attractions appealed to June, also.

A week later, Meredeth was out of town, and I attended church alone. Shortly after the church service, I met June in the church foyer. On this occasion, she did not walk away or avoid my eye contact. She asked to speak to me, and we stepped outside.

With tears in her eyes, she acknowledged the effect the sermon had had on her and apologized for the way she had acted toward me. (The sermon was about forgiveness and the price one pays for holding grudges.)

She acknowledged that an e-mail I had written to her more than a year earlier had greatly offended her. I listened intently. As the tears welled up in my eyes, I hugged her and apologized. "I had no intention to hurt you. I am truly, truly sorry."

When I released her from my embrace, I felt free—free to give my heart completely to Meredeth. It was not time to look back, and I secretly thanked June for setting me free.

I finally asked Meredeth why she had waited so long to respond to my proposal and was surprised by her response. "Well, I thought you would have proposed to me while we were in Minnesota."

"At that time I . . . "

"And I didn't like the way you proposed to me," she continued.

"You didn't like how I proposed to you?" I asked in disbelief.

"No! Darn, Skippy! You told me over the phone, and now you wonder what happened and why I was not more enthusiastic?"

"I am sorry. But wait a minute, let me make sure I understand. Over the last eleven months, we have spent a lot of time together, more than some couples do in two years. We love each other. However, because I was not creative in my proposal, you were prepared to forfeit our lives together?"

Meredeth did not respond. And I would mistakenly assume that she had seen the superior logic of my question. However, as time went on, several older and wiser men in successful relationships would caution, "if you win an argument with a woman, you lose. It does not matter if she is rich, poor, educated, liberated, you will still lose."

The observation was important. No matter how non-traditional and modern a woman claims to be, she still values some traditions. The difficulty is that men like me must figure out which of these traditions to keep and which to dispel. This will continue to be the dilemma of contemporary men trying to find a girl.

Unfortunately, I had not given a lot of thought to how I would propose. One reason was that Meredeth had already signaled that she did not want to wear a ring. Meredeth chose not to wear a wedding ring for religious reasons. Religious preference in our church allowed women to decide on their preference. I didn't complain at the prospect of not buying a ring.

However, I should have anticipated that Meredeth wanted some symbolism for the occasion. In retrospect, it appeared obvious that I had a lot to learn, not only about women, but also about the language of love. Style sometimes matters over substance. Women like to be chased and wooed. If things worked too well, some would start to sabotage the relationship, believing that manufactured conflicts test a man's tenacity and interest. My very calm and unpretentious qualities that attracted Meredeth could also provide fuel for resentment when I appeared emotionless. How do I adapt? I asked myself. When will I learn? How would I learn? Did I want to?

Whenever I ask myself soul-searching questions, they usually trigger personal reflection. I wondered if Meredeth had only responded out of fear of my moving on. Or, had June finally talked with me only when it was apparent that I was moving on? I never understood these behaviors from women. These behaviors reminded me of a story one of my brothers told about Lassman (cutlass man).

Lassman was a mentally ill man who carried around a sharp machete. At times, he created terror by chasing people with the machete raised above his head. One day, Lassman chased a man who appeared to be a strong runner. The man ran until he tripped and fell, not only from the loose gravel on the road, but also from fatigue and exhaustion. While on the ground, the tripped man held up his hand to defend against chops from Lassman's machete. Instead of chopping him, the insane Lassman handed him the blade. "Here," he said. "It's your turn to chase me."

Meredeth planned and executed a wedding in less than four months. I am not sure what motivated the date. Was it the good package deal that she had found for a cruise to the Mediterranean, which would be our honeymoon? Was it the understanding that my job was likely to extend another opportunity for me to move to another state soon? Was it that her college friend was getting married, and she had solicited several ideas from their wedding planning?

In addition to marriage counseling, which included compatibly testing, I suggested that we talk to a few couples to get a more realistic view of married life. We invited a number of couples to lunch. One of my favorite couples was Brenda and Keith. They had busy lives, yet they seemed to accomplish a lot together. In addition, Keith had Jamaican roots. The lunch took place after church at Meredeth's apartment, and I hurried over to prepare.

When Keith and Brenda arrived, they did not disappoint. They were a delight to spend time with, and they shared intimate moments of their lives, from a discussion of morning breath to flatulence. The experience left me admiring them even more because they were less concerned with pretences and more with realism.

When I attempted to joke about how I had proposed, and Meredeth's subsequent delay, Keith shared with me the importance of symbolism.

"Symbols are going to help you get through the difficult times. Wedding dates, engagement dates, and anniversaries are all symbols. It is not the cost, but the vividness of memories you create around symbols."

The wedding date was approximately two months away, and we had just met the pastor who would do our counseling. Meredeth's former pastor in Florida was unable to perform the counseling. The new pastor took us through a battery of compatibility testing.

"That is kind of late, isn't it, pastor?" I asked jokingly, since our wedding was already planned.

He agreed it was late, but helpful nonetheless. A week later, when the results came back, he informed us that we were a "vitalized couple." I loved the term and proudly told my boss and colleagues that we were a vitalized couple. Very soon, the words became a humorous punch line for office humor. From it emerged jokes of the vitalized man, vitalized employee, and vitalized company.

My bragging continued at church until an elegant lady pulled me aside for a chat. She had heard me boasting about my vitalized woman. She had been divorced for a year, and she cautioned me to be careful not to place too much value in those tests.

"I know," I told her. "I am just maximizing the symbolism," I said jokingly. Our gaze locked, and she wasn't amused. Her elegance, beauty, and poise did not mask the pain of her recent divorce, which she was revealing to me telepathically and in her sad eyes. I broke the gaze, and I took her hands, thanked her, and assured her that I understood what she was communicating; she too had been part of a vitalized couple.

I went to talk with Keith. He had made an unguarded statement that he didn't think our marriage would last for more than three years.

"What did you mean?" I asked. "Why do you think I will not be committed to Meredeth?"

"Well, it is not you that I am worried about!" he said. I wanted to press him, but he was called away. What had he seen in Meredeth that he didn't think we would survive together for a lifetime? Keith was usually careful, and I was pressed to find out what triggered that perspective.

I was confident enough to make up my own mind about whom I would marry. However, I wondered, what Keith—a psychiatrist—saw that I didn't? I certainly wanted to press him on the subject, but there was not much time. My wedding was in one week.

Wedding day with the boys. Left to Right Dale, Darlick, Joseph, Brian, Andy, and Hallbrooke.

ii.

At our wedding, I had a surreal feeling of being a spectator. Several times before the wedding, I had joked that all I had to do was show up. However, during the procession, I never actually believed that I would feel like a bystander.

Wedding Day, Atlanta. Left to Right Beverly (sister) Joseph, Adora (Mother) Rickey (Brother).

I saw my mom beaming. She had jumped at her first opportunity to travel abroad, and she loved it. She joined two of my siblings—Bev and Ricky—on her flight to the wedding. A day before the wedding, she took me aside for a little heart-to-heart.

"I am sorry I was not able to provide for you, but I am happy about the way you persevered to improve yourself."

"Don't worry, Mom," I said, trying to comfort her. "God has been very kind to me."

I wanted both Mom and Dad to attend, but the big man was not keen on traveling. He was nursing arthritis in his knees and decided that it was too much of a hassle.

"Show me the pictures," he countered.

Aunt Eunice and her contingent made a road trip from Maryland, and she and Mom reunited. After the wedding, they all went to Maryland and had a great time before Mom returned home weeks later.

Jenny was noticeably absent from the wedding. She and Shelly were planning to attend. I was told that they had booked the flight a week earlier. Jenny provided no explanation, but I suspected that Mom was the reason. She resented Mom for being absent from her life as a child. (She was raised by her grandmother and uncle.) Jenny also shared in my success and didn't think Mom played a pivotal role. I did not have those concerns, and apparently she felt betrayed.

My out-of-body experience was not only the result of personal reflection of a life-changing event. This congenial and vitalized woman I was marrying could also be inflexible. In many ways, she was like a train on a track. The only way to change directions was to switch the track or derail the train.

Meredeth was beautifully adorned, and everyone stood as she entered. We had come a long way in a year. I had watched her closely when I took her to Jamaica and visited with my family. I had laughed when my mom took her hands and tried to guide the city girl on a narrow dirt path near her home.

I had cringed when she initially opposed my only recommendation to add a couple of reggae songs to the songs to be played at the reception. Now, as she glided toward me, I fought hard to hold back tears.

The ceremony went smoothly. My best man, Brian, matron of honor, Fuchsia (both attorneys) presented oral arguments for their clients. I was reminded that I had a right to leave the toilet seat up, which was followed by a chorus of laughter. Fuchsia was equal to the task in defending her client's right to shop and store excess shoes and other merchandise in the trunk of her car.

iii.

The ceremony and reception took place at a hotel near the airport. This made it easy logistically for guests coming from out of town, and for our departure for our honeymoon.

I was more excited about our honeymoon. We would cruise the Mediterranean for fourteen days, stopping in Greece, Croatia, Egypt, Turkey, and Italy. It was my first time crossing the Atlantic, and I was excited.

We were exhausted when we arrived in Athens. It was more than twenty hours since we'd left home and since our last shower. As soon as we boarded the ship, we showered and went to bed. Hours later, we awoke fully rested and famished. It was near 11:00 p.m. local time, and we hurried to the deck and were surprised to find it empty. On this cruise, nothing was available except room service with the simplified menu of sandwiches. On the flight, we had noticed that we were in the company of mostly over-forty adults, and we felt out of place. Only one other couple was of similar age.

After much cajoling, I was able to persuade Meredeth to get off the ship and find a local restaurant.

"Do you speak Greek?" she asked mockingly. "How can we get around without a tour guide?"

"You are talking to a guy who spent four months in the Dominican Republic and four months in New York City starting out with less than one hundred and forty-five dollars."

"And your point is?"

"We will find a way," came my calm assurance.

I didn't have to learn Greek. We found a taxi driver who was fluent in English. He took us to a restaurant frequented by locals. The food was great, and we knew we were overcharged when the check came.

"What did you have?" the cab driver asked when he heard us talking.

"Well, the menu was in Greek. But we followed the waiter and pointed at a fresh catch of fish that was sautéed in authentic sauce plus the best Greek salad I ever tasted."

The 2004 Olympics in Athens were three years away. However, numerous projects were under construction. On our second day in Athens, our guide warned people to be careful and avoid becoming victims of pickpockets and other criminals. Several vendors made their way onto the tour bus, selling souvenirs and other trinkets.

An enterprising young man placed his product in each hand as he walked the bus aisle, making his sales pitch. As he exited, he collected money or his merchandise. He walked past a couple from Mobile, Alabama, who still had the merchandise and had not paid. The husband called after him in an attempt to return it.

"Hola, señor!"

My smile prompted a question from Meredeth. "What's so funny?" she asked.

"Hola, señor? We are in Athens, Greece, not Mexico City!" I whispered.

Rodney and Mika were the other young couple on the cruise. Rodney was an ex–football player and very congenial. He joked that we were the only blacks on the cruise; we had better get to know each other.

"After all," Meredeth chimed in, "We are already assumed to be related."

While we laughed, I realized how much America had changed me. When I entered the room of an event, it was now not uncommon to subconsciously scan it to determine how many other blacks were present. Or when watching the news, to secretly hope that the culprit in some incident was not another brother.

However, there was something distinctly different about the cohesiveness of this group of Americans more than five thousand miles away from home. Everyone on the trip, regardless of ethnicity, looked out for each other in ways that were not typical of life in the homeland. It was as if we all had a collective epiphany that we not only resided in the same country, but also shared same targets on our backs. We were literally and figuratively all in the same boat.

Whenever we stopped at different ports, Rodney and I found ourselves playing security by lingering an extra minute to make sure members of our shopping party got their change or ended transactions with vendors on the street without incidents. I noticed that while I engaged in conversations with my wife, my peripheral vision constantly surveyed my surroundings. I reminded myself that I did not have any security training. However, while I felt relaxed and was enjoying my honeymoon, I had a heightened sense of my surroundings and was noticing things I typically would miss. Every time we ventured off the recommended path, I found myself mentally asking a question that no one had appointed me to ask or answer: If something went wrong, how would I get my wife and any of these people out of here?

The coast of Dubrovnik, Croatia, was beautiful, and I was pleasantly surprised. At first, I was not sure why I was surprised until I realized that it was my first time in a country that was formally under Communist rule. Somehow I had bought into the propaganda that life was gray and dreary in the lands of Communism, as if that system of government affected the landscape.

We surveyed old forts and different sites. Bullet holes from the recent Bosnian war were still visible in the sides of different buildings. The realization that I was standing in a recent warzone was a reminder of how fragile and tenuous the process of achieving peace could be. Diplomacy and the understanding of people from different cultures were necessary. So, too, was capacity and ferocity of your firepower.

When a US warship docked alongside our vessel, it brought me a sense of relief that I had never before felt in the presence of a warship. From the deck, I waved and saluted the naval officers on board. They smiled and waved back. Subconsciously, I felt relieved of my security concerns. They had sent a telepathic signal to be at ease; the navy and the marines had our backs.

It would be nice to be off the boat for a full night, I thought. On our way to Egypt, the seas were rough, and the ship swayed. At breakfast, a number of people repeated the refrain that all that rocking that the ship experienced the night before was directly related to the activities of the newlyweds. I watched from the deck as the immigration officer joined the ship before it docked. By the time we had docked, our passports were already stamped to enter Egypt.

The news of tourist attacks in Egypt was still on people's minds when we docked in Alexandria. However, this did not deter our new friend Rodney, a software engineer, from locating a cheaper overnight tour of Cairo than was offered by our cruise line. People inquired what activities we would be doing, and by the time we docked, over forty people had signed up for the tour that Rodney had found. On this tour, we would see the pyramids, Cairo Museum, mosques; dinner on the Nile; and spend a night in Cairo.

The bus ride to Cairo from Alexandria was uneventful. An armed guard sat in the front. It seemed a more tranquil atmosphere than the sight of men dressed in military fatigues and high-powered weapons guarding the port in Alexandria.

One didn't need to be an Egyptologist to appreciate the richness of history of one of the world's oldest civilizations. At the same time, the abject poverty of the masses was striking. With millions of tourists flocking to the country each year, creating a massive inflow of revenue, it was sad that the basic needs of the people were not met.

Garbage piled up in the backyards of apartments and businesses. Sometimes, it overflowed the ten-foot walls that surrounded them. I couldn't dispel the cynical thought that one reason archaeologists had to dig for everything was, not only because centuries had passed, and some buildings laid in ruins, but also because everything seemed to be covered with garbage.

As we stopped to observe the sights, I was struck up in a conversation by a papyrus vendor after he refused payment for his product in Egyptian currency, favoring instead US dollars. He echoed a familiar refrain that I had heard in Jamaica. "My friend, everything here is owned by a few wealthy families. The very papyrus that I am selling came from a factory of one of those families. Very little of the money that comes in from tourists is spent on the people here. There are two types of people here. The very wealthy people here who think everything is wonderful in Egypt, and then there are the rest of us."

I was struck by how flawless his English was, and suspected that he was a university graduate. I was aware of the aid that the US government gave to countries such as Egypt and wondered if we were giving a lifeline to regimes that did not feel the need to be accountable to their people. With such wealth disparity, people's quest for the meaning of life resulted in greater religiosity, resulting in religious extremism and the undermining of women.

Not surprisingly, the afterlife was given more prominence, demonstrated by the elaborate and well-kept cemeteries. In some cases, the cemeteries were in better shape than the available houses for people to live in. I was not surprised when our guide told us that people had taken up residences in those cemeteries because they could not afford rent. By the time the pyramids came into view, I had a greater understanding of the culture's past-and-present appreciation for the afterlife.

I was looking through the opposite side of the bus and taking in the magnificence of the Great Sphinx of Giza, with the Pyramid of Khafre in the background, when my gaze shifted to the window on my side of the bus where a camel stood less than a foot away peering at me. He was ridden by a boy who was trying to get a head start on selling camel rides to tourists. I observed the face of the animal, which told the story of its daily toil to feed the family of its owner. I was jolted by the familiar sight behind the camel, Kentucky Fried Chicken.

I was amused and saddened by the irony. I had traveled back in time to see great wonders of the world. The pyramids were on my right, and Kentucky Fried Chicken, Hard Rock Café, and other western stores were on my left.

Following our tour in and around the Sphinx and pyramids, Rodney and I decided to go for a camel ride. He moved toward a camel, and the beast looked at him from head to toe as if determining the appropriateness of his size to ride him. Then, it bolted. I laughed heartily, as I joked that the camel had decided not to mess with this linebacker.

After a long day visiting different sights, we freshened up in the hotel that our tour package had secured for the night. Later that evening, we returned to the pyramids to see the laser lights show. As we entered an area for seating, an Egyptian boy said, "Welcome to Alaska." We were all amused by the statement, and in half an hour, it was clear what he meant.

The desert that was scorching hot only hours before was getting cold very fast. The spectacular story of the show competed with the cold desert wind for our attention, and since we were not appropriately dressed, we were relieved when the show ended.

Dinner on the Nile would follow, complete with belly dancing and other spectacular dances. Rodney found himself the pick of almost every performer. One male dancer, who twirled himself for over ten minutes without getting dizzy, picked Rodney up, to the amusement of the crowd, and twirled him before putting him down again. The big man was immediately dizzy and stumbled back to his seat to the laughter of the crowd.

Cairo was a delight, and we ended our tour of the museum the next day. From Taria Square, we took the long ride back to the ship in Alexandria. We had an exhilarating feeling that we had tasted a piece of history. The queasiness in Meredeth's stomach was not from tasting history, but from something she had eaten. She would require the service of the ship's doctor before he made it to Venice, our final stop on the fourteen-day voyage.

Before we reached Venice, I commented on how my allergies were gone. I was at sea away from pollen, and all symptoms had disappeared. In addition, my sight had improved to the point where I didn't need glasses. I had found the antidote to my need for prescription glasses; a permanent vacation or voyage could cure me of all ailments, I joked.

A voyage of several months at sea would remain a mystery to me. After our experience in Venice, we flew into New York City; and despite a great trip, I was happy to be back in the USA. I realized this was the feeling I used to have when I returned to Jamaica. Now, slowly, the USA was becoming home.

I watched as fellow passengers from our cruise hurried to get their bags and scurry back to their regular lives: jobs, children, businesses, and other commitments. We exchanged contact information with a few. Some avoided eye contact. I smiled at the realization that the lesson of the trip was already lost to many. While we traveled abroad, we became a community. We ate together, laughed together, and looked out for the safety of each other.

At home in the USA, things were more complicated. Some were not too keen to expand their circle of friends beyond their existing hyphenated demographic cliques. There would continue to be little contact with people of other groups, unless required by law to do so. Jobs and schools were examples of where the law encouraged integration. Voluntarily, many Americans were more comfortable living segregated lives.

The euphoria of our trip would not last very long. A month after we returned from the trip, we were packing to move to Raleigh, North Carolina, where I would continue my current job in a new location. Before we departed Atlanta, Meredeth became a casualty of the deflating dot-com era. As with many in that industry, her remunerations had increased with the increasing fear of Y2K. When those doomsday scenarios did not materialize, a number of people in the industry lost their jobs.

iv.

Suddenly, there were challenges ahead. Meredeth had been the leading wage earner, and now my salary was the only salary. In addition, she felt exhausted and decided that she would take a break and would not look for a job immediately. I became concerned.

I was concerned not because I feared financial ruin. We were in temporary housing provided by my company, and were getting our finances ready to buy a house. My concern was that my new wife was not ready to modify her tastes, despite her desire to simplify her life.

My suspicion was confirmed when I had the audacity to suggest that while I enjoyed meeting her for lunch, cooking might be more cost-effective than going to restaurants for lunch and dinner.

"You didn't marry a domesticated woman and you are not about to get one!"

"I was not asking for a domesticated woman, but rather one who could adapt."

I found it incomprehensible that anyone would find preparing a meal for the family so objectionable. Isn't that what partnership is about? I had no difficulty cooking, cleaning, and doing whatever it took to make our house a home.

To smooth the feathers I had ruffled, I decided to prepare a Jamaican meal. We had eaten several times at Jamaican restaurants in Atlanta or when we traveled to Jamaica. However, I realized that I had not prepared a Jamaican meal specifically with Meredeth in mind.

One of the reasons was that when I met her, she was following a vegan diet. However, before long, she was enticed by steaming oxtail, jerk chicken, and curried goat, and abandoned her diet.

My wife entered the kitchen as I prepared my ingredients for dinner and insisted on helping. Soon after, I was receiving instructions on how to prepare Jamaican-style curry chicken. I lost my cool.

"How the hell can you be telling me how to cook a Jamaican meal?"

The various differences in our background had finally collided. I did not consider myself a strict traditionalist. In fact, I was angered when my sister Bev returned from work and set about preparing dinner while her husband (who arrived the same time or earlier) sat, read the papers, or watched television.

In addition, I had learned frugality and fiscal conservatism from my eldest sister Jenny and Patrick in the way they operated their business. They prepared meals and took their food with them, even when they traveled for the day. They saved and did not spend unnecessarily.

The situation reminded me of an episode of the *Cosby Show*. One of the Cosby daughters decided that she was going to "dump" her child on the father and go to medical school. I was a big fan of the show, but was disturbed by the suggestion that the child was a burden and an interruption of careers, rather than a blessing. Were my beliefs to be considered sexist? Could I really consider fathering a child with someone who did not see the necessity to provide for the nutritional needs of her family? Maybe I should have taken Meredeth at her word when she said she did not want children. Maybe that was the right decision, and I needed to be reconciled with that decision.

Meredeth and I did not discuss the issue again. However, I suspect that she gave up the idea of relaxing for a few months, especially since she was not prepared to perform a domestic role. She found a temporary job soon thereafter.

While in Raleigh, we decided to visit Meredeth's dad on a regular basis. He lived in the rural town two hours away. He had lost his legs to diabetes, and it was decided that it was a good time to spend more time together. On the first of one of these visits, I took him shopping and cleaned up his house, among other chores. I didn't mind, but I was bothered when Meredeth sat and made no effort to help. Why was she not helping? I wondered. This is *her* father's house! Did it have to do with our domestic discussion?

Shortly after we left, I inquired about the reason. She could not articulate it clearly, but I understood that it was not related to any discussion we had had about domestic chores. She did not have a great relationship with her dad, and developing one would take time.

The next few weeks went by quickly, and so did the decisions that we made. Meredeth's temporary job assignment ended, and she was restless and wanted to return to Atlanta. We had not fully moved from Atlanta and was still in a temporary apartment provided by my company. It was time for a decision about what to do next.

Some of the decisions that were made, in retrospect, appeared ill advised. Even though Meredeth wanted to stay in Atlanta, she interviewed for jobs in Pennsylvania and Florida. After her second interview for the Pennsylvania job, I quit my job to demonstrate my readiness to support the move to Atlanta. She concurred with the decision before I submitted my resignation. In fairness, I did not find my job intellectually stimulating, and the decision was easy.

But then we found ourselves with no jobs and a declining economy. An offer came for Meredeth before the tragedy of September 11, 2001. We had accepted the offer, and after a day of watching the most vicious terrorist attack on America, live on television, we set out by car for a new life in Pennsylvania. We had an eerie feeling that America was suddenly a different country.

CHAPTER 16: **PENNSYLVANIA**

i.

We settled in York, Pennsylvania. York is known as the Factory Tour Capital of the world. A number of national and international manufacturing companies such as Harley Davidson, Susquehanna Glass, and Hershey Chocolate are located in or near this city. Like many manufacturing towns, York has suffered and benefited from globalization, free trade, and outsourcing.

Free trade provides the advantage of finding new markets for local products. Disadvantages include losing jobs to new or emerging economies able to produce cheaper goods.

We made an effort to settle in York and visited a number of churches before deciding on a church home. Members, as I expected, were pleasant and welcoming. On a visit to a predominantly white congregation, I was again reminded of America's lingering issue of race. After church service, I was in conversation with some of the church members before I was interrupted by a charming elderly white lady.

"Your family is looking for you!" She chimed in.

"Really?" I asked. She invited me to follow her to meet members of my family. My wife, who was in a discussion nearby, saw me walking away and asked, "Are you ready?"

"My family is looking for me," I said as I winked at her.

Meredeth excused herself from the conversation and followed as we were pointed in the direction of another black couple. I thanked my guide, and I proceeded to greet the couple.

"My lost brother," I said, laughing while simultaneously making our introduction. They played along, and humor dispelled my surprise.

After reflecting on the situation, I was reminded of Colin Powell's advice to consider people's intent and meanings rather than their words. I believe that the lady who led us to the couple wanted us to be comfortable and make friends. Other members of the congregation had demonstrated a sincere concern for our comfort by inviting us to make their church our church home while they simultaneously and diplomatically alerted us to where the black congregation worshipped.

I had no reason to doubt their sincerity. As a member of the church family, I understood the selfless desire to consider the needs of others. Would it therefore be selfless to stay away from church and minimize the possibility of discomforts that my presence may cause? Should I do better research in learning the makeup of a congregation before I visit?

The easy answers to those questions were tempting. However, I reminded myself that my move to the USA and to different states within her borders demonstrated my openness to new opportunities, ideas, experiences, and friendships. Comfort zone was not my only concern, nor did I harbor any latent unhappiness or discomfort in my skin color or racial identity. I believe openness is not only liberating but underscores the concept that we are all of God's creatures. Openness means freedom and liberty—the essence of America.

Bob Marley's lyrics to "emancipate yourself from mental slavery" are intrinsic in King's dream. Perpetual mental emancipation by the sons and daughters of slaves and slave owners must continue.

Several months passed in York, and my search for a job seemed futile. While I conducted my job search, I had a contingency plan to become a financial advisor and obtained the required certification. My new wife remained supportive, but after three months, our marriage was tested when she revealed to me her innermost feelings.

"I am not in love with you . . . " I didn't hear the remainder of her statement. She continued, "I don't think I ever was . . . "

When I recovered, I calmly mustered the question, "Why did you marry me then?"

"I think I wanted to get married," she replied reflectively.

We were silent for what seemed like an eternity. I reasoned that if I wanted total honesty, I must be open to taste the product of her thoughts even if they were not palatable.

My focus shifted to me. Was the fact that I was out of a job the reason for this behavior? We were not hurting for money. A scene from the movie *Soul Food* sprang to memory. "You don't tell a black woman that you have no job," one of the characters had cautioned.

This woman, however, had supported my decision to quit my job. How would my immigration status be affected now that I had left my previous company and filed for permanent residency as the spouse of a US citizen? Was she saying this to test me or manipulate me? It was then I recalled the experience related by the Browns during the *Songs of Solomon Series* months before I had met Meredeth. The wife had made a similar reservation during their first three months of marriage. I was comforted by that shared experience since they were still married.

As unsettling as the situation was, I remained composed, and I thanked Meredeth for her honesty. I expressed regret that those feelings were not shared before we were married. However, we were now married, and I didn't want us to look back. Silently, I vowed that I would do whatever I could to make her happy. However, while I believed in my marriage vows, I decided that I would not fight to keep her in a relationship in which she was not fulfilled.

Days turned into weeks, and the routines of married life became the norm. I was still unable to find a job, and so performed daily household chores out of a sense of duty rather than desire. When it was time to fly to Meredeth's family gathering, I declined. While I loved traveling and visiting with friends and family, I did not want to incur additional costs for flying. If we were able to drive, I gladly attended. I had secretly vowed that beyond the cost of servicing our apartment, I would not add a dime to our family's budget.

After eight months, the economy started improving, and I found a job as a commercial insurance underwriter. I was happy to be working again and did not care that the commute was in another state more than forty miles away. I had not planned to continue in insurance operations, but I found out that many HR departments had only the capacity to see a candidate for what they last did.

I settled quickly into my new role and found instant synergy with my boss and colleagues. The job was demanding, but I had enough latitude and flexibility, and I excelled and set the pace. Since almost all businesses required workers' compensation insurance, the job provided an open window into how highly regulated and costly it was to do business in America. I was amazed to find out that some firms in the construction industry and other high-risk jobs could pay $2 or more of insurance premiums for every $1 paid in salary.

Companies doing business across state lines faced the burdensome responsibilities of obeying and filing various documents to different jurisdictions such as federal, state, and municipalities. The cumbersome process made compliance one of the most costly drivers for doing business in America. Investors seeking to operate inside the US are often surprised at regulations' costliness and duplicative nature.

More surprising to me was how businesses and individuals seemed to support actions not in their self-interest. Occasionally, I would ask business leaders what they thought about federalizing insurance to promote ease of doing business across state lines. Many were torn between the ease of doing business and the loss of state rights. One of my fellow underwriters provided a more enlightened self-interest answer. More regulations meant more underwriting jobs, the same way tax laws fueled the need for more accountants and tax preparers.

Ironically, while inefficiency and bureaucracies can be costly and reduce competiveness, they also create jobs.

ii.

Weeks after starting my new job, we purchased a home. The decision to purchase was delayed for me to find a job, so I could have a reasonable commute. In addition, we decided that our mortgage should be able to be supported by each of our individual salaries.

The housing market was heating up nationally, and even though increases in York were modest, it was no exception to the national trend. Baltimore's suburbanites searched for deals that extended north of the Maryland/ Pennsylvania line deep into York County.

Our first offer was made on a duplex to be constructed close to the Maryland line. Before it was accepted, the builders raised their preset price. We balked, and then walked when they refused to budge. It was a matter of principle for us. For the builders, it was a seller's market. Weeks later, we closed on another house fifteen miles north of the Maryland line. My commute would be a little longer, but we had more square footage as a consolation.

Two years later, the price of the house on which we made the initial offer had doubled. I started to second-guess myself about whether we had made the right decision when we walked away after the builders asked for $3,000 more. I concluded that we had. Unless a house that has appreciated in value is sold, there is no true gain. High equity could encourage cashing out and deeper debt. Besides, I was convinced that it was only a matter of time before things would come crashing down. After all, the dot-com bubble was still fresh in our minds. With that focus, we started a serious effort to become debt free.

Despite Meredeth's love for shopping or "retail therapy," we adopted a debt reduction strategy. Our new house remained sparsely furnished, and we clashed occasionally, mainly from my objection to go deeper into debt. To avoid clashes over the number-one issue about which couples fight, money, we devised the following arrangement which I have since termed "two individuals and one joint (2IJ)."

We would have three bank accounts. Each of us would keep our individual bank accounts over which we exercised discretionary control. We opened a third account that would be used jointly to finance the household budgets, including paying down the debt. The bulk of our salaries went into the joint account, and the predetermined discretionary spending went into the individual accounts.

I insisted on keeping all credit cards in separate names. This had two effects. First, it avoided the credit rating agencies reducing both our scores with the same balance and held us accountable to observe our agreed plan. Very soon I was credit card debt-free. At times, however, I took advantage of the zero percent offers (no transaction fees). In some cases, I would draw the cash deposits to earn interest or play the market. For a change, I could make money on the banks' money or avoid the margin on my trading account.

I learned the hard way that good fiscal managers can be perceived as heartless and cold, which is not conducive to a sustainable relationship. Before we met, Meredeth lost one of her aunts. Her aunt's husband was still in love with her years after she had died. He described how they had racked up tens of thousands in credit card debts as they traveled the world before she passed. He did not regret a penny. It was a great love story. I watched Meredeth as she listened intently to the story she had, no doubt, heard before. With her indulgence in shoes and clothes, I feared that she was taking the wrong lesson from the story about credit card spending.

Days later, she asked, "Joseph, would you have done the same for me?"

My response was aimed at our current situation. "We don't have to run up tens of thousands in credit card debt. We can make better plans now, and if, God forbid, that you have a terminal illness, I'll do whatever it takes to make your last days as enjoyable as possible." Obviously, that was not the most romantic thing to say, and I received the silent treatment.

While we monitored our finances, I watched in amazement as the "conservative" congress got rid of the pay- as-you-go system that the "liberals" had implemented. In addition, the Congress raised the debt ceiling, and the debt clock in New York that was dormant because of declining national debt was soon to be reactivated. "Deficit does not matter" was the catch phrase from the vice president, a "true conservative."

We were in two wars, and Congress financed them with supplemental funding instead of the regular budget process. These behaviors defied the principles of conservatism that I had learned in early accounting class. Fiscal conservatism suggests that when forecasting and dealing with uncertainties, one should err on the side of overstating expenses and understating revenues. The Bush administration and Congress did the exact opposite.

iii.

Alan and Kate introduced their family to us. They were our neighbors closest in proximity, and had moved in only two years earlier from Ohio. Other neighbors exchanged polite waves. It was nice to be meeting the neighbors, especially since we were about to leave the new house and head to Jamaica for our first vacation since the honeymoon.

In Jamaica, my family treated Meredeth like royalty, and I was delighted to show her the island, meet friends and family, and also visit places I'd never had an opportunity to visit. On this trip, Meredeth just wanted to rest, and a resort in Ocho Rios was just what the doctor ordered.

The bright, sunny days rekindled memories of carefree childhood days. I loved the serenity of the beach. Every time I exhaled, the cares of the world were minimized. As I walked, I felt the soft sand cushioning my feet and caressing my toes. I sat on the shore and gazed across the ocean and was treated to a sparkling light show created when the rays of the sunlight along the ocean were broken up by the gentle swaying waves.

The waves carried to the shore a gentle wind that rustled the tiny hairs on my body. With the wind was the scent of the woman, lying next to me, whom I had vowed to love until death. "I want to love you, love and treat you right. I want to love you every day and every night." The words of Bob Marley captured my feeling and were instructive as my wife and I set out to rekindle the passion that we hoped would endure for a lifetime.

We boarded the plane bound for Baltimore. The flight attendant joked to everyone that we should take a good look at the sunny sky and blue waters because snow awaited us in Baltimore. She was right.

In Baltimore, we spent nearly an hour digging just to get out of the airport parking lot. It was already after midnight when we crossed into Pennsylvania. I could not bear the thought of what our driveway would look like. How would we get in tonight with more than two feet of snow on the ground? When we neared our driveway, I thought I was hallucinating. The huge driveway was cleared all the way to the garage, courtesy of our neighbor, Alan, and his son. With gratitude, I pulled into the garage. I was grateful for great vacation and good neighbors.

That night, as I cranked up the heater, got under the comforter, and secured the comfort of my wife's bosom, a smile lingered on my face as I recalled my first blizzard in Washington, DC. People had eyed me suspiciously as I offered my help. My neighbors' gesture in clearing my driveway reminded me that it was okay to be neighborly, and my experience in DC was not the accepted norm throughout the country.

iv.

As the 2004 general election approached, I was still not able to vote. I had written to the immigration office several times only to receive the same response: "The normal processing time for this office is ten months." I circled the ten months plus my initial application date (three years earlier) to show that we had already exceeded that. I mailed it back along with an explanation, only to receive the same form letter response three weeks later. Finally, I visited the office and provided another copy of the application, which apparently had been lost.

Months later, we were called in for an interview, and my residency card was processed. When it arrived in the mail, there again was an error. It had a conditional two-year limit for spouses of US citizens not married for more than two years. We were now married for more than three years and pointed out this error. It would be another two years, and the expiration of my resident card, before the immigration service corrected the initial error. My participation as a citizen would have to wait for another three years. Did Uncle Sam want me?

My neighbor, Alan, mounted a Bush-Cheney sign in his yard.

"Can you tell me why you are supporting this ticket for re-election?" I asked.

"I don't really care about anything else, but I am a fiscal conservative," he replied.

"Well, I believe in fiscal conservatism also, but this administration is not," was my reply.

I left wondering why so many people concluded that lower taxes equaled fiscal responsibility. Sometimes, raising revenues was the fiscally responsible thing to do, especially when fighting two wars. It is not that I liked paying higher taxes. The millage on our house provided the county school taxes of over $6,000 each year, and we did not have children in school.

With federal income tax, state and county income, plus sales and real estate taxes, we were paying over 40 percent of our income in taxes. As an accountant, however, I knew that the course of the administration was not sustainable. We were developing structural deficits, and soon revenues would have to be increased.

Before the invasion was ordered, I presented a speech at my local Toastmasters club explaining why it was not a good idea. I had supported the war in Afghanistan and the first Gulf War, but was opposed to invading Iraq. After the speech, I spoke to a number of local leaders and CEOs in attendance. Most supported the decision to invade.

Even if one supports an administration's decision, it is healthy to question it. Questioning helps to sharpen focus and improve the quality of government's decisions. On this, the media and the democratic opposition failed, not only the administration, but also the country.

As a commercial underwriter, I learned about general contractors and the multiple layers of subcontractors. It was not uncommon for general contractors to win the bid on projects and then subcontract all or part of them. After the Iraq invasion, the administration made it policy that only companies in countries that supported the war would be allowed to be general contractors. While this sounded like music to the ears of supporters, it was bad news for the taxpayers.

US general contractors would take on millions in contracts and then subcontract the same projects for a fraction of the cost to contractors who were not allowed to bid on the original contracts. In addition, insurance carriers that provided insurance coverage for US workers in the newly occupied Iraqi territory gained a chunk of these contract dollars for the risky coverage.

To create the illusion of a smaller size of government, the administration subcontracted many functions typically reserved for military personnel. Sometimes the ratio of contractors to military personnel was more than two to one.

As Halloween and the election approached, it seemed likely that President Bush would be re-elected. I had no voice, but the election was on my mind when I prepared a piece for Halloween that I kept in my home office. I printed a copy of an art piece recently seen in the news (reported stolen), *The Scream*. I added the caption "Bush Again?"

V.

I had grown disillusioned, and my attendance at church became more infrequent. I remained active by volunteering in events that helped people directly. I valued the community that church provided, but my heart was not in the weekly rituals. I was not pleased that my church had continued to accept an organizational structure that facilitated race preference (black and white conferences).

I resented the Iraq war, the Arabs' obsession with the destruction of Israel, and religious organizations that became cheerleaders instead of a conscience to a nation pursuing preemptive war.

My disillusionment intensified when I suspected, but did not want to believe, that my wife was having an affair. Before long, my suspicion was confirmed, and we decided to end the marriage. I knew we were beyond reconciliation when, instead of remorse, there were feelings of vindication and justifications.

I confided the likelihood of our breakup to a female friend, but was not prepared for her question. "What did you do?" she asked almost instantly. I was crushed.

"What did I do? It is always the man's fault, isn't it?"

It didn't matter what caused the breakdown. It didn't matter that my wife's best friend had cautioned her that she was going to destroy her marriage. I had to accept responsibility. Maybe I did not do all I should have done, but now the question was what should I do?

vi.

As my world fell apart around me, I became intimate with the biking trails of the Susquehanna valley. I rode for miles each week to drown the pain. Very few recognized that we had problems. On one of my long rides, I found myself laughing. My laugh was drowned out by a chorus of happy cicadas, the object of my laugh. The thought had occurred to me that I was alone in the woods surrounded by horny bugs that emerged from the ground to mate every few years. As the cicadas got louder, I pedaled faster. It didn't matter that the cicadas had no interest in humans; I had to get away. The joke was now on me, and it was not funny anymore.

Home. Left to Right Joseph, Jenny (sister)
Christine (niece) Collin (in-law)

I accepted a job in Florida and decided that it would provide me a clean break. Meredeth had flown with me to Sarasota and made a weekend vacation out of the trip during my second interview. The plane was delayed for more than five hours and it was after 4:00 a.m. when we checked into the Ritz Carlton. I was glad to survive the interview four hours later.

Two weeks earlier, we had been in Las Vegas together. After the trip, it was clear we would not be together, but would remain close friends. Meredeth worked meticulously with online divorce software to be equitable and fair.

"Why do I feel like this is a mistake?" she asked.

"Well, we had a great run together! However, I sense that your heart wants to be free. I care for you too much to try to fence you in," I told her.

Ironically, I felt guilty. My guilt was not from infidelity. I had lost the will and tenacity to fight to preserve the union. I did not fight because I was not sure I wanted to win. I had made a tepid attempt at marriage counseling and I felt relief when the effort was not embraced. I rationalized that what we were doing after the first three months of marriage (when she said she didn't love me) was delaying the inevitable. I wanted a new life, and the sunshine state was calling.

CHAPTER 17: **FLORIDA**

i.

"Did you know that we are fully divorce?" Meredeth called to ask.

"Yes," I replied. "That was two months ago." I had contacted a lawyer to find out what was holding up the process after Meredeth ran into some stumbling block. I received a notice in the mail and assumed she was also notified. The process was completed on what would be our sixth and final anniversary as man and wife.

Months before the process was completed, I had already decided it was time to consider dating again. I wasn't looking forward to it. Not that I was concerned about my readiness. Of major concern to me was the dating process: the miscommunication, misunderstanding, and deception that one endured on the path to compatibility.

Not the typical emperor, Bejing

Posing with tourists, Tiananmen Square

Joseph in Egypt

I considered myself a simple, frugal, unpretentious, average guy who had a vision to develop and maintain a successful family. Attracting drama was not my style. Excitement for me meant weekend getaways, or the occasional travels to distant lands. I had a goal to visit every continent, and I looked forward to continuing the journey with someone who shared a similar passion for travel. My travel to Brazil proved therapeutic, and added South America to my list of continents. I was ready to move on.

Relationships are difficult, and I believe people should form a union with a person with whom they are comfortable. I had been in America for more than twelve years, and I somehow started accepting social norms. During a discussion with my niece, Christine, I talked about acceptable racial dating preferences in America. She reminded me that she was from a mixed union, and her husband was the same racial stock that I was.

The reminder was sobering, because I realized I was allowing this aspect of America to change me in the wrong direction. I was starting to conform to someone's idea of what the norm should be. For the first time, I started an attempt to segment my family into racial groups and realized the impossibility of this task. This was one thing about me that I decided not to let my new country change. I did not grow up viewing life through a racial prism. I would not blind my eyes to how the world worked, but I did not have to change to be accepted.

Recognizing the similarities between financial investments and investing in a relationship, I consulted my finance textbooks to formulate a dating strategy. I extracted some of the factors that affected investment decisions: liquidity, investment returns, diversification, and use value.

I cannot claim to be an expert on women, but I understand that most women (regardless of status) like to be wooed and made to feel special. The wooing process requires resources (liquidity).

All investors expect a return on investments, and my expected return was to kiss some LIPS (Loyalty, Interdependence, Perseverance, and Synergy). My return would be to find someone who is loyal, who would not seek the nearest exit when we were faced with a challenge.

She would share my belief that interdependence—not independence—is the highest form of human relationships. She would be perseverant and tenacious since anything worth having is worth fighting for. Finally, a return on investment would produce someone with whom I would find emotional synergy (one plus one is greater than two). I had difficulty using diversification in this construct.

In the early dating stage, it helped when considering options. However, unless one is in a polygamous setting, exclusivity is the focus. To truly experience the synergy, vulnerability is the first necessity. This spreading of oneself to allow a new unit of both lives to emerge is how diversification is considered in this context. It also meant that I would not seek all my emotional support from a mate, that I would include family and friends. Don't be content with independence; diversify to interdependence.

When considering "use" value, it was not my intent to ask any of my dates about the operational useful life of her ovaries. However, in the context of a relationship, use value would ask the question, "What do you want from a relationship?" Acting on Stephen Covey's advice on developing mission statements, I had a mission to develop and maintain a successful family. My challenge then was to find someone who shared a similar mission and goals.

After considering factors that affect a relationship investment decision, the next step was to consider methods for acquisition. I considered the following: hostile takeover, lease with an option to buy, and merger.

As unpleasant as this may seem, hostile takeover works for some who have to be dragged into a relationship. This dragging usually involves some emotional or economic manipulation, or even physical manipulation. For example, if someone decides to trap her mate by getting pregnant, one is using this method. The hope is that later, the trapped mate might decide, like a kidnapped victim with Stockholm syndrome, that this is not so bad after all, and then a successful relationship develops. The risk is great, and a pleasant outcome usually does not result from this strategy.

Lease With an Option to Buy occurs when both parties are not sure or do not think it is practical to go the distance of a lifetime. It is then less threatening to take the relationship out for a short- to medium-term test drive. From this union, it is easy to move on without the baggage of a nasty separation.

Merger occurs when both parties are committed to a union that will last a lifetime. Come what may, they are prepared to make it work. There is little hedging, because the belief is that the unit is for a lifetime. While a marriage might appear synonymous with a merger, the mind set of the participants is the difference. With the high rate of divorce in America, it is clear that some enter a marriage with a "lease" mind set. My hope was to find a mate with a merger mind set.

After considering the method of acquisition, the medium of implementing a strategy was next. In the case of investing, a broker or online trading are typical mediums.

I selected eHarmony and found it to be a non-invasive and efficient medium for meeting like-minded singles. The site has a track record of producing successful matches using dimensions of compatibility and a series of questions that one can select to break the ice before actual conversation begins. The site allows you to choose a nearby radius or anywhere in the world. I first started my search internationally. However, I found it impractical to my situation and modified my searches to a one hundred–mile radius of my home.

ii.

I was off to a great start and met some intriguing possibilities. However, timing and chemistry and the intensity of attraction cannot be successfully programmed into a computer. One of my possibilities was an attorney with whom I had talked and had instant chemistry. We set a dinner date, and I made sure I was on time and reserved a table. She had posted some pictures online and was sure I could spot her when she arrived.

When she first walked in, I saw the resemblance and wondered why she had sent her mom or maybe her sister to meet me. It was during dinner that she acknowledged that her online pictures were fifteen years old, the way she likes to remember herself. Despite the additional pounds, she was still a very attractive woman. However, I couldn't understand why someone, knowing that we would meet, would encourage that deception. After all, a relationship should focus on acceptance just-as-we-are, not who-we-were.

I was very intrigued with one lady who communicated with me online for some time. After a long discussion, I volunteered to call her and noticed she was hesitant to give me her number. She finally volunteered that even though Venice, Florida, was the city she said she was from, she was actually living in Ghana. When the same thing occurred with someone else living in Ireland, I realize that I had again wasted my time.

It would take months before I was again intrigued. She was a charming, attractive woman named Chloe. Her sweet accent gave a hint of her Nigerian background. Her native name translated as a prized eagle's egg. I wanted to learn everything about her, and I listened to her every word and absorbed them like desert soil absorbing droplets of water.

I was anxious to learn Chloe's story. She was divorced from a man she truly loved, but who became abusive. She had attended medical school in Nigeria, but had opted to get married and follow her husband while he pursued his career. She had lived in London, Canada, and now Florida. Chloe was living with an uncle who still saw her as a little girl. She was anxious to get her life back on track and had applied to a number of schools, so that she could do her residency in the USA. Chloe was forthright and didn't mince words; she didn't drive and depended on her relatives to get around.

Both of our lives were in transition. I had lost my job, and Chloe's life seemed to have one adversity after another. Several weeks passed before we reconnected, and I was anxious to meet her. I drove two hours to Orlando. I had waited for more than forty minutes, and passed the time at a coffee shop on my computer. Chloe's nephew dropped her off and shook my hand and went home. I thought it was a smart strategy since we were meeting for the first time, and she could identify me and my car if something happened to his aunt.

Chloe's picture did not do her justice. She was incredibly gorgeous, and she knew it.

"I am sorry to be late," she said.

"That is fine, I was on the computer most of the time," I replied.

"I am sure I am worth the wait," she said confidently.

I laughed and acknowledged that she was incredibly attractive and self-assured.

We both laughed as she got in my car, and we went in search of a restaurant. It was after closing time when we left, and we decided to continue our conversation in a sports bar. It was the weekend, and even though I would be helping my niece and her husband move into their new home the next day, I found every moment with Chloe intriguing.

At three 3:00 a.m., I dropped Chloe home. She hugged me good night, and I watched her disappear into her uncle's house, and then I set off on my three-hour drive to help my niece move.

Over the next few weeks, Chloe wanted to move into her own place and get accepted into a residency program. She had money troubles, and I thought about helping, but resisted offering. There were too many examples of middle-aged knights in shining armor who became victims. Several weeks passed before I saw Chloe again. She was now in her new apartment, and she accepted my invitation to pick her up and visit Sarasota.

I had a dilemma. That same day, I had committed to attend the seventieth birthday celebration of Rene. Rene and his wife Barbara were the closest to family that I found in Sarasota. When I needed a taste of a good Jamaican home-cooked meal and a sense of family, they had an open arm. When I was to be sworn in as a new citizen, this was the family that attended the ceremony.

I communicated this dilemma to Chloe, and we agreed that if she was uncomfortable attending, then we would spend the day in Orlando and I would head back to the party that night.

I got to her apartment and waited while she got dressed. As she emerged partially dressed, she remarked that her roommate and her roommate's boyfriend would be happy to have the house alone for a day.

As I drove away from her apartment, she asked to see my driver's license.

"I thought we were beyond that," I said as I reached for my wallet.

"We'll, you can't be too careful," she remarked. "After all, you are someone I met on the Internet." I complied.

"Well, I agree we must be careful, and I want to make sure you are comfortable before we leave your city, but isn't it a little late since we are already in motion?"

"Not at all," she said confidently as she texted my information to someone.

Oh, the joys of modern dating, I thought.

We spent the day in Sarasota, and she loved the city. We talked about several things, religions and friendships, including a transvestite friend with whom she had spent most of the previous evening. The conversation shifted to terrorism and the Nigerian Christmas bomber. She was visibly upset by his behavior and was happy that people were not using his behavior to make a broad judgment about Nigerians. She obviously had a privileged childhood and had that in common with the bomber.

I reassured her that I had attended college with many Nigerians and had found them to be incredibly smart and confident people. I was also aware of the numbers of scams that permeated the Internet out of Nigeria; however, Nigerians in America are positive, upwardly mobile people. The actions of a few should not paint the reputations of the many.

"I hope you don't find it disappointing that I don't know how to bobsled," I quipped. "Since Jamaica is now known for bobsledding."

Before the day started, we agreed that neither of us was in a good place to start a relationship. Chloe was looking to start her residency, and she was not sure in which city she would be. I was looking to find a new job. Despite these obstacles, we decided to develop a friendship.

Chloe helped me pick out a wine for the upcoming party. I was impressed with her knowledge of liquor. I recall that she told me about her early habit of sneaking liquor into her high school boarding dorm, which she drank to relive menstrual discomfort. All seemed to be going well until I called ahead to let our host know that I had a friend with me.

Chloe started talking about transvestites again, and then told me that she was one. I didn't believe her and thought that this was her idea of a practical joke. We were on the same subject several minutes later when it finally occurred to me that she might be telling the truth.

"This is not something that someone would joke about, is it?" I asked, wishing that the joke was on me. Chloe acknowledged that it wasn't. We were now back at my house, and she encouraged me not to miss the party. She wanted to remain at my house while I attended. That option was out of the question. I did not know this person. Her identity was in doubt, and I would not allow her/him to remain in my house. I would do the honorable thing and get her back home safely, but she would not be left in my house.

"Would you like me to drop you at a movie theater while I drop in for a few minutes at my friend's party?"

"So you are kicking me out of your house?" she said sorrowfully, feeling wounded. "You should know that I was joking. Look at me! How can you believe that I am a man?"

"A moment ago, you were trying to convince me that you were a man; now you are suggesting that I am naïve for believing you? You are somebody I met on the Internet!"

I dropped Chloe at a bar and proceeded to the party. Twenty minutes later, I was leaving and my host didn't understand what happened to my friend, and why I was leaving after only a few minutes.

I was in a serious state of confusion. I knew that I couldn't have an honest conversation with Chloe. And she would feel that she was under duress since she depended on me for a ride to get back home. If she was a woman, she had already started to hate me for entertaining the belief that she was a man.

"Good God!" I yelled to myself. "What the hell is going on?" The incident had demonstrated the uncertainties that were now my life. Over the past three years, I had lost my wife, my job, and my religious conviction as I questioned God and organized religion. I had embraced my new identity as American, but now I couldn't be sure about someone's gender. Who am I? Why am I here? Are there any absolutes anymore? I wondered.

I went to the bar where I left Chloe. She was the only black woman in the bar. Having lived in major cities over the world, she was not uncomfortable in such settings. The bartender was alert and realized that she was not in the mood for conversation and decided to find her someplace where she could be alone. She had had more than her fair share of guys trying to make conversation. She was an attractive woman, and Chloe did not like being hit on. From previous conversations, she had expressed her displeasure at the general belief that women from the Atlantic Coast of Africa were promiscuous. The AIDS epidemic in Southern Africa had only strengthened that belief.

A bartender came by to find out how we were doing. Chloe was now in "high spirits" and insisted that I have one of the drinks she was having. I opted for iced tea instead, adding that I wanted to get her home safely. She pulled little bottles of liquor from her purse and improved the proof of the drinks she had purchased from the bar. She had developed a high tolerance for liquor from her earlier days of smuggling liquor into her Catholic dorm.

As I drove her back to Orlando, I felt sad. We talked politely. She expressed surprise about getting into a car with someone she knew very little about. I knew I did not know her full story and probably never would. The truth is I was scared and resentful. I was scared that someone I knew so little about could make me so vulnerable and resentful that I could feel attraction for someone whose gender I was no longer sure of. What was she thinking for making a joke like that? Was it a joke?

As I dropped Chloe off that night, a feeling of uncertainty washed over me. It was clear that the search for a new life partner was not going to be quick. I had covered the full range of emotions in one day with this woman—or was she? The only consolation I could find is that I had not kissed her.

CHAPTER 18:
ISSUES FACING AMERICA

i.

My life appeared emblematic of the changing America, with growing and morphing pains, sometimes dramatic and chaotic. Such changes forced the sharpening of survival instincts, and evaluation of belief systems and life's purpose. In my continued pursuit of happiness, I am forced to look inward and confront my fears, biases, and understand my limitations and relationships to God and country.

I have a greater appreciation for the people of America. I was eager and optimistic to play my civic role as

I cast my first vote in a local Sarasota election. Later, I volunteered as a local county tax advisor. As a citizen, I believe that I have a duty to inform myself about current affairs and to hold my leaders responsible and to join the debate. I continue to support the president and other leaders, and I hope that they succeed.

I think it is short-sighted to wish that our leaders to fail when we disagree with their policies in solving existing problems. The success of any administration is not measured in a president's ability to implement policies, but rather the effectiveness of those polices in bettering the lives of people. Hoping that a leader fails so our preferred leader can win a future election is not a good recipe for nation building. Successive leadership failures will only hasten the demise of a great country.

The alternative view is to hope that our leaders succeed. If the success is not good enough, then we change leaders with better ideas. With this approach, America gets increasingly better rather than regressively worse. Any policy directive of any administration costs money that comes from my pocket as a taxpayer. Why, then, would I be rooting for failure?

After months of being laid off, I regained employment. It did not take getting laid off to understand the benefits social services play in preventing citizens from falling through the cracks. Working in the financial services industry, I am aware of the lobbying that takes place behind the scenes for insurance, banking, real estate, and other services. It is simply naïve for ordinary citizens to conclude that a *laissez-faire* concept will eventually work to the advantage of the masses. What makes anyone think that private industry would gladly pay the environmental costs of their actions if not required by the people through their government to do so?

When I moved to Florida, I started my third job since graduate school and my second private sector job. The job I was leaving with the state of Maryland had dispelled a number of myths I had held about public sector employees. I had lost the belief that public sector employees were clock-watchers who cared little for the people they served. I found my colleagues to be highly accomplished and motivated. Some had worked in the private sector, but had opted for stability rather than positions that required almost daily justification of one's role. This survivalist behavior in some private sector firms created some results, but also mistrust and short-term focus that sacrificed the team for the more ruthless individuals and the mind set to get yours now before you are out.

I was grateful for my first private sector job in the US. It provided me the opportunity to work legally in the country. The fact that I was more academically prepared than anyone in that role did not stop others from concluding that I had gotten the job based solely on affirmative action. Initially, my own lackluster performance did not help. I was concerned about how I had managed to snag probably the lowest-paying job of members of my class after leaving graduate school. This lack of focus resulted in silly mistakes, which my colleagues were eager to amplify as evidence that I was not qualified. I snapped out of it and started employing a more thankful spirit. Within months, I was the pacesetter. Interestingly, when my performance was consistently above average, it was dismissed as "to be expected" since I was overqualified for the position in the first place.

My second private sector job was more challenging and taught me things about corporate culture that many take for granted. Relationship networks are sometimes more important than hard work, merit, and paying the "black tax" in ensuring your survival. (The black tax is the notion that African Americans must add twice the value of the average white person in the department of his company to be considered successful.) I also learned that if you are passionate and assertive, you risk being unfairly labeled as threatening or the "angry black man." If you are too calm, then you risk becoming a victim and a stepping-stone for the more aggressive.

ii.

While our country has shown an openness to change, it is not without risk, as people question if the country is losing its moral boundaries and identity. I recall a business trip to Fresno with a former boss. We got into a taxi that took us to our hotel. The driver was a sheik who wore a turban. The next day, my boss proceeded to tell other senior leaders that she was picked up at the airport by Al Qaeda. After attempting to explain the difference between an Indian sheik and Islamist Al Qaeda, I realized that she preferred the Al Qaeda narrative, and continued to repeat it. It was clear that this was not a punch line, but what she believed. Efforts such as these to oversimplify issues can lead to demagoguery and fear.

iii.

Obama's election was heralded as an end to racial barriers and the start of a new post-racial and post-partisan era in America. However, the racial prism continued to shape how issues were viewed by many. Racial classification forced many with mixed racial heritages to choose identities not fully representative of their backgrounds (the president included).

After Obama's election, I asked the following questions of some friends: Would Barack Obama's campaign for president be as successful if the color of his wife Michelle was the same as his mother's? Soliciting response to my question was not scientific. However, it illustrated how sensitive the issue of race continues to be in America.

My conclusion from this casual discussion is that Obama's 34 percent support from whites and 60 percent support among Latinos would remain unchanged. Blacks, however, may have taken a longer time to embrace him. A number of professional African American females echo this sentiment. It is the sentiment expressed in *Essence Magazine* by Jill Scott explaining why it hurts to see black men with white women. In addition, during the campaign, Obama had to address questions such as "was he black enough?"

The question of the color of a black man's spouse and his political acceptance might bear some relevance to two prominent Republicans, Justice Clarence Thomas and Secretary Colin Powell. They have different degrees of political acceptance across America. Former Secretary of State Colin Powell is married to an African American. Supreme Court Justice Thomas's second wife is white. The difference is not simply the colors of their spouses, but it is undoubtedly a political factor. One of the advertisements against Harold Ford, Jr., in his failed bid for senator of Tennessee indicates that strategists believed that. Ford was depicted dating white women.

Racial politics and other divide-and-conquer techniques might appear more striking to new immigrants. I now understand why blacks overwhelmingly support the Democratic Party. However, I don't believe that African Americans and the country are best served by having a monolithic voting bloc for the Democratic Party while being ignored by the Republican Party. Competition of ideas is good. George W. Bush, while Governor of Texas, and Mayors Giuliani and Blumberg of New York demonstrated that when Republicans compete for the African American vote, it can be had. As a presidential contender, one of the reasons for Bush's failure was the early loss of the inclusiveness message and symbolism when he launched his campaign at Bob Jones University. Fairly or unfairly, the university was portrayed as a symbol of non-inclusiveness, and this reminded blacks of Ronald Regan's launch of his campaign in Philadelphia, Mississippi.

Divide-and-conquer politics is painful, as Justice Thomas suggested in his book, *My Grandfather's Son.* In trying to understand my role as a new citizen, as a hyphenated American, I read this book along with Obama's *Dreams of My Father* and *The Audacity of Hope.* I came away with the impression that the justice felt mistreated and misunderstood. Surprisingly, I found a lot more agreements between the views of President Obama and Justice Thomas than disagreements.

What are strikingly different are their tones and styles. The tone of Justice Thomas' memoir is combative and confrontational, which may be a relic of the bitterness he still feels from the bruising confirmation process. However, if one waits long enough to wade through the inartful and sometimes caustic comments of Justice Thomas, it is evident that he, like President Obama, believes in personal responsibility and upward mobility.

It is a historical fact that years of conditioning created a feeling of low self-esteem and learned helplessness among many blacks. Blacks exposed to other cultures, away from the black–white paradigm, and new immigrants of color usually do not have this mind set and are aggressive in striving for upward mobility. Affirmative action sought to break the historical conditioning by creating positive symbols of success for the younger generation to see. The objectives are commendable. Having full participation in American society benefits America by making citizens more independent, less dependent on the state.

Unfortunately, the by-product of affirmative action is a belief, especially held by a number of whites, that blacks in positions of authority are somehow not qualified. This is the gist of Justice Thomas's concern. He argues that African Americans' hard-earned accomplishments are devalued by this unfair conclusion.

The distinction I have with Justice Thomas' view on the issue of affirmative action is what seemed to be his focus on the side effects of the medicine of affirmative action, rather than on the benefits of treating the endemic illnesses of racism. Justice Thomas, Secretary Powell, and others who were clearly talented may not have achieved their degrees of success without the "affirmative" opened door.

Opened doors traditionally existed for whites through networks and entrenched traditions in American life. Affirmative action may have made the patient, America, better. But, like many medications, affirmative action must cease to be administered as the patient (society) heals. The end of affirmative action is therefore not a question of *if*, but *when*.

Another interesting experience with America's obsession with racial issues presented itself while I was volunteering in Obama's election campaign. As we waited to get started, a retired couple engaged me. The husband asked, "What happened to your people?" I knew what he meant as I looked around and realized that there were not many African Americans present.

"My people?" I asked. His wife was clearly uncomfortable with the question, but he was a man who spoke his mind. He proceeded to explain why he thought African Americans should be volunteering in droves to elect Obama. I thanked him for openly expressing what he thought "my people" should do. I, however, reminded him that while I understood the historical significance of what an Obama election would mean, we were all working to help elect the next President of the United States, not an African American president. We had concluded that Obama's unique skills made him the better candidate. I was, however, relieved when a number of African Americans gushed in as the event got started.

My learning was not over. Many of the new entrants sought the company of other African Americans, including me. Some engaged me in conversations, sometimes oblivious to the white members of the group already in conversation. I found myself repeatedly attempting to ensure that no one felt excluded. It was refreshing to see the ice melting and people stepping out of their comfort zones, building new relationships as we worked with a common objective.

The objective was, of course, bigger than Barack Obama. As America progresses toward a more perfect union, some behaviors must be unlearned and new ones learned. One guiding principle is found in many philosophical, biblical, and parental teachings worldwide: to treat others the way you would like to be treated. This is necessary if you believe in the motto "E pluribus unum."

Months into the new administration, Attorney General Holder commented that, "When it comes to discussing race, America was a nation of cowards." His intent apparently was to stimulate conversations; the timing, however, could not have been worse. When people are losing jobs, this is not the discussion people want to have.

As the racial discussions continue, whites and blacks must be open to listening to insensitive and ill-informed speeches. If we are inviting the discussions, we must be prepared to hear views with which we disagree. It is only when people are allowed to expose their beliefs that those beliefs can be challenged and disinfected by the purity of competing thoughts.

I find it appalling when politicians are not able to listen to opposing views without attempting to devalue an opponent. I must confess that there are a number of politicians and "yelling heads" from both political parties to whom I listen, but can no longer hear. I see their lips moving, but I have acquired a barrier against talking points and intellectual dishonesty.

It is a constant struggle to remain respectful and open-minded as I wade through the barrage of intellectual dishonesty, false choices, and contempt for the intelligence of the populace. I am not naïve to think that logic and persuasion will moderate all views. But I understand the need to keep trying and avoid arrogance, since all of us hold inconsistent positions and biases.

The danger, if we stop trying, is to assume that our position is intellectually superior, when sometimes, it is our views that need informing. Sometimes, we simply have to agree to disagree.

iv.

Debts and deficits concerned me before I moved to the US. In order to repay debt, I saw how the Jamaican government and other developing countries adopted austerity measures prescribed by the IMF. Those prescriptions wreaked havoc on people's lives. It reminded me of the King Solomon Proverb that the borrower is a servant of the lender. When the Tea Party movement and other conservatives amplified the concerns about the growing national debt, they had my undivided attention.

As someone whose profession encourages professional skepticism, I considered the makeup of the movement and its selectivity in identifying the problems as dependent on the makeup of our government. Despite that, there is agreement that the growing debt burden is threatening the fiscal security of the United States.

After identifying a problem, we must address the causes, suggest solutions, implement the solutions, and monitor the solutions to make sure they are working. Some seem incapable of acknowledging the causes of the structural deficit problem. This, of course, presents a dilemma because if the causes are not correctly identified, the solutions are not likely to be effective. To correctly understand the debt and deficit issue, I looked at the historical debt and deficit since the Great Depression.

From this research, I can conclude that every administration increased spending and/or cut taxes during a recession, which temporarily increased debt and deficits. When President George W. Bush succeeded Clinton, he found a budget surplus and a declining debt. At that time, the national debt was five trillion dollars. President Bush argued that since we had surplus, it was an indication that we were taking too much in taxes from the people, and that we should return their money.

Later, when there was an economic downturn, President Bush argued that we should cut taxes again to stimulate the economy. As we prepared for war in Afghanistan and in Iraq, actions that would dramatically increase spending, President Bush initiated tax cuts without putting in place any programs to pay for wars or tax cuts.

These actions were financed by simply charging the expenses to the national credit card, and the debt was nearly twelve trillion dollars when President Bush's term ended. Paying for these actions would be the problem of his successor, of any successor.

Cutting taxes is a vital fiscal tool when viewed in context. Before the Great Depression, the highest individual tax rate was 25 percent. After the Great Depression and

World War II, it was 94 percent and 91 percent when President Kennedy reduced taxes. It was 70 percent when President Regan reduced taxes, and 39 percent when President George W. Bush reduced taxes.[2]

At the start of President Obama's term, the highest individual tax rate was 35 percent. One can conclude then that President Obama did not have the same fiscal tools and conditions available to President Regan or Kennedy. The closest conditions mirrored the Great Depression when President Roosevelt took office.

Everyone who loves the idea of lower taxes should seek to avoid wars because history suggests that increased tax rates are usually required to finance wars. It is irresponsible to push for wars and then run away from financing them. In spite of the question of who is responsible for our current debt situation, solutions are required.

As citizens, we have a legitimate right to be dissatisfied with the current state of our country. But simply being angry is not a solution. Anger can be pivotal for change but can also result in bad decisions.

V.

As a new citizen, I am concerned with a number of other issues, including: gerrymandering, the length of campaigns, free speech, security, and demagoguery. Gerrymandering defies the basic premise of democracy, of people choosing their leaders. After each census, partisan leaders choose their constituents by drawing districts based on the support of residents. I would hope for electoral reforms that empower the populace.

Campaigns are too long; many Americans now confuse campaigning with governing. Instead of starting the process of governing after an election, the campaign for the next election starts.

Media conglomeration and an unlimited supply of money in campaigns threatens free speech, and not only in politics. Since we started paying for cable television, we pay for the privilege of watching more advertisements, and I am disappointed that I don't get to vote with my dollars on what channels to support. The cable companies do that for me, bundling their services.

It is comical to see how far some have taken the free speech when it comes to advertising. Businesses and politicians have the right to promote their products and platform, but I have the right not to listen, and the right to my own thoughts. Recently, I walked out of a movie theater frustrated at the number of advertisements I had to endure after I had handed over a bundle (my date and I) for that privilege. I visited the restroom to relieve my mind and bladder and could not believe my eyes when a screen above the urinal lit up with video streams and jingles. When did I lose the right to an advertisement-free leak?

Why are Americans comfortable with businesses monitoring our buying habits, tracking our online behaviors, selling personal information, and calling us at odd hours of the day and night to sell us products when we would not tolerate these same behaviors from our own government?

If businesses get a pass, what is to prevent governments from outsourcing data collection to businesses and gaining access to all the information that we would not want government to have directly? The concept is so inverted that we have to sign Do Not Call lists asking not to be called, rather than the reverse.

There have been a number of complaints, especially from the right, that the media has a liberal slant. The result of this criticism has sent the media to overcompensate by moving to a more rightward slant. That approach, I believe, is a mistake, since a conservative free press is an oxymoron. If the press is to be truly free, it must be truly liberated (not left wing or right wing). Therefore, in the denotative sense of the word, we should demand a media that is liberal in disseminating information without ideological slanting.

vi.

"Our flight is going to be delayed!" Annemarie repeated to the members of the group. We had just completed two days in Shanghai and were in line to board a flight to Beijing, China. As we waited, I started a conversation with a nearby traveler. He introduced himself as Jason and produced a business card.

"You are English?" I asked.

"Yes, but I live in Beijing."

"Really, how long?"

"Actually, I just moved! Funny you should ask. I was living in South Korea, but I found it too conservative for me and jumped at an opportunity from my company to live in Beijing."

"You found South Korea, an open democracy, too conservative? And therefore you are moving to Communist China?"

Jason laughed heartily before responding, "Funny, isn't it?"

My question to Jason underscores a question many Americans are asking. Why are so many capitalist and western companies beating down the door of a government-controlled Communist country to get in, while decrying regulation in countries like the USA? Does cheap labor trump all other risks? Will America's dominance be eclipsed?

vii.

A day after Christmas, and a year before I became a citizen, Big Mac passed away. He was still mentally agile. His upper body was strong, but he was immobile due to arthritis in his knees. I saw him for the last time one month before his death.

Our conversations followed a typical pattern each time we spoke. Big Mac made requests, and when possible and realistic, I accommodated them. On this occasion, however, he asked me about my divorce, marriage, and my church attendance. The questions sounded accusatory and I responded with brief non-answers.

During the funeral, I was concerned with efficiency and sought to get it started on time. I had forgotten that locally things operated on a different schedule. Before the church service ended, I slipped out and made my way to the gravesite in the church plot where Big Mac would be buried. While surveying the gravesite, McKewan's voice soared from the pulpit in her solo rendition. She too had had come to pay her respects. It was then that it occurred to me that I was the only one of Big Mac's offspring in attendance. Sure my siblings Jenny,

Bev, Marlene, Collin, and Conroy were all there and very supportive and provided comfort to Mom, but they are not from Big Mac lineage. Kenny was in New York and unable to make it. Val and Jasmine lived in Britain and did not make the trip.

Several months later, I visited London for the first time. I watched the USA versus England in soccer at Wembley, but I also wanted to meet my brother's family. After spending a day reuniting with Val, who was more than twenty years older, he invited me to church. The most delightful time of the trip, for Val, came when a member of the church came up to us and asked a question.

"Val," he said. "I can see that you are both brothers, but which of you is older?"

"Could you repeat that please?" Val said, laughing.

I watched Val as he walked to the pulpit. His mannerisms reminded me of the dad I wanted to remember, one gentler, measured, and more refined. The softness and gentleness when he touched and conversed with his wife comforted me. It was clear that Val and Jasmine had moved past the Big Mac years and had no desire to talk about or to relive them. I had to do the same.

Uncle Sam and the world are undergoing changes at a rapid pace. For some it is exhilarating, and for others it is painful. Only the adaptable will succeed. Uncle Bengy has taught me that we don't get to choose our family the way we do our friends. But we can choose how we embrace, forgive, sacrifice, and love.

In writing this memoir, I have gained a better appreciation for my family and Jamaica. I understand better my own weaknesses and I am now more forgiving. Uncle Bengy has helped me to understand that the numerous mountains and rolling hills are not stumbling blocks, but are barriers to slow the violent wind during a storm. When it rains, the awesomeness of the cascading waterfalls is only enhanced. On a sweltering day, the pristine beaches and refreshing waters are only better appreciated.

Uncle Sam has welcomed the ambitious and the downtrodden and provided conditions for one to thrive and grow. As new citizens, we all have an interest in keeping that beacon shining. My new country will be better off, one life at a time. My life is my responsibility. Hello, Uncle Sam!

Notes

[i] New Test of Ability for High School Entry in the Caribbean, Corinne Barnes, Inter Press Service

[ii] www.taxfoundation.org

INDEX

C

D

E

F

G

H

I

J

K

L

M

N

O

P

R

S

T

U

W

Y